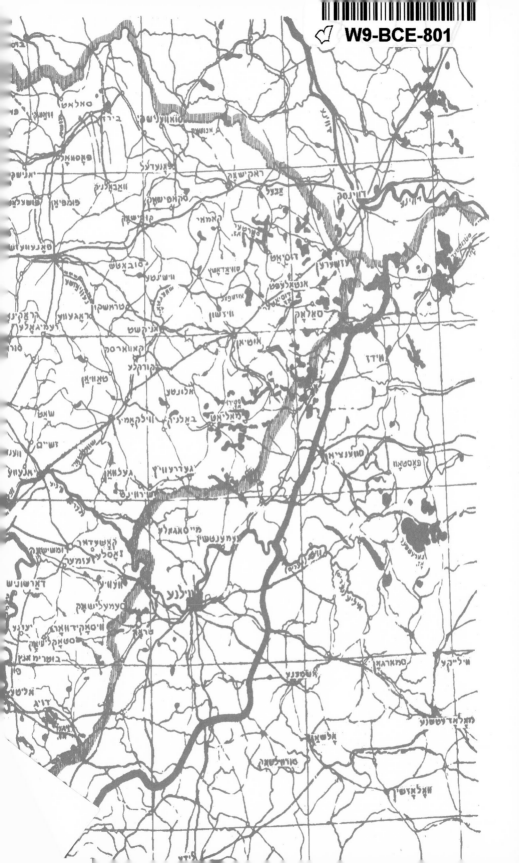

THE ANNIHILATION OF LITHUANIAN JEWRY

BY RABBI EPHRAIM OSHRY

Translated by Y. Leiman
from the Yiddish book "Churbin Lita"

THE JUDAICA PRESS, INC.

© Copyright 1995 by Ephraim Oshry

All photographs are from Rabbi Oshry's personal collection.
Editors: B. Goldman, E. Nauen **Editorial assistant:** Malky Tannenbaum
Indexer: Yitzy Kret **Typesetter:** Michael Brown

ISBN 1-880582-18-X

Library of Congress Cataloging-in-Publication Data

Oshry, Efroim 1915-
   [Hurbn Lite English]
   The annihilation of Lithuanian Jewry / Ephraim Oshry
   p.   cm.
   Includes bibliographical references and index.
   ISBN 1-880582-18-X
   1. Jews—Persecutions—Lithuania. 2. Holocaust, Jewish
(1939-1945)—Lithuania—Personal narratives. 3. Oshry, Efroim,
1915- . 4. Lithuania—Ethnic relations. I. Title.
DS135.L53083613 1995
940.53'18'09475—dc20   95-22907
                             CIP

THE JUDAICA PRESS, INC.
123 Ditmas Avenue
Brooklyn, New York 11218
718-972-6200   800-972-6201

Manufactured in the United States of America

TABLE OF CONTENTS

♦ Part I ♦

THE KOVNO GHETTO 1941-1944

◆ Part II ◆
THE ANNIHILATION OF LITHUANIAN JEWRY
The Cities and Towns of Jewish Lithuania

AUTHOR'S INTRODUCTION

In publishing *The Annihilation of Lithuanian Jewry*, I propose to raise a monument to destroyed Lithuanian Jewry, to the holy and unde-filed ones, the *gaonim* and *tzaddikim*, to our dearly beloved relatives and friends who were murdered by the Germans and their Lithuanian assistants during the years 1941-1944.

More than half a century has passed since the systematic destruction of Lithuanian Jewry began. The Germans and Lithuanians killed all kinds of Jews—geniuses, righteous people, and ordinary people who served G-d wholeheartedly.

Recently, the Jewish world has been alarmed by outbursts of anti-Semitism and racism in a number of European countries. "The troubles begin from the north," says the prophet, quoting G-d (Jeremiah 1:14). Neo-Nazi groups began by inciting and carrying out acts of violence against Jews in Germany. From there anti-Semitism has spread throughout the former Soviet Union and even the American diaspora. Nazism is like the python, which swallows its victim whole, then digests it over days, even weeks of lethargy, when the snake appears to be dead but is actually dormant. After its lengthy digestive rest, the snake awakens hungry, seeking fresh prey. So it is with anti-Semites the world over.

◆ ◆ ◆ ◆

In Deuteronomy 25:17-19, our Torah teaches, "Remember what Amalek did to you" (referring to the Amalekites, who brutally attacked the Israelites in the desert from the rear). The paragraph closes with the command, "Do not forget." The obvious questions are: Why command us not to forget when we have already been commanded to remember? If we remember, how can we forget?

My answer, based on contemporary events, is that Jewish elementary school and high school students, in yeshivos and elsewhere, are kept from hearing firsthand reports by survivors of the Holocaust. These survivors are not given the opportunity to tell the next generation what happened to our great scholars, our righteous *tzaddikim*, our yeshiva deans, our plain folks—to men, women, and children—because people would rather forget those horrors. The Almighty commanded, "You are not to forget. And if you try, I won't let you forget."

Writing is not my vocation. I am a rabbi and the dean of a yeshiva. My duty is to spread Torah knowledge. Had times been normal, I would surely not be writing any book other than one on *halachah* (Jewish law), as I have in fact done with G-d's help.

But when the great world tragedy befell the Jewish people and I, thank G-d, was miraculously saved from the hell I lived through—where my own eyes saw "Take revenge!" written in human blood; where my own ears heard more than once martyrs cry out just before their execution, "Whoever survives must tell the world what the Amalek-Nazi has done to us!"—I decided to fulfill this sacred last will of the martyrs. I decided to tell the world in simple words what I personally witnessed and what I heard from other witnesses, so that it will be permanently on record.

There are several other books documenting the agonies and horrors of the Kovno Ghetto. None, however, focus on the religious community's relentless dedication to the Torah and halachah. *The Annihilation of Lithuanian Jewry* emphasizes the everyday heroisms in the ghetto—studying Talmud, baking matzah for Pesach, donning *tefillin* every morning, davening, learning in Tiferes Bachurim groups, wearing tzitzis, eating kosher, finding a shofar to blow on Rosh Hashanah, an esrog and lulav for Succos or a menorah for Chanukah. It is these martyrs' sacrifices which lend truth to the term *"Kiddush Hashem"*, the sanctification of G-d's name.

I have listed every name I can remember of rabbis and Torah scholars in Lithuania. Jews who came from these Lithuanian towns but left before World War II remember the communal leaders of their home-towns. Every holy, undefiled Jew from these old Jewish communities represents, to those who remember him, a permanent memorial of Jewish life in Lithuania as it used to be.

◆ ◆ ◆ ◆

It is for this purpose that I wrote *Churban Lita* in Yiddish, publishing it in 1951. Now I have had it translated into English by Rabbi Yehoshua Leiman, who condensed and translated my *Responsa from the Holocaust* a decade ago. Along with the skilled editors of Judaica Press, we have updated wherever necessary the information in this book. We have also changed the order of the book from the original Yiddish to facilitate the narrative.

I gratefully thank my dearly beloved cousin, Harold Oshry, a philanthropist who does great things for Eretz Yisroel, and his wife, Claire, for sponsoring this vital work. May G-d bless them with a long, healthy life so that they can continue their good and holy works.

Ephraim Oshry
New York, October 1995

THE HISTORY OF LITHUANIA
AND LITHUANIAN JEWRY

My beloved Jewish Lithuania, how can I forget you? How can I live in peace when your horrifying destruction stands before my eyes!

Like the prophet Jeremiah I cry out, "Would that my head were water and my eyes a fountain of tears, so that I could bewail day and night the corpses of my people!"

May this work be a small monument to the immeasurable destruction of our Jewish Lithuania.

◆ ◆ ◆

When czarist Russia collapsed in the First World War, independence and freedom were restored, in 1918, to Lithuania.

This small country, which lies along the east coast of the Baltic Sea, has as its capital the city of Kovno (known as Kaunas in Lithuanian). Including Vilna, which it annexed in 1939, the population of Lithuania reached approximately 4 million, including some 250,000 Jews.

For over 700 years Jews had lived in Lithuania, where they suffered far fewer pogroms and outbreaks of anti-Semitism than Jews had in many other lands. The exception was the sudden forced baptism that began in 1495 and ended eight years later with the full rehabilitation of all the converts.

The reign of the grandduke Vytautas the Great, from 1386-1430, was a golden era for Jews, who were granted many rights and privileges. From the 16th through the early 18th centuries, Lithuania became renowned as the greatest center for Torah and Jewish knowledge in Europe. Among the great sages and scholars who taught in Lithuania or were associated with Lithuanian teachers were the influential Polish-Lithuanian commentator Rav Shlomo Luria (1510-1573, known as Maharshal); his disciple Rav Mordechai Yofeh (d. 1612) (author of *Levushim*, a 10-volume encyclopedia of codifications and commentaries); Rav Yoel Serkis (author of *Bayis Chodosh*); Rav Yehoshua Heschel (d. 1648); Rav Yehoshua Falk (1550-1614 author of *Peney Yehoshua*); Rav Shabsy Cohen (author of *Sifsey Cohen*); and Rav Moshe Rivkes (author of *B'eir Hagolah*).

In the second half of the 18th century rose the Gaon of Vilna, Rav Eliyohu ben Shlomo Zalman, the greatest spiritual leader of Lithuanian Jewry. He was succeeded by his greatest disciple, Rav Chaim of Volozhin, who established Yeshiva Eitz Chaim in Volozhin, the prototype of all Lithuanian yeshivos.

Scholarship continued to flourish in Lithuania through the 19th and 20th centuries. Prominent sages included the *gaon* Rav Yisroel Lipkin of Salant, the founder of the *mussor* movement; Rav Yitzchok Elchonon Spector of Kovno; Rav Naftoli Berlin of Volozhin; Rav Yosef Dov Soloveitchik of Slutsk; his son, Rav Chaim Soloveitchik of Brisk; Rav Meir Simcha Cohen and Rav Yosef Rosen of Dvinsk; Rav Yisroel Meir Kagan of Radun (author of *Chofetz Chayim*); Rav Eliyohu Boruch Kamei of Mir; Rav Moshe Mordechai Epstein of Slobodka, and Rav Boruch Ber Leibovitz of Kamenitz. The tragic fates of many of these holy martyrs will be discussed later in this book.

The Torah was the life-breath of the world in which the Lithuanian Jew functioned. Raising children to study and fulfill the Torah was the desire of every father and mother. Lithuanian Jewry's pride was its yeshivos. Lithuania was known as "the cradle of the yeshivos" during the 17th, 18th, and 19th centuries. Students came from all over Europe and England, as well as from the United States, to study in the renowned yeshivos of Volozhin, Mir, Slobodka-Kovno, Radun, Telz, Kelm, and Ponevezh. Small wonder that Lithuania achieved renown as the world's greatest Torah center and was nicknamed "The Second Eretz Yisroel," with Vilna earning the sobriquet "The Jerusalem of Lithuania." These yeshivos produced true *gaonim*—Torah masters— yeshiva deans, rabbis, and knowledgeable lay leaders. Even boys who were not naturally gifted developed and ripened in the yeshivos.

The Lithuanian Jew was not haught. The desire to stand out, to show oneself better than others, was not typical of the Lithuanian Jew.

Major scholars served as rabbis of small towns and did not desire a big-town rabbinate. Lithuanian Jewry possessed many people skilled in self-deprecation, whose humility was genuine. They had brilliant minds with simple demeanors, and were masters of personal integrity and wholeness with G-d.

Lithuanian Jewry was famous for its hospitality, generosity, devotion, and love of fellow Jews. A vivid illustration of this appears in the chapter "Lithuanian Jews—Embodiment of Torah and Chessed" in *Operation: Torah Rescue* by Rav Yecheskel Leitner:

The Lithuanian Jews extended their proverbial hospitality to the refugees from Poland. Although they had lost most of their means of livelihood due to the Soviet occupation of Lithuania in June 1940, they often shared the very last of their supplies with their unfortunate brethren, the refugees from neighboring, devastated Poland. This generosity took place under circumstances and conditions so trying, that if not personally witnessed and experienced, one could never have imagined them. No hosts were ever tested as severely as these Lithuanian Jews. Propelled by superlative Jewish principles, they performed unparalleled deeds of hospitality for their Polish brethren.

Kaisiadorys, the one-time border station of the Vilna-Kovno (Lithuania) railroad line that brought the refugees from Poland and Vilna into the Lithuanian heartland, was for many refugees a gateway to the Free World in tiny Lithuania. Trains packed with refugees would sometimes wait on the tracks of this former Polish-Lithuanian border town for hours, even after the incorporation of Vilna and its environs into Lithuania.

A Jew from town approached one train, shouting desperately, "Help! Help! Jewish brothers, please, help, please!"

People stuck their heads out of the train's windows; some even got out of the train in apprehension. "What's the matter, what happened?"

The man replied, "I live just opposite the station, on the other side of the Station Square."

Two, three, five, and more refugees followed the man out of curiosity and compassion. "Reb Yid, what's the matter in your house?" someone inquired. "Is somebody sick there? Tell us, please, what happened?"

"Oh no! Nothing of the kind, thank G-d," the man answered. "But you still must come and help us. We prepared the best things that we could offer you. You must come in for a short while to have a bite and rest," he insisted. "Please, don't turn us down." This man's "problem" was typical of the average Lithuanian Jew. The poor refugees were treated to a hot meal. A sumptuous table was set, and the host, his wife, and his family invited their guests to sit down and eat so that they could strengthen themselves for the next stage of the journey into an unknown future. The refugees did not have to search for synagogues and schools to get food, shelter, and housing. Their fellow-Jews willingly shared their modest homes and their food; they even gave up their own beds, sleeping on the floor or on makeshift beds made of boards so that their guests would be comfortable. Five, even 10, guests might be welcomed into a poor three-room apartment. The more guests, the happier the hosts, because their satisfaction would be greater at being able to fulfill the *mitzvah* of hospitality and of helping to bring relief to fellow Jews in distress.

In Slobodka, a suburb of Kovno, Lithuania's capital, the Com-munists had confiscated a bakery that had been built up through a lifetime of hard work. They permitted the baker to continue working in his former shop, but only as an employee and only until new workers and apprentices could be trained to take over. Even his savings had been appropriated by the local *Soviet* workers' council.

Yet this man's faith in G-d and the depth of his Jewish commitment sustained his strength and enabled him to overcome adversity. He continued to be a shining example in the practice of Torah and *mitzvos* as before, when his house had been known for its exceptional hospitality. Every Sabbath morning after services he continued to invite guests to his home—not just one or two people, but as many as he could persuade to join him for the Sabbath meal. He performed this act of generosity even on weekdays, prodding refugees at random to come to his house "for just a plate of hot soup." An army kettle filled with rich, hearty soup was the main "equipment" of this extraordinary hospitality. His guests assumed that such mass feedings had the support of a Jewish relief organization or some local charity fund. They were startled when they later learned that their host had used his meager financial reserves to feed the refugees, notwithstanding his family's own desperate plight in those days. Countless instances of such great selflessness and absolute devotion to humanity were encountered throughout Lithuania, even in the most remote Jewish settlements.

The wealthiest man and leader of a *shtetl* (a small, mostly Jewish town) had a number of servants and maids in the house as well as in the fields. But the lady of the house insisted, "I would not let anyone deprive me of the privilege of giving room and board to such people!" And so (as witnessed by this writer) she personally involved herself in all phases of hos-

* Abridged with permission from *Operation: Torah Rescue* by [Rav] Yecheskel Leitner (New York: Feldheim, 1987).

pitality—preparing delicious, home-baked bread and all kinds of fancy pastries, using her best resources: flour from their own mill, fresh vegetables from the family's own farm, and fruits from the garden, served with fresh milk—flavored with chocolate—from the family's own cows. All these delicacies were served personally on exquisite china by the rich lady of the house.*

This was Jewry in Lithuania: Torah, wisdom, and love for a fellow-Jew. And it has all disappeared.

The Germans, together with their Lithuanian assistants, uprooted the vineyard of Jewry, the Jewish communities that over the course of more than 700 years had taken root and flourished in Lithuania. A bloody stream of fearsome mass murders gushed through Lithuania and wiped out nearly all of Lithuania Jewry, its yeshivos, Torah institutions, and secular institutions. Terrible deaths were the lot of many.

◆ ◆ ◆ ◆

When Lithuania became an independent state in 1918, the Jews of Lithuania rejoiced wholeheartedly. They had deep sympathy and respect for their newly liberated land. They applied their energy and spirit to assist in building up the land, and they had a major share in its progress.

The Lithuanian people seemed to appreciate this, and it seemed that the good relations then established would create a new epoch of friendly cooperation between the Jews and the Lithuanians, who for generations had lived side by side, sharing good times and bad, until they at last arrived together at the moment of Lithuanian liberation.

At the outset of her independence, Lithuania gave the Jews autonomy in the form of independent communities with a national governing body and an independent school system where subjects were taught in Hebrew and Yiddish. This school system was funded by the government and supervised by a Jewish ministry, directed by a Jew. Lithuania could have served as a model for many other countries in dealing with minorities.

But the sweet time did not last. The anti-Semitic element in the Lithuanian government destroyed these institutions. By the time World War II broke out, all that was left was cultural autonomy for both religious and secular school systems. The Lithuanians also pushed Jews out of long-held positions and made their lives difficult, forcing many to emigrate.

But the climax came in 1941. On June 22, 1941, when the war between Germany and Russia broke out, Jews panicked. The Jews of Abel, a town directly on the border of Lithuania and Russia, sought to save themselves. They packed their meager belongings, climbed into their carts, and headed their horses toward Russia.

As they traversed the fields, German parachutists and Lithuanian farmers attacked them, murdering women and children and forcing the men to bury their dead. Then they herded the men to a town where frightened Jews from surrounding villages had fled for their lives.

These sadists put the Jews through cruel tortures and then led them to the nearby Antenas forest, where they forced them to dig pits. Men, women, and children were thrown alive into these pits and then shot at. Thus were the Jews of Abel and its surrounding villages put to death *al kiddush HaShem*—because they were Jews.

May this remain an eternal mark of Cain upon the Lithuanian murderers: how they treated the Jews who had contributed their marrow and blood to building Lithuania and with whom they had lived for over 700 years.

◆ ◆ ◆

"I am the man who saw the oppression by the rod of His wrath" (Lamentations 3:1). I witnessed the destruction and demise of Lithuanian Jewry. I witnessed the horror of individual Jewish homes being destroyed, and I personally traversed the entire hell of suffering and anguish that Amalek-Nazi had prepared for us Jews. I, too, drank from the cup of bitterness.

Thank G-d, Who saved me from the murderers, I am one of the very few surviving Jews of Lithuania. Why was I saved? I don't know. It was G-d's will. In what merit, I surely do not know, it was G-d's will that I would survive and walk out alive from that hell.

And it really was Hell. No person who did not also live under German domination at that time can imagine it, or can comprehend what happened to us in Lithuania in the terrible years between the German invasion and the liberation of Lithuania by the Red army on August 1, 1944.

That hell lasted three years. In the course of those horrible years almost the entire, blooming Jewish world of Lithuania was wiped away. The yeshivos, the citadels of Torah and *lomdus* (learning), disappeared. The centuries-rooted Jewish communities and their social and cultural institutions were destroyed. The Jewish newspapers disappeared; the Jewish libraries went up in smoke. The ancient family tree of Lithuanian Jewry was chopped down and its roots torn out.

There remained "one from a town and two from a family" (Jeremiah 3:14), surviving witnesses of the overwhelming destruction, orphaned and mourning—surviving, no doubt, to replant elsewhere the Torah of the Lithuanian yeshivos so that that Torah would not be forgotten by Jewry. And perhaps, too, they survived to tell what happened, so that their children and grandchildren would remember, and never forget, what the Amalekites—Lithuanian as well as German—did to us.

Yes, I am a witness to this destruction, a destruction without equal in the history of the Jewish people. I feel it is my duty to read aloud the scroll of this terrible destruction of Lithuanian Jewry. We must recount it. We must let everyone know what happened!

ACKNOWLEDGEMENTS

The editors of The Judaica Press wish to thank Ms. Elizabeth Kessin Berman, Director of Special Exhibitions at the United States Holocaust Memorial Museum, for her assistance in verifying factual information about the Kovno Ghetto.

Ms. Tina Lunson, historian at the United States Holocaust Memorial Museum, also gave generously of her time. Rabbi Moshe Kolodny, Chief Archivist at Agudath Israel of America graciously assisted us in finding additional photographs for this book. Mr. Thomas G. Declaire of the Library of Congress Geography and Map Division provided us with reliable maps of pre-WWII Kovno.

We also would like to thank Rabbi Mayer Z. Mann, Executive Director of the Rabbinical College of Telshe in Wickliffe, Ohio, and Rebbitzin Chaya Ausband of Cleveland, Ohio, for providing us with additional information about the Lithuanian towns of Tavrig and Telz. Lastly we thank Rabbi Zvi H. Shurin, Rabbi of Congregation Sons of Israel in Jersey City, New Jersey, for contributing the remarkable story of the Rav of Riteve.

◆ PART I ◆

THE KOVNO GHETTO

1941-1944

View of Kovno

THE KOVNO GHETTO IN SLOBODKA

Ghetto map key:

1 Block A
2 Block B
3 Block C; the Delousing Institute;
   Rabbi Oshry's bunker.
4 The Central Jewish Police
   Department.
5 The pottery workshops.
6 The ghetto school.
7 The hiding place for the books.
8, 9, 10, 11, 12 The ghetto gates.
10 The main ghetto gates.
13, 14 The German ghetto guard.
15 The old Slobodka Yeshiva and beis hamidrosh.
16 The bridge between the Little ghetto
   and the Big ghetto.
17 The ghetto baker.
18 Soup kitchen.
19 The new Slobodka Yeshiva.
20 Children's Home; furniture workshops.
21 The hospital in the Little ghetto.
22 The hospital in the Big ghetto; the
   Ghetto Health Department.
23 The German Ghetto Guard; the ghetto
   pharmacy.
24 The ghetto courthouse.
25 The Housing Department; the Social
   Aid Department.
26 Graphics Workshops; Criminal
   Department of the Jewish Ghetto
   Police.
27 The Jewish Council of Elders
   ("Altestenrat") Building; Jewish
   Labor Office; Nutrition Department.
28 The sight of Mek's execution.
29 The ghetto firehouse.
30 The large ghetto workshops.
31 The Abba Yechezkel kloiz, later
   turned into the ghetto jailhouse.
32 Public bathhouse.
33 The ghetto gardens.
34 Vegetable gardens.
35 The Jewish cemetery.

· 1 ·

THE DESTRUCTION OF KOVNO BEGINS:
THE SLOBODKA POGROM

Even to this day I cannot rid myself of my first impression of the German occupation of Lithuania. More than 50 years have passed since the 25th of June 1941, when the Lithuanian fascists, who had been looking forward to Hitler's invasion and the resulting withdrawal of the Russians from Lithuania, celebrated with a Jewish bloodbath in the old, majestic Torah town of Slobodka (called Vilijampole in Lithuanian), a mostly Jewish suburb just across the river from Kovno, Lithuania's capital city.

It was a Wednesday night several days after the outbreak of the German-Russian war. We had expected serious trouble, but none of us had imagined the horrors that would happen to us under the German occupation.

We were also shocked by the attitude of the Lithuanian populace, our "good Catholic" neighbors. I cannot remember a single person among all our Gentile neighbors in Slobodka who openly defended a Jew when more than 6,000 Slobodka Jews—with whom they had lived all their lives—became victims of a terrifying pogrom.

It is not possible to relate everything that happened the night of June 25th in Slobodka. But what I will relate is enough to show the extent of the Germans' cruelty. They were things the world had not yet seen.

We, a group of 12 rabbis and a few yeshiva students, were hidden

1

that night in the home of the dean of the Slobodka Yeshiva, Rav Avrohom Grodzensky. With us was the great *gaon* (genius), Rav Elchonon Wasserman. We spent that night praying and weeping. But we also discussed what we could do.

Rav Avrohom Drushkovich, an elderly man and former *mashgiach* (dean and spiritual mentor) of the Volozhin Yeshiva, one of the greatest Lithuanian yeshivos, came in to join us. From what he told us he had seen happening on the streets of Slobodka and had heard was going on in Kovno, it became clear that the Germans and Lithuanians seemed intent on killing all the Jews. What were we to do? Could we devise some sort of plan? That was the issue that wearied us that night while Jews were dying in the streets of Slobodka.

That Wednesday evening at dusk, Lithuanian Nazis, accompanied by mobs of ordinary Lithuanians, marched into the Jewish section of Slobodka with axes and saws. They began the Slobodka pogrom on Yurborger Street, moving from house to house, from apartment to apartment, from room to room, killing every Jew they encountered, old and young alike. They chopped off heads with axes, sawed people in half and—we learned afterwards—they took their time doing it in order to prolong their victims' agony.

The first stop the butchers made was at the Yurborger Street home of Mordechai Yatkunsky and his wife, Dr. Stein-Yatkunsky, a dentist. They chopped off their hands, feet, and organs, killing both of them as well as their son.

From Yurborger Street the Lithuanians headed into Yatke Street and other streets. Indiscriminately they killed every Jew they encountered—rabbis, professionals, Zionist activists, intellectuals, Communists. The butchery was overwhelming. From the streets rose horrifying screams, and rising above those screams one could make out the ancient Jewish death cry, "*Shema Yisroel*" ("Hear, O Israel"), the prayer that affirms G-d's existence.

We, the Jews who had hidden, squirmed in our hideouts. How we felt—we "lucky ones" who were not murdered that night—cannot be imagined.

One of the most terrible instances of savage butchery was the death of the venerable rabbi of Slobodka, Rav Zalman Osovsky— may G-d avenge him. The Germans bound

Rav Zalman Osovsky, rabbi of Slobodka.

Rav Zalman hand and foot to a chair, then laid his head upon an open volume of *gemora* (volume of the Talmud) and sawed his head off. Their brutality did not end there, for afterwards they murdered his son, the young genius Rav Yudel Osovsky, and then shot Rav Zalman's wife.

The rabbi's five-year-old granddaughter, Esterka, was the only person at home who survived; she hid under a bed. Tragically, Esterka was subsequently killed together with her mother, Rochel, three months later on Friday the 26th of September, 1941.

When we later entered his residence, Rav Zalman's body minus its head was still "sitting" in his rabbinic chair at his desk, his *gemora* open before him at tractate *Nidah*, folio 33. The holy rabbi had been interrupted in the middle of his studying. We found his head in a window with a sign: THIS IS WHAT WE'LL DO TO ALL THE JEWS.

During that night of horrors, Reb Gershon, the sexton of the Slobodka Yeshiva, was also killed, his throat slit. As he lay dying, he gasped to someone who discovered him, "When you are liberated, relate our suffering and hell."

Another dying Jew, in his last throes, wrote on a wall with his

Found written in blood on a wall in Slobodka: "Jews! Take Revenge!"

own blood, "Jews! Take Revenge!" His writing remained on that wall for a long time.

Some Jews jumped off the bridge into the Viliya River in order to escape. And Germans stood on the bridge and used the Jews for target practice.

Many other well-known Jews were slaughtered that night, among them the *iluy* (prodigy) Rav Yona of Minsk. The Lithuanians tore out his intestines, wrapped them in a *tallis* (prayer shawl) and set it down next to the murdered *tzaddik* (righteous person). On that dreadful night dozens of Slobodka Yeshiva students were also murdered.

When the Lithuanians finished their dirty work in private homes, they went to the main commercial streets. At the corner of Yurborg Street and Shosaika, they shot the blacksmith, then lined 26 Jews against a wall and shot them. They let no Jew pass—man, woman, or child. Near the bridge leading to Kovno they buried 34 Jews alive.

The following morning along with many of the other survivors I went door to door. We gathered the dead and buried them in a mass grave in the Slobodka cemetery. We decided to do this despite the danger from the still-roving gangs of Lithuanians.

I believe I will never be able to erase the memories of that terrifying night from my mind, the night on which the annihilation of Lithuanian Jewry began.

· 2 ·

JEWS GO TO THEIR DEATHS
WEARING *TALLEISIM* AND *TEFILLIN*

M y hand trembles as I write this. How does one recount such a tragedy, such a catastrophe? How can one even mention such horrible things? And yet it is imperative to narrate those events. Everyone must be told about the final days and hours of our Jewish brothers and sisters martyred al *kiddush HaShem* (in sanctification of G-d).

After all, if one has emerged from that hell, one is obliged to pass on the final regards from those martyrs. And they sent horrible regards. These are not mere reports of murder, rather they are holy pages of Jewish martyrology, of *kiddush HaShem*.

Jews did not merely die, they sanctified G-d. They fought for Jewish honor and Jewish worth. There were others who could not fight; I will tell you about them later.

◆ ◆ ◆

What Lithuanian Jew does not recall the old Kovno *beis hamidrosh* (place of study and prayer) next to the Viliya River? Much has been written about this holy synagogue where over the course of many generations Jews studied and prayed. It also served as the home of Yeshiva Ateres Tzvi, named after Rav Tzvi Hirsh Rabinovich (1848-1919), the *maggid* (preacher) and *dayan* (judge) of Jewish law in Mitow and son of the renowned Rav Yitzchok Elchonon Spector (1816-1896), and Rav Spector's successor as Kovno's chief rabbi.

The old synagogue stood next to the Jewish hospital. Kovno's Jews remember well how much sanctity was connected with this *beis hamidrosh*. It was where Rav Spector, the great rabbi and *posek* (scholar who rules in halachic issues) of his generation, had prayed and studied. It was where both community members and *perushim* (scholars who separated themselves from their families and hometowns in order to study) who were great in Torah and in fear of G-d studied. It was also where Rav Yeruchom Y. Perelman of Minsk, father-in-law of Rabbi Avrohom DovBer Kahana-Shapiro—who was Kovno's chief rabbi before and during the War—studied in his youth. It was also where Rav Spector's vast library was housed.

Into this holy synagogue, early Thursday morning on June 26, 1941, marched Lithuanian and German Nazis. They found Jews there in the middle of the *Shacharis* (morning) prayer. Despite the risk, despite what had transpired the day before in Slobodka and in the center of Kovno, 25 Jewish men had gathered to pray. Some were Kovno's leading citizens. There were elderly men, and even children. Because of the shocking events of the previous day, most men prayed with greater intensity than usual. Several studied *gemoros*. Almost all the men wore *talleisim* and *tefillin* (phylacteries).

When the Lithuanians and Germans entered, their first command was, "Stop praying!" The most shattering part was that the Lithuanian who gave this order was Kovno's Shabbos-*goy* (a non-Jew who performs services for Jews on Sabbaths and holidays), a man who had been born among Jews and ostensibly had been a friend of Jews all his life. No one could believe that this man was capable of such perfidy!

When this man entered the sacred synagogue, he showed off his Yiddish for the Germans and Lithuanians accompanying him. He spoke Yiddish very well, for he had lived among Jews all his life. First he introduced the leading townspeople. He demonstrated to the Nazis that he was no mere "pogromchik," but rather a man who could be indispensable. He knew the Jews well, he knew who was who. He knew the Jewish spiritual leaders—in other words, he knew who it would be practical for the Germans to kill.

In general, the German policy in Lithuania was that the first people to be killed were the spiritual and intellectual leaders of the Jews: the rabbis, the writers, the professionals. The Lithuanians helped them greatly in this respect. The Germans would not have been able to so thoroughly destroy Lithuanian Jewry if they had not had the active assistance of the local Lithuanian populace.

The Lithuanians offered their assistance enthusiastically. This coop-eration was so unthinkable that both Jews who were there and those who heard about it later were stunned. How could it have happened? we asked ourselves repeatedly. How could we have been so deceived? How could our neighbors, with whom we had lived side by side for hundreds of years, sink to such degrading betrayal? To this day I can-not fathom it. I cannot comprehend how the Lithuanian non-Jews liv-ing in Jewish cities and towns such as Kovno and Slobodka could have become the murderers and accomplices to the murder of their Jewish neighbors. Although the Lithuanians clearly hated the Russians and were thrilled to be "liberated" from the Russian occu-pation by the Germans, their slaughter of the Jews was incomprehen-sible.

This Shabbos-*goy* wanted to show off his usefulness to the Germans. He clearly expected great panic to break out in the syna-gogue. When he gave his order for everyone to stop praying (this was related to me later by a Jew who escaped), he stood there officiously, waiting for the Jews he had served all his life to fall at his feet and beg him to take pity and not harm them. But the Jews remained standing. Not one of them cried or even moved. Instead, they prayed silently, moving only their lips. Many of them had probably begun reciting *Viduy* (a confessional prayer said before dying).

The Germans and Lithuanians were armed; the Jewish men were unarmed. The Jews stood there, proud, courageous, wrapped in their billowing *talleisim*, crowned with their *tefillin*, looking straight into the murderers' faces. The Germans and Lithuanian Nazis seemed momentarily taken aback by the fearlessness of those men. But all too soon they attacked. Exactly how long the Jews were beaten and tor-tured, I do not know. But shortly after this senseless attack, the Jewish men were led through the streets of Kovno—in anguish, blood stain-ing their *talleisim*. Yet even in this condition, not a single one broke down. They walked upright, wrapped in their *talleisim*, still wearing their *tefillin*—G-d's soldiers.

They were led to the bank of the Viliya River, which runs through the center of town, where they were ordered to dig ditches. Still wear-ing their *talleisim* and *tefillin*—reminding them of the *echod*[1]—they stood digging their own graves. They stood so tall and brave, eyewit-nesses later said, it seemed as if the Germans were the captives and the Jews were the victors.

---

[1] *Echod* ("one") is the last word of the verse that begins with "*Shema Yisroel, HaShem Elokaynu, HaShem Echod*—Hear, O Israel, *HaShem*, our G-d, *HaShem* is one." This is usually the last verse a dying person recites on his or her deathbed.

Not one of those men had any illusions about what was in store for him. But even in the last minutes of their lives, they did not break down. A crowd of Lithuanian anti-Semites gathered around them. Jeering, enjoying the spectacle, they tried to provoke the helpless Jewish men, but to no avail. The Jews remained firm and recited their prayers—with greater intensity, with more passion, with more sanctity than ever before. They stood and said *Viduy* as they dug the soil for their own graves. At that moment they were no longer part of this world of falsehood—they had transcended to a higher world, the world of truth. The Germans with their machine guns, the Lithuanians with their axes and iron rods, no longer existed for them. They were part of the dirt in the corridor that is this world.

As the Germans mowed them down, the tune of Lithuanian Jewry—the heartfelt, soulful *Tehillim* (Psalms)—was heard. And so the music of the sweet singer of Israel accompanied the martyrs of the old Kovno synagogue as they fell into the graves they had been forced to dig for themselves.

After our liberation in August 1944, I returned with other survivors to the bank of the river. We dug up those graves and reinterred these martyrs in the Jewish cemetery. Some were still wrapped in the remnants of their *talleisim*. May their mention be a blessing.

· 3 ·

YESHIVA KENESSES YISROEL
OF SLOBODKA

To understand Jewish Lithuanian life, we must turn to its center, the town of Slobodka. Slobodka was not merely a Lithuanian-Jewish town with traditions and a style of its own. Slobodka was a world unto itself. It became famous on account of its *yeshivos*, its centers of religious study, on account of its Torah, and on account of one particular yeshiva, Yeshiva Kenesses Yisroel, known as "the Slobodka Yeshiva."

The Slobodka Yeshiva, at that time one of the world's biggest *yeshivos*, is now gone. It was wiped out together with the Jews of Slobodka. Gone too are its scholarly members, rabbis and bright students who came from all over Lithuania. And alas, I witnessed its destruction. How can one recount it! How can one forget the destruction of this precious community! Fortunately, its spirit rolls on through those of its students who left before the war broke out, and those students whom Providence saved from the German gas chambers and crematoria. Many of those students found their way to Israel and to the Tel Aviv suburb of Bnei Brak, where they carry on the traditions of Slobodka guided by Rabbi Moshe Hillel Hirsch, Rabbi Noson Tzvi Shulman, and Rabbi Amrom Zaks, as they were guided by the late Rav Isaac Sher (who managed to escape Slobodka in 1941).

Before I begin my detailed recounting of how the yeshiva was destroyed; how the *gaon* Rav Avrohom Grodzensky, its spiritual dean, was put to death; how Rav Shraga Feivel Hurvitz, dean of Talmudic studies, and the precious students of the yeshiva were killed—I want to relate the history of this world-renowned Torah center.

For more than 50 years the old wooden building at the corner of Glezer and Furman Streets in Slobodka was a place where the light of Torah burned with inextinguishable fire; where generations were trained in the pure Jewish ethic of Slobodka *mussar* (the study of rebuke to improve one's character). *Mussar* meant integrating Torah study with personal character development. *Mussar* teaching obliges students to engross themselves in the depths of Torah study while at the same time fulfilling the commandments with thoughtfulness derived from Torah thinking. The greater one's scholarship, the more refined one's character and behavior must be. One must serve as an example for others in the practical fulfillment of Judaism's ethical principles.

In 1932 when I was 17 years old, I left the Ponevezh Yeshiva in the north of Lithuania to study at Slobodka. I recall how on Shabbos (Sabbath) evening after *sholosh seudos* (the third meal of the Sabbath, eaten before sunset on Saturday), the yeshiva students gathered to study *mussar*. Each student would draw up his own spiritual balance sheet. A Slobodka yeshiva student did not think only about himself. He thought about the entire world, about Jew and world, about true spiritual purpose, about love of G-d, and about love of fellow-Jew.

This atmosphere of sanctity and purity permeated the students in their Shabbos spirit as well as the less scholarly men from Slobodka and even Kovno who would drop in to warm their souls. As Rav Nosson Tzvi Finkel, founding dean of the yeshiva, who was respectfully nicknamed *Der Alter* (the Elder), used to say, "The bridge leads from Kovno to Slobodka, not the other way." Slobodka yeshiva was a glowing spiritual fire that attracted Jews from all the surrounding areas. To these bright young men, Rav Nosson Tzvi Finkel's son-in-law, Rav Isaac Sher, the rosh yeshiva (dean of rabbinic academy), would give a *mussar* discourse. There were approximately 360 students 17 years old up to 25 years old at the yeshiva. The majority came from out of town and lived, as I did, with local families. To gain admittance to the yeshiva one had to pass a difficult oral exam with the rosh yeshiva.

◆ ◆ ◆ ◆

The Slobodka yeshiva was founded in 1882 in the spirit of the world-renowned *gaon* Rav Yisroel Lipkin (1810-1883) who came from the small Lithuanian town of Salant. Known as Rav Yisroel Salanter, it was he who introduced the study of *mussar* to the Torah-world. And it was for him that the yeshiva was named Kenesses Yisroel. He was a spiritual giant, a master educator of thousands of yeshiva students. But it was Rav Nosson Tzvi (Nota Hirsh) Finkel, who founded the yeshiva along with one of Rav Salanter's disciples—Rav Yitzchok Blazzer, the former rabbi of St. Petersburg. The immediate pressure that led to the establishment of this yeshiva was the closing by the Russian government of the "mother of all *yeshivos*," Yeshiva Eitz Chaim of Volozhin in 1892, along with the steady decline in Torah scholarship among Jews in Lithuania.

The broad scope of the yeshiva was clear immediately upon its opening. Thanks to the extraordinary energy of its founder, who had thoroughly mastered the *mussar* system, and thanks to the financial assistance of Ovadya Lachman of Berlin, a well-known philanthropist, the Slobodka Yeshiva quickly became renowned in the Jewish world.

When the name of Slobodka is mentioned, the insignificant Jewish town fades out of sight, and the lighthouse that for 50 years illuminated Jewish life by producing hundreds and hundreds of students who became spokesmen for Jewry stands tall: famous rabbis, deans of *yeshivos*, and leaders—Jews who have welded further links to the golden chain that links our generations, from Sinai through Yavneh, Nehardea, and Pumbadisa, to Volozhin and Slobodka.

At the end of World War I, when the Lithuanian government came into existence, the significance of the yeshiva as a major center for Jewish studies was acknowledged, and the yeshiva was granted the same rights the government accorded secular institutions. By that time the yeshiva population was an "ingathering of exiles" of the best students from Lithuania, Poland, Germany, Czechoslovakia, Hungary, the United States, England, Israel, and other lands.

Slobodka Yeshiva had two preparatory schools for the younger boys. Or Yisroel had an enrollment of 70 to 80 boys 16 through 18 years old. Its principals were Rav Yosef Farber and Rav Yechezkel Bernstein with Rav Boruchson as *mashgiach*. The second preparatory school, Ohel Moshe had approximately 100 boys 11 through 16 years old enrolled. Rabbi Yosef Chaim Zaks was the Rosh Yeshiva of Ohel Moshe, and Rabbi Shmuel Marak and Rabbi Yitzchok Geffen were his assistants. The Slobodka *Kollel*—the seminary of advanced talmudical studies for married men—was directed by Rabbi Zalman Permut and had about 16-18 men in attendance.

Yeshiva Kenesses Yisroel, known as the Slobodka Yeshiva.

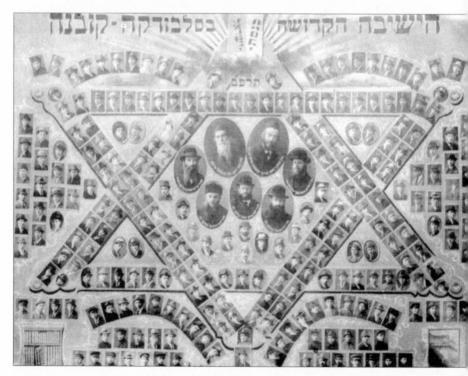

Slobodka Yeshiva, 1922.

Slobodka Yeshiva had the great merit of being guided from its inception by a rare personality, a spiritual giant who has not yet been fully appreciated in the Jewish world. Rav Nosson Tzvi Finkel was not only the founder of the yeshiva and its director for 40 years but he established or helped establish nearly all the *yeshivos* in Lithuania. The greatest rabbis and yeshiva deans of the twentieth century were once his disciples. Among the heads or former heads of *yeshivos* in the United States—in the order of their arrival on these shores—were these disciples of *Der Alter* of Slobodka: Rav Yaakov Yitzchok Ruderman of Ner Israel Rabbinical College in Baltimore, Rav Yitzchok Hutner of Yeshiva Rabbi Chaim Berlin in Brooklyn, Rav Aaron Kotler of Beth Medrash Govoha in Lakewood, New Jersey, and Rav Yaakov Kaminetsky of Mesivta Torah Vodaath in Brooklyn.

Der Alter was an extraordinarily gifted teacher whose genius in Torah and fear of G-d enabled him to burrow into the hidden recesses of the human soul and draw forth the student's own powers so that he could raise himself to his greatest potential. *Der Alter* was his students' economic patron as well as spiritual guide. He provided them with everything they needed on the road to personal achievement.

◆ ◆ ◆ ◆

Until the 22nd of June 1941, when the Germans invaded the Soviet Union, the yeshiva operated in all its glory. Even on Monday morning, the 23rd of June—just before the Slobodka pogrom—the yeshiva still functioned normally. That morning I was in the yeshiva. As the Germans approached Kovno, war planes could be heard flying overhead and bombs were sporadically dropped. Suddenly the learning was stopped and the students and their teachers began to recite *Tehillim*. Wailing and weeping broke out as they prayed. At the verse "Save me from my pursuers, for they are mightier than me" (Psalms 142:7), the yeshiva students sobbed loudly, while the windows fell out of the walls.

The students kissed their *seforim* (sacred books) goodbye, running their fingers over the *shtenders* (study stands) where they had learned Torah and Talmud over the course of so many years. They took one last glance at the holy walls that had absorbed the sanctity of their Jewish study.

Many students gathered around the great genius, Rav Avrohom Grodzensky, then an elderly man, and looked into his deep and wise eyes. Although his eyes were calming, simultaneously, we saw an unsettling question in them: "When will G-d take pity on us? When will we gather again inside these holy walls to continue our study of Torah?"

*Rav Yitzchok Blazzer,
renowned as Rav Itzel
Peterburger, founder of the
Slobodka Yeshiva.*

*Rav Yechezkel Bernstein,
rosh yeshiva of
Or Yisroel in Slobodka.*

*Rav Zalman Permut,
director of the
Slobodka Kollel.*

Slobodka Yeshiva, 1929.

I remember one student saying to Rav Grodzensky in confusion, "Farewell, Rebbi, I'm going. But where should I go?" Moments later he changed his mind: "Maybe I should stay?"

Although it was difficult to stay in Slobodka, no one knew where to go. Many Jews had already left, following the fleeing Russians. But we had heard that many had not made it. If we tried to make it to the Russian border we feared we would be killed by the Lithuanian mobs we heard were rampaging through the countryside. Everywhere Jews were hated and in danger. Many of the roads were blocked and German pilots were firing machine guns from the air at fugitives. Everyone felt helpless.

But we had to disperse.

Never will I forget that last morning, the 28th of Sivan 5701, June 23, 1941. On this day, we stopped learning in the Slobodka Yeshiva; the sound of Torah study was heard for the final time on the corner of Glezer and Furman Streets.

Several days later, on Friday the 27th of June—2 Tamuz 5701—the Germans killed the *gaon*, Rav Shraga Feivel Hurvitz, one of the young instructors in the yeshiva, a son of Rav Boruch Hurvitz, the former rosh yeshiva of Slobodka Yeshiva and the rabbi of Alexot, a town near Slobodka. That was on the third day of the horrible Slobodka pogrom, during which hundreds of Jews, including many yeshiva students, were murdered. Rav Shraga Feivel Hurvitz, a vibrant man in his early 40s, was sitting in his apartment in Reb Chaikel the *shochet*'s (ritual slaughterers) house on Boiner Street, studying Torah with a yeshiva student from Germany named Wolff. Rav Hurvitz's wife and five-year-old daughter were also at home.

Earlier that morning Mrs. Hurvitz had noticed three Lithuanian fascists being shown her apartment. Now it was too late to escape. Several men entered the apartment and without saying a word, took the rabbi together with his student and led them out to the courtyard. At the door to his apartment, in front of his wife and child, they shot him. Wolff the yeshiva student they also cold-bloodedly killed.

So died one of the best young teachers of Torah.

This is the awful regards, the horrifying regards from Slobodka that I must deliver.

Many other teachers and students were brutally murdered by the Germans, including, at a later date, the great *mussar* authority Rav Avrohom Grodzensky.

· 4 ·

THE KIDDUSH HASHEM OF THE SLOBODKA YESHIVA STUDENTS

To facilitate the genocide of the Jewish people, the Germans first sought to destroy the Jewish spirit. They reasoned that by removing the head—i.e., the spiritual leadership—it would be easier to annihilate the then-helpless body of the Jewish people. To this end, they systematically went about destroying the beautiful Lithuanian Jewish intelligentsia in all its panorama—the religious and the secular, the Torah authorities and the cultural leadership.

We received daily reports from villages and towns throughout Lithuania of Germans killing rabbis, Torah scholars, yeshiva students, and intellectuals. In Slobodka too, yeshiva students and the men who were members of the Kovno *kollel* were regularly grabbed off the streets or pulled from their homes and taken to the Seventh Fort or to the Ninth Fort for detention or to be killed immediately. Rav Simcha Gitelevitz rabbi of Greenem Barg and rosh yeshiva of Ateres Tsvi, was among those martyred at the Seventh Fort.

These forts had been constructed at the turn of the century in anticipation of war with Germany. The Russian czars who had ordered their construction wanted this chain of forts to serve as a sort of Maginot Line against the Germans. These forts were built on hills and in valleys along Russia's Lithuanian border with Prussia. Thousands of people had been employed in building them and millions of rubles spent on them. The Seventh and the Ninth Forts were built on the outskirts of Slobodka-Kovno. During the First World War, those forts were as helpful to Russia as the Maginot Line was to France—meaning, not at all. After World War I the forts were used as prisons. When the Germans invaded they found them suitable for imprisoning Jews and Russians, but mostly used them as sites for mass murder. They killed thousands upon thousands of Jews there.

Of the many Slobodka yeshiva students murdered, one particularly horrible story made us shudder, that of the tragic death of 20-year-old Chaim Luft, known as Chaim Litiyaner because he came from the Lithuanian town of Litiyan.

Chaim Luft was arrested during the first days of the German occupation when Jews were seized off the streets or taken from their houses. This was known as *chappenish* ("the grabbing time").

When two Lithuanian Nazis entered his room, Chaim was standing wearing his *tefillin* in the midst of praying *Shacharis*. At the sight of the *tefillin* on the young man, one of the Germans said venomously, "So you are a rabbi? Come for a walk with us and we will show you how we treat rabbis!"

Chaim Luft replied coolly, "Please wait until I finish praying. Then I will go with you."

The men of course did not wait. Enraged, they tore the *tefillin* from Chaim's head. Then they dragged him out of the house. Ignoring the pain they were inflicting on him, Chaim continued his prayer aloud all the way to Ninth Fort where some time later, he was murdered along with dozens of other yeshiva boys.

Among the Slobodka yeshiva students martyred along with Chaim Luft in the Ninth Fort were Heshel Fuhn, son of the rabbi of Trisk; Rav Avrohom Grodzensky's son Zev Grodzensky; Leibel Lebidaver; Leib Ehrlich; Yitzchok Kotler; Aharon Reichman; Yisroel Segal of Pozevla; Chaim Shitzkus; Leib Yavnelovitz; Avrohom Yitzchok Zaks; Shmuel Rolba; Rav Lipa Zilber; Rav Chaim Vetzerebin; and Rav Chaim Gilman, cousin of former Israeli Chief Rabbi Isaac Herzog.

Not long after, when another group of students was imprisoned, Rav Avrohom Grodzensky, director of the Slobodka Yeshiva, asked me to send Rabbi David Itzkovitch, secretary of Agudas Harabonim (Union of Orthodox Rabbis), to try and persuade the Lithuanians who he knew from before the war to free the yeshiva students. We knew we had to do everything in our power to save the students.[2] And following the dictum "whoever saves one life it is considered as though he saved the whole world" (Sanhedrin 4:5), Rabbi Itzkovitch risked his life. He courageously approached the Lithuanians, and succeeded

---

[2] For an in-depth explanation of the halachic question of endangering oneself to save another, see my *Responsa from the Holocaust* (New York: Judaica Press, NY, 1981), page 1.

Soon after the German occupation of Kovno, about 10,000 Jews were seized in various sections of the city and taken to the Seventh Fort, a part of the city's ancient fortifications. Between 6,000 and 7,000 of these Jews were murdered in early July 1941.

The Ninth Fort, near Slobodka, was the end of the road for the inmates of the Kovno Ghetto and thousands of Jewish deportees from Germany, France, and other German-occupied countries. Jews imprisoned in the Ninth Fort were either murdered on the spot or sent away to death camps.

in getting the students freed. Rabbi Itzkovitch later died in an extermination camp.

But most of the Slobodka Yeshiva students weren't saved. Another terrible story concerns the deaths of Yitzchok Patinsky and his brother Kuppel Patinsky, who was called Kuppel Pilvishker because he came from the Lithuanian town of Pilvishok. Kuppel was one of the most gifted students in the yeshiva. When the Germans were about to enter Kovno in June of 1941, Kuppel and his brother Yitzchok fled to their hometown, two hours away by train. When the Germans murdered the Jews of Pilvishok, both brothers managed to hide and survive in the attic of a non-Jew's house.

Yekusiel Friedman, a fellow Pilvishoker (who survived and later settled in Israel), used to bring the brothers food. He noticed, however, that even though Kuppel was obviously famished, he did not eat any of the food. Yekusiel asked why. Kuppel replied that he could not touch the food because he had no water for washing his hands. After that Yekusiel provided him with water and he ate.

For two months the brothers remained hidden in the attic. Eventually they were discovered, shot, and buried near Pilshivok's river. The following spring, when the ice melted and the river overflowed, their bodies washed out of their shallow graves.

Yekusiel discovered their bodies partially eaten by dogs and despite the risk of being seen by the Germans, he managed to bury them again.

· 5 ·

KIDDUSH HASHEM

Every day it became clearer that everything around us was collapsing. Everything?

The word may be a bit too strong. Some Jews refused to yield to their fate and escaped into the forests to fight the Germans. Others fled to small towns, hoping that there they would be safer. Still others attempted to reach the Russian border. But among the people who stayed put we had the righteous sages of Lithuania who, in the midst of the blackest darkness, kept the eternal lamp of Torah burning. Despite the German defilement everywhere around them, they always managed to reserve a small corner for Torah, for sanctity, for purity.

In those difficult times, when the darkness around us thickened and became increasingly unbearable, when daily more Jews were beaten or murdered, we thought everything was coming to an end. During this time, wondrous acts of sanctification of G-d (*kiddush HaShem*) would occasionally take place, fortifying our trust in G-d and driving away the confusion that clouded our innermost, unshakable faith in the Eternal One of the Jewish people.

As I noted in earlier chapters, as soon as the Germans entered Lithuania, it was open season on Jews. Thousands of Jews throughout Lithuania were pulled off the streets or out of their houses and tortured to death. This preceded the German's systematic elimination of Jews in the ghettos.

When the Slobodka Yeshiva closed, the Torah sages refused to give up their Torah study. The home of my revered teacher, Rav Avrohom Grodzensky, the yeshiva's director, became the home of Torah in Slobodka.

As soon as the Germans marched into town, many rabbis, Talmud instructors, and students took up quarters in Rav Grodzensky's apartment at 15 Poneru Street. It was extremely crowded in that apartment. Living conditions were very unpleasant. I know because I lived there. But despite the horrible living conditions, the study of Torah in that apartment did not cease for even one minute. Although the *yeshivos* were closed, the "four cubits of halachah (Jewish law)" remained active in that apartment.

◆ ◆ ◆ ◆

It would be incorrect to leave the impression that only rabbis and great scholars kept the spark of Judaism and Torah alive in those dark days. No less a degree of *kiddush HaShem* was demonstrated by the less educated.

I will never forget the great *kiddush HaShem* demonstrated by two men. One was Yerachmiel, a Jewish porter, and another was a shoemaker of Slobodka named Itche Moishe.

On the Shabbos morning of June 28th, the fourth day of the Slobodka pogrom, I weighed the risks that going to synagogue entailed, and decided that on Shabbos *Mevorechim* (the Shabbos before the start of a new month), when we ask G-d for life on the occasion of the coming new month, it would be appropriate—especially in this Jew-hunting season—to do so with a *minyan* (quorum of ten men). Who could be certain another such opportunity would arise? I figured the safest synagogue to attend was the Shoemakers' kloiz (small synagogue) on Shosei Street, because its entrance was not visible from the street. I left for synagogue early in the morning, when I hoped the Nazis would still be in their beds.

Upon entering the kloiz, I found a *minyan* in progress. Itche Moishe the shoemaker was leading the service with the usual Shabbos melody at the typical slow Shabbos tempo. I walked over to him and whispered, "Reb Itche Moishe, this Shabbos requires a different melody, a sadder one, with a quicker tempo, because the murderers may enter at any time."

We were reading the Torah when we heard shouts of discovery. The Torah scroll was immediately returned to the ark so that the Lithuanians would not force us to desecrate it. Four Lithuanian soldiers burst into the kloiz and one of them shouted, "We've caught you plotting a rebellion against the Germans to escape to Palestine!" Two

Lithuanians stood guard at the door while the other two approached and clubbed us left and right with their rifle-butts. After we were bloodied enough to satisfy them, they lined us up two-by-two. We understood that our next—and last—stop was going to be the Ninth Fort. Itche Moishe whispered to me, "Rebbi, is it permissible to recite *Viduy* on Shabbos?"

I whispered back, "If you die on Shabbos, you also say *Viduy* on Shabbos."

One of the Jews in the kloiz was Yerachmiel the porter, a big, solidly built man who usually could be found in the major shopping area of Kovno, on Meatmarket Street, where he earned his living carrying and delivering heavy packages for local businesses and their customers. As we were being led out of the kloiz, Yerachmiel said to us, "I will not let you be led from the kloiz to death. I will show the murderers that you don't put Jews to death because they are praying. This shames G-d and the name Jew. Do you hear me, Jews? When I move into action, run for it!"

With that Yerachmiel jumped on the Lithuanians and began hitting and punching them. A powerful man, he managed to keep all four Lithuanians busy while the rest of us fled. Late that night several of us returned, in great fear, and we collected Yerachmiel's remains. They had literally cut him to pieces. We buried him in the Jewish cemetery and put up a wooden marker that read: "Here lies holy Yerachmiel the porter."

Itche Moishe the shoemaker, the *gabbai* (synagogue official) in the Shoemakers' kloiz, also refused to be intimidated by the Germans or the Lithuanians. He continued going to synagogue to pray as usual in quest of his Divine reward for praying with a *minyan*.

Itche Moishe walked through the streets openly, his *tallis* bag under his arm, and the Germans arrested him. As they led him through the streets, Itche Moishe walked between his German captors not as if he were their prisoner, but as if they were his escorts on his way to perform a *mitzvah* (good deed).

Whoever saw Itche Moishe the shoemaker walking proudly and courageously through the streets between his German captors witnessed greatness and *kiddush HaShem*.

May the mention of these holy martyrs bring blessing to their souls.

◆ ◆ ◆

One startling occurrence about which Jews in Lithuania spoke for a long time was the martyrdom of the *gaon* and *tzaddik* Rav Elchonon Wasserman, along with other rabbis and yeshiva students in the

Ninth Fort on 11 Tamuz, Sunday the 6th of July 1941.

Let me pause to tell you about one of the Torah giants of Poneru Street during this period of German terror, a man who was one of the great personalities of the Jewish people.

Rav Wasserman was born in 1875 in Birzh, Lithuania. His parents later moved to Boisk in Latvia, which is why he became known in the yeshiva world as *der Boisker*, earning a reputation as a young *iluy* and *tzaddik*. He studied intensively in Telz for several years and then in Brisk under the great rabbi Rav Chaim Soloveitchik. In 1899 he married the daughter of the sage, Rav Meir Atlas, the rabbi in Salant and later in Shavl.

In 1903, Rav Wasserman became a lecturer in Talmud at the yeshiva of Amtchislav. In 1907 he went to study in Radun under Rav Yisroel Meir HaKohen (Kagan), renowned as the author of *Chofetz Chayim*, an important and influential work on Jewish law. (In fact, Rav HaKohen's book attained such immense recognition that he soon became known by the name of his book—the Chofetz Chayim.)

In 1910, with the Chofetz Chayim's consent and blessing, Rav Wasserman accepted the position of *rosh* yeshiva in Brisk. During the war years, 1914-1918, when the fugitive students of the Chofetz Chayim's yeshiva were divided among several towns, Rav Wasserman was the rosh yeshiva for the Chofetz Chayim's students in Smilovitch. After the war, Rav Wasserman founded and headed Yeshivas Ohel Torah in the little Lithuanian town of Baranovitch, where he taught hundreds of students from all over the world.

Rav Wasserman never wanted to be the rabbi of a community. Under no circumstance did he wish to undertake what he considered the yoke of the rabbinate, not even when the city of Shavl in 1926 offered him the very respectable rabbinate that his father-in-law had occupied for the previous two decades.

Rav Wasserman was the Chofetz Chayim's most prominent disciple and was considered

Rav Elchonon Wasserman

the second Chofetz Chayim. His noble personality traits and his lofty deeds; his unbending character, his caution, his alacrity, and fiery zeal; his simplicity, uprightness, and integrity reflected the life and effect of the Chofetz Chayim.

Rav Wasserman's published works include *Kovetz Heoros*, elucidations on tractate *Yevomos*; the 3-volume theological *Ohel Torah*; the halachic *Divrei Soferim*; and *Kovetz Shiurim* on the *gemora*. He published many Torah and *mussar* articles in Torah journals, and many essays on current events in the Yiddish press. Two of his sons survived the Holocaust, the late Reb Dovid Wasserman who lived in New York, and the late Rav Simcha Wasserman, whose Torah-teaching led him from France to Los Angeles to Jerusalem, and a host of points in between.

◆ ◆ ◆ ◆

Let us return now to the makeshift yeshiva at the home of Rav Avrohom Grodzensky at 15 Poneru Street: Rav Elchonon Wasserman—his long, patriarchal, white beard framing his luminous, wise face; next to him sat Rav Yosef Chaim Zaks, an instructor of Talmud and a dean at Yeshiva Ohel Moshe in Slobodka; Rav Yisroel Yaakov Lubchansky, *mashgiach* of the Baranovitch Yeshiva; Rav Moshe Reiz, an instructor of Talmud at the Slonim Yeshiva; Rav Shabsy Vernakovsky, *mashgiach* of the Lomza Yeshiva; Rav Dovid Goder; Rav Yitzchok Geffen, a dean at Yeshiva Ohel Moshe; the present writer; and other rabbis and yeshiva students.

All around the assemblage the sanctity was noticeable; you could really see that the righteous were enjoying the glory of G-d's presence. Tragically, however, this new home for Torah lasted less than two weeks.

Late Sunday afternoon, 11 Tamuz, the 6th of July in 1941, was in effect a day of mourning, a Tisha B'Av (day commemorating the destruction of the two great temples in Jerusalem) for this tent of Torah, because thousands of Jews in Kovno, in Slobodka and throughout Lithuania had been arrested and tortured or murdered. We were sitting around a table in the backyard of Rav Grodzensky's house on this hot summer afternoon. Rav Wasserman was teaching the daily leaf of Talmud in tractate *Nidah*, and the sages and students present were immersed in the intricacies of a complex talmudic discussion.

It seems eminently appropriate that we should have been discussing laws of defilement at a time when the atmosphere around us was being so horrifyingly defiled. Suddenly the gate to the yard was pushed open, and in marched four Lithuanian Nazis.

Their shout was at first ignored because almost no one heard it. Certainly not the sages present, whose ears were attuned solely to the words of Torah.

When the Lithuanians noticed that the rabbis had not reacted to their shout, they drew their revolvers and fired off a few shots. This sent a tremor through the group of learners, and everyone rose to their feet.

The cynical laughter of the Lithuanians greeted their rising. One of the Lithuanians called out, "We know you were trying to organize a rebellion to go to Palestine. But we caught you. You won't get away with it."

Another Lithuanian ordered, "Line up and follow me!"

The rabbis and scholars stepped into line, but the Lithuanians rearranged their captives. They placed Rav Wasserman at the head of the line and next to him Rav Zaks and the other rabbis with the most patriarchal visages. I was placed last and managed to slip away.

As Rav Avrohom Grodzensky was then in bed with a foot ailment, they decided not to take him along. They wanted people who could walk, so that they could parade the Jewish leaders triumphantly.

While the Lithuanians made their plans, Rav Wasserman spoke to the arrestees. His voice retained its evenness, and his face displayed the same solemnity as always. He spoke as if he realized these were his last words. There was nothing personal in his words; he did not even ask to say farewell to his son Naftoli who was in bed inside with a broken leg (as was Rav Grodzensky. There were also women in the house, but the Lithuanians were only interested in the rabbis now, and so they didn't go inside the house.) He addressed everyone, *all of Jewry*:

"Heaven apparently considers us righteous people, for it wants us to atone with our bodies for Jewry as a whole. So we must repent now, on the spot. Time is short, the Ninth Fort is near. We must make up our minds that we truly wish to sanctify G-d. If we repent, we will thereby save the remaining Jews, our brothers and sisters, so that they will be able to carry on as the remnant of Jewry."

Rav Wasserman had returned to Lithuania in June of 1939 after visits to the United States and to England. His life since had been a series of harassments by the hostile Russians who were occupying Lithuania followed by the threat of death at the hands of invading Germans. It was apparent when he spoke that he was referring to our brethren in England and the United States.

He continued, "Let us walk with heads held high. Let no one think a thought that would disqualify his sacrifice. We are about to fulfill the greatest *mitzvah*—the *mitzvah* of *kiddush HaShem*. The fire that consumes our bodies is the fire that will rebuild the Jewish people."

The line of martyrs marched forward. Proudly, courageously, they walked on, about to atone with their own bodies for Jewry as a whole. These holy Jewish sages—may G-d avenge their blood—were killed that night in the Ninth Fort.

Women who were freed from the fort the next day related that over the clacking of the machine-guns they heard the piercing wails of the rabbis as they recited *Shema Yisroel*, the prayer that affirms G-d's existence, the last prayer said before dying.

· 6 ·

KOVNO'S JEWS ARE DRIVEN INTO THE GHETTO

June and July of 1941 contained the bloodiest terror in the long history of Lithuanian Jewry. In the course of those two months thousands of Jews were beaten, tortured and murdered. Day and night, men, women, and children were pulled out of their homes and out of stores, off the streets and out of synagogues, and they were savagely butchered. This was accompanied by large-scale looting and robbing. The Jewish communities of many Lithuanian towns were obliterated during the initial few months of the German invasion.

Nevertheless, despite the blood-letting, those two months were an idyll compared to what happened subsequently. Although Jews were murdered and robbed and their businesses looted during the first two months of the German occupation, the bloody terror was an unorganized pogrom carried out by our Lithuanian neighbors, rather than a systematic slaughter following the German plan.

During the first week of July, 1941, the Germans spread the word that they intended to restore order. The chaos and terror following the Russians' departure and the arrival of the Germans was to end. All of us knew that the Germans were orderly people. They openly declared, "We Germans consider you Jews our enemies. Therefore we will strip you of your rights and make you pariahs and slave laborers. You will work for us as for masters, and if you obey us nothing terrible will happen to you." Although we were skeptical, we had little

The Altestenrat (Council of Jewish Elders). Seated in the center is the chairman, Dr. Elchonon Elkes. After the ghetto was liquidated, Dr. Elkes was deported to Dachau where he died on July 25, 1944—just one week before the liberation of Kovno.

George Kadisch

Jews with the mandatory Star of David plainly visible on their outer clothing.

The Altestenrat building.

choice, because it had become evident that the Lithuanians would surely kill us, whereas it was still unclear whether the Germans would do so.

That's how the Germans spoke to the new Kovno leaders of the Council of Elders (*Ältestenrat*), a Jewish community council that the Germans told the Jews to appoint. At the time neither the Jews nor the Council suspected that the Council was to be nothing more than an instrument for carrying out the Germans' nefarious plans.

Almost no one was able or willing to believe that the Germans were capable of slaughtering a whole people, as they very nearly did. Jews believed and hoped—in the midst of the bloody Lithuanian terror—that despite all evidence to the contrary, the killing would stop. "It will have to come to an end," we said. "How long can such a blood-bath go on?" All the believing Jews prayed and sought Divine intercession. Among the Jews who believed in G-d, was a strong feeling that an irreversible decree had been issued, for which there was no recourse, no hope for a quick ending. Our sense was that the worst was yet to come, but that salvation would ultimately follow. We perceived our suffering as the birth pangs of redemption.

The period of chaotic and bloody street terror by mobs and Lithuanian Nazis *did* end. Here and there assaults and murders kept occurring but the widespread brutality of those first weeks tapered off, and the Jews slowly left their homes, timidly walking the streets of Kovno and Slobodka once again. The Lithuanians enthusiastically continued to help the Germans root out and kill Jews, as they had from the onset of the occupation, but in this new phase they worked under German orders. As we realized later, Germany's master plan for the destruction of all of Europe's Jews had begun to be put into effect in Lithuania.

For the Jews of Kovno it began, as it did everywhere in Europe under the German's murderous domination, with *Aussiedlung*.

Aussiedlung was the term the Germans created to mean resettlement. What it meant in practice was moving the Jews out of their hometowns and settling them in work camps and ghettos. Soon enough it came to mean taking them to extermination camps.

At the outset, as I recall, the term used was *Übersiedlung*, meaning transferring. In other words, the Germans merely transferred Jews to other dwelling areas. On July 10, 1941, Kovno's Jews received an edict from the German military commander of Kovno ordering all of Kovno's Jews to move into the suburb of Slobodka by August 15. The Jewish Council would be responsible for supervising the transfer. He

Moving into the ghetto: On July 11th an order was issued that between July 15 and August 15, 1941, all of Kovno's Jews were to move into a ghetto set up in Slobodka.

Entrance to the ghetto: The Kovno ghetto initially housed a population of almost 30,000.

The barrier in the ghetto.

also issued a decree that as of July 12 all Jews were to wear a yellow star of David patch on their clothing on the left side of their chest. The Jews were also given a curfew—no Jews could be on the streets after 8 p.m. or they would be put under arrest.

During this period two ghettos were created in Slobodka. Young Jewish men, forced laborers, built them, unaware of what they were putting together. The two ghettos in Slobodka were called the Big Ghetto and the Little Ghetto. Penned into the Big Ghetto were to be 27,500 Jews, and in the Little Ghetto, another 2,500 Jews. The two ghettos were connected by a long, high wooden bridge. The *Übersiedlung* into the ghetto was set to begin on the 15th of July 1941.

By this date Kovno's Jews had already registered with the Labor Bureau, the *Arbeitsamt*. The Germans were extremely efficient in compiling a registry of all the Jews by name. What the Germans didn't explain, of course, was that this was done so that they could efficiently murder us and ensure that no one escaped.

An electrified barbed-wire surrounded both ghettos, which were under strong guard by both German and Lithuanian soldiers stationed in two towers. A huge searchlight lit up the entire area surrounding the ghetto.

♦ ♦ ♦ ♦

The Jews left Kovno and entered the ghettos like, G-d forbid, animals going to the slaughter. And as they walked, their tormentors poked fun at them. Day after day, in rented or borrowed carts pulled by horses and filled with whatever could be carried, rich Jews and poor Jews, educated Jews and noneducated Jews, secular Jews and religious Jews all wound their way from Kovno over the Slobodka bridge into the Slobodka ghetto.

Even then, when we moved into the ghettos, many believed that G-d might yet take pity, that we might yet be saved. The Germans told us that it would be good for the Jews. They said that we would have our own government, that we would be among our own kind. They said we would be safe from Lithuanian gangs hunting Jews. The only requirement was that we work. Some Germans spoke earnestly, others sarcastically, but the unfortunate Jews latched onto every last straw of hope. "Maybe...perhaps...possibly...we will survive this difficult time. Maybe there will be nothing worse than hard labor."

That was how the Jews reacted. Very few sensed that a rope was being tightened around their necks.

Other edicts had been issued in Kovno making it impossible to stay there. Jews were forbidden to go on Kovno's sidewalks or use public

The Kovno Ghetto was divided into two parts, the Big Ghetto and the Little Ghetto. The two parts were linked by a wooden bridge that was heavily guarded by Germans and Lithuanians.

The bridge connecting the Big Ghetto to the Little Ghetto.

transportation or go into parks. At least in the ghetto they wouldn't be harassed by the local Lithuanians.

The two ghettos totaled only about 45,000 square yards. Thirty thousand people were moving to a place where only 8,000 had lived previously. Slobodka was poor compared to Kovno—many of the old wooden houses had no running water or sewage system. In order to make room for Kovno's Jews, the local Lithuanians were told to exchange their homes in Slobodka with the homes those being vacated by the Jews of Kovno, or else move into homes along Slobodka streets not included in the new border of the ghettos.

But there was still not enough room in the designated areas of the two ghettos for the 30,000 Jews who then lived in Kovno. Most of Slobodka's synagogues were therefore turned into living quarters. Every hole, every tiny nook, was grabbed and occupied. Whoever could afford it bought out the original occupants for a vast sum to gain larger living quarters.

Worst off were those without means who were unable to find themselves any shelter. They had to store their belongings with friends or acquaintances. Throughout the ghetto pieces of furniture, piles of sacks, and assorted household objects littered the streets—the property of poor Jews unable to find even an attic or a cellar in which to store their worldly goods.

On the initiative of Kovno's chief rabbi Avrohom DovBer Kahana-Shapiro, and with the help of a few others we made a concerted effort to save and transfer to Slobodka Torah-scrolls, sacred books, and other religious objects.

I managed to obtain a special permit from the Germans to move the Torah scrolls from Kovno's approximately 60 synagogues as well as volumes of Talmud and other works. We also transferred Rav Yitzchok Elchonon Spector's large library from the *Alte* (old) *Beis Midrash*. His personal set of Talmud with his original hand-written glosses on every

Kovno's Old Beis Hamidrosh, where Rav Yitzchok Elchonon Spector used to pray and where his library was kept.

page was of inestimable value. In addition, the library contained many priceless antique volumes of the works of early sages. We also transferred other books from the communal library. Everything was temporarily stored in the Agronomists' Synagogue inside the ghetto. I was appointed by the Jewish Council as custodian of the book archives. It became my duty to guard our precious treasures. And although I had a special permit to move the books, while doing so one day I was arrested by the Germans and jailed for a day. I was quickly released, but to this day I know neither why I was arrested nor why I was let go.

By the end of the first week of the *Übersiedlung*, the majority of the Jewish population had moved into the ghettos.

Behind the barbed wire, life quickly took on a "normal" pace with all its bitter contradictions. People lived for the moment. They had managed to escape catastrophe. So many Jews from Kovno had already been killed! Their only hope was that the next day would be better. Countless edicts were issued to confuse and frighten us. Every day we would ask each other, "What's the latest rumor? What's new today?"

The *Übersiedlung* of the Jews into the ghetto lasted until August 15th. Only 30 days were necessary for the entire Jewish population of Kovno to march away forever. Stumbling, falling, they made their way into the two connected ghettos in Slobodka, surrounded by a barbed-wire fence.

And so came to its end the history of Jewish Kovno, Rav Yitzchok Elchonon's Kovno, the city of Torah, of *yeshivos*, and of Jewish culture. The Jews were driven out. By the 15th of August, 1941, not one Jew was left in Kovno. Who knows if there will ever again be a Jewish Kovno? I suspect it is gone forever, for the post-Holocaust returnees are dry bones, small groups of Jews who cannot rebuild the Jewish Kovno that was.

There are still some Jewish monuments in Kovno: the Choir-Synagogue is still there, as are Hoizman's kloiz, put to use by my small post-war congregation, and some other buildings. But the vibrant community of yesteryear is gone forever.

· 7 ·

THE FIRST MONTHS IN THE GHETTO

The first months in the ghetto were difficult. We were afraid to stay inside and afraid to go out, but nonetheless there was a *minyan* every day at Halvoyas Hameis. After *davening* (praying), we would study for an hour or so. The Germans supplied the Jewish Council with food which was usually distributed through the work groups. Mostly it was a warm, watery black soup made of horse meat and other bones called *yushnik*, and bread. Occasionally we also received a little meat and sugar.

By the first weeks in August the Germans had told the Jews to choose a leader. A Jewish Council was assembled, headed by Dr. Elchanan Elkes, the former chief of internal diseases at the Kovno Jewish Hospital. The Jewish council was instructed to appoint a Jewish ghetto police force and supervise food distribution.

Despite our fears and the crowded conditions, we felt that at least the chaos of the Lithuanian mobs was in the past. Terrible things had happened to the Jews before; this too would pass.

But we were wrong. One horrible event that happened a short time after we had arrived in the ghetto occurred on August 27th, when the Germans captured stray dogs and cats, herded them into the Neier kloiz and shot them to death. Then they forced a number of Jews to rip apart a Torah scroll with their hands and use the sheets of parchment to cover the carcasses of the animals. Other Jews were compelled to watch.

Ghetto inmates reading an appeal for used clothing: "Jews, donate for the poor and for the naked the old winter clothing and shoes you no longer need! Do not stint! Give generously!"

Carrying an ailing person to the Ghetto Hospital.

Things soon got even worse. On September 19th, slave labor was imposed upon the Jews of Kovno. The Germans needed laborers to transform a small country airport into a modern military airport in Alexot, a suburb of Kovno. The majority of the slave laborers for the airport came from the two ghettos in Slobodka. Two shifts of 1,000 laborers had to be provided daily.

Day and night Jewish men dug channels, carried sacks of cement, mixed concrete, and so on. At the outset the Germans would take Jews for night work. "Taking" meant that a band of soldiers entered the ghetto, randomly grabbed the required number of Jews, and led them off to Alexot.

Eventually, the Jewish Council's Labor Bureau had to accept responsibility for providing the required number of workers for both shifts at the airport. The night shift usually replaced the Russian prisoners-of-war who worked all day and were driven back to their camp at night.

Among the captured Russians there were also Jews. By nearly supernatural effort some of them managed to get into the ghetto.

The work was extremely difficult. Sporadically I was forced to join those working out at the airport. Mixing the concrete was particularly laborious, for the Jews had to keep pace with the mixing machines. Dozens of wagonloads of cement would be delivered and had to be unloaded quickly. Iron and other heavy materials also had to be unloaded. To make it worse, the nights were cold and damp, and we had no shoes. In order to protect ourselves from frostbite, we would wrap our feet in any rags we found.

Hygiene was close to impossible. There was no soap. There was a constant shortage of water, and there was certainly no hot water. We all suffered from boils and lice.

The German officials who supervised the work made it even more intolerable. At every opportunity they verbally and physically abused the Jews. "You gorge yourselves on German bread!" they would say to the famished Jews. "So work, make yourselves useful!" They would also sneer contemptuously, "We are turning you into productive people!"

Often their insults were accompanied by beatings with clubs.

The "enough food" the Germans gave us was 100 grams (less than five ounces) of bread a day per person. Later they gave us a little *yushnik* as well.

One work rule forbade men from leaving their place of work even for a moment. This was to prevent us for looking through garbage heaps for scraps of food——we got barely enough to keep us alive and we had to struggle for food every day. One man sneaked away for a few minutes and went into the fields during the potato harvest to gather food for himself and his fellows. When the Germans caught him, they beat him so viciously that he lost his ability to speak or hear.

Even without beatings, several Jews collapsed every day as a result of the strenuous pace imposed by the Germans as they herded Jews to their workplace—forcing them to run miles—then working to exhaustion. The first to drop dead that way was a man named Shpieler, who collapsed on one of the first days of forced labor.

As if the forced labor were not enough, the Germans developed a brand-new idea to wear the Jews out. As they herded one shift of Jews back from their slave labor before daybreak, the armed guards cocked their rifles and ordered them to run. "Faster! Faster!" they screamed. And hundreds of Jews, after a night of heavy labor, would have to gallop downhill from the airport, over the Alexot bridge, to Council Square, which was the collection point from which the Jews were led back into the ghetto. It's no wonder that people collapsed.

The Germans used to boast that their goal was to turn the Jews into animals. I remember one German who used to say, "Perhaps some Jews will survive. But those who do will be two-legged beasts."

One way they went about this was by targeting Jewish leaders. The Germans ridiculed and harassed anyone with a beard as being filthy and carrying disease. Intimidated, bearded ghetto dwellers—even rabbis and scholars—removed their beards. Beards were seen by the Germans as identifying rabbis, who were hounded mercilessly or killed outright. To protect their lives they had to remove their beards. Only two men kept their "emulation of the Divine image." One was Rabbi Avrohom DovBer Kahana-Shapiro, because he was known by the Germans to be a rabbi and had nothing to gain by hiding in this way. The second was a *chosid* of *Chabad* (a follower of the chassidic sect that emphasizes the intellectual and emotional aspects of a person in serving G-d) named Rav Feivel Zusman, who managed to keep his beard until he was murdered in 1944.

To facilitate transportation of laborers, the Germans set up a camp near the airfield. One of the Jews confined to this camp asked me what to do about his beard since there was no implement there to remove it other than a razor blade, which Jews are forbidden to use. He come to me and asked if Jewish law permitted him to use the razor because of the danger to his life. I agreed that he could indeed shave with the razor.

The Germans issued many orders in the first month further constraining us. The ghetto was sealed and no one could leave. Under threat of death the Jews in the ghetto were ordered to give up all money, valuables, and animals. There were guards everywhere. People who had permission to leave for a work detail outside could not bring back any newspaper or any food. If they were caught smuggling food to their hungry families they would be beaten or shot. One man hid a piece of bread between his thighs, hoping to sneak it past the guards. He was caught when the Germans stripped him, tore apart his garments, and made a thorough body search. When they found the bit of dried bread, they kicked him repeatedly until he was left with permanent physical damage.

One night, a man died in his room. It was so cold that the people who shared his room couldn't eat outside, and if they didn't eat before going to their slave labor, they would surely die. So they were forced to eat in the presence of the corpse.

On October 3, 1941, a rumor reached the ghetto that all women without husbands were to be murdered. Many single women found men willing to marry them, and asked the rabbis to arrange for their Jewish marriages. Since the ghetto didn't have a *mikveh* (ritual bath), the rabbis weren't sure they could honor the requests of these unfortunate women. Would their lives be saved at the peril of *kareth* (being cut off from the Jewish people in this world and in the next)? But since these desperate women would marry in a civil ceremony if they could not have a Jewish marriage, which could lead to even more complications, the rabbis decided to bless these unions. This rumor turned out to be unfounded.

In their attempt to dehumanize the Jews, the Germans especially focused on the children. I cannot forget a scene I witnessed. A German soldier called a group of starving and weary children to him, and slowly cut up a potato and threw the pieces down in front of them, the way one throws food to hungry dogs. He wanted the Jewish children to squabble over a piece of potato. That killer was well aware that the children were starving and would be incapable of keeping themselves from falling all over the bits of raw potato.

After their work day, teenage boys used to gather in groups and I would study Torah with them. The evening immediately after I witnessed this revolting incident, I tried to clarify things to the youngsters. "The Germans are seeking to take away from us what they cannot conquer within us—the Divine image. Dear children," I begged them with tears in my eyes, "I know you are hungry. But remember,

Children going to study at the Tiferes Bachurim in the ghetto.

The Ghetto Police: The Jewish police force responsible for maintaining order in the Kovno Ghetto under the supervision of the Altestenrat. This police force helped some 250 armed Jewish fighters escape from the ghetto and join partisan units in the woods outside Kovno.

The Kovno Ghetto Children's Home.

we must show the murderers that we Jews, even when hunger wracks us, refuse to lower ourselves to their level."

One boy, Meir Abelow, the pale, reddish-blond son of the rabbi of Azeran, stood up, a serious expression on his face, and asked in a choked-up voice, "Rebbi, do you think that we are unaware of this? But what can we do if we're starving?" And he quoted the text of the Talmud in tractate *Baba Basra*, "Hunger is worse than the sword." (Meir, his mother, and his younger brother were later tragically murdered.) I had no answer for him.

I saw the sword of the angel of death hanging over us. How could I try to convince him, convince them all, that on their way to martyrdom we should not give up our Jewish faith.

Kovno Ghetto emblems and insignia.

· 8 ·

ROSH HASHANAH

During the Days of Awe—the period beginning with Rosh Hashanah and ending on Yom Kippur,—when Jews render their spiritual accounting to themselves and then stand before their Creator, *machzor* (holiday prayer book) in hand and prayer in their hearts, many of the prayers speak of recalling, of remembering. Yet there are many things that a person prefers not to recall, things he'd prefer to forget.

Suffering and pain are two things thought better forgotten. Subjects like ghettos are pushed out of mind. It is natural to avoid memories that evoke pain in order to be able to function well.

But it is irresponsible to escape some memories, particularly those of the awesome destruction of European Jewry that still shocks me—one who was there—but I must continue to tell what I witnessed.

At the end of August, in Elul 1941, we began preparations for our first Rosh Hashanah behind the ghetto's barbed wire. But where could we find room to pray and pour out our hearts before G-d? Slobodka's empty synagogues—the New kloiz, the Old Beis Hamidrosh, the Gemilas Chessed kloiz—were all outside the ghetto. Within the ghetto were the Katzovisha kloiz, Abba Yechezkel's kloiz, Halvoyas Hameis, and Poel Tzedek—all of which had been divided into living quarters for families. Because of the crowding, no person was allowed more than two square yards. Where could a *minyan* meet?

A committee was established to undertake the job of finding places where prayers could be held. I was a member of that committee. One day I was walking, absorbed in my thoughts while seeking an empty place—an attic or even a barn—that could be used for our holy purpose. I encountered Feivel Gapanovich, who greeted me cheerfully and announced the good news, "Rebbi, don't worry so much. I have a place for several dozen people."

"Where?"

"At my apartment."

"How—"

"I'll put my things out into the yard, and there will be room for Jews to pray."

Chayim Shaffer, too, made room for praying in a lumber storeroom. And in the ghetto hospital, room was made. We found competent people to lead the services, soaked *shofaros* (rams' horns blown on Rosh Hashanah) in vinegar, and found qualified people to blow them. We even prepared *kittels* (white shroud-like robes) and *machzorim* for each location.

The committee discussed with the Jewish work-command the possibility of freeing the prayer leaders and *shofar*-blowers from their slave-labors several days before Rosh Hashanah. That would enable them to conserve some energy for leading Jews in asking G-d for a year of salvation and redemption, and for a powerful blowing of the *shofar* so as to drive away Satan and his attacks on the Jewish people.

The Germans, not surprisingly, tried to disrupt our Holy Days. It seemed they wanted to deny us the opportunity of asking G-d for our lives on the day of annual judgment when it is decided "who will live and who will die."

They were as punctual as the calendar. It seemed as if they were aware of the Jewish laws regarding the day before Rosh Hashanah. As time went on, it became clear that they were well aware of all Jewish observances since we were especially harassed on holidays. As the Jews were preparing to walk to their respective places of prayer, the Germans went into action.

How can one forget that Sunday night, September 21, 1941, the eve of Rosh Hashanah 5702? Because it was Rosh Hashanah, only a small number of men showed up for slave labor. When the Germans discovered the shortage of manpower, they went on a Jew-hunt. Under the direction of a rather unimportant German soldier named Sergeant Neumann, soldiers entered the ghetto and ran through its streets, seizing Jews from their houses and synagogue. In those very synagogues Jews were beaten and shot to death.

Baum, the iron dealer from Linkeva Street, carrying his prayer book, was on his way to pray and was shot. After him fell Berel Mendelevitz, son of Rav Eliezer Salanter of Yurborger Street. He was carrying food to the ghetto hospital for Rochel Rochelsohn, who had lost a leg during the Slobodka pogrom of June 25th.

At the same time groups of Jews were returning to the ghetto from their German-assigned jobs. Sergeant Neumann greeted them at the entrance to the ghetto with derision, hastening them along with the cry, "Hurry up!"

While his men were hunting Jews, Neumann gave the order to fire on the returning workers. Killed were Meir Weiner and Binyomin Klugman, both of whom had just returned from their work at the mill. A woman who had returned with another brigade was killed too. Klugman was buried half alive in a garden next to the ghetto entrance. Seven Jews were killed that night.

That was our first Rosh Hashanah in the ghetto. Nevertheless, Jews prayed to G-d on this Rosh Hashanah with greater intensity than ever. The Germans could not extinguish their spirit.

Rabbi Oshry's ghetto identification papers.

· 9 ·

YOM KIPPUR

Nine days later on October 1st was the holy day of Yom Kippur, the Day of Atonement. No matter how far removed a Jew may be from Jewish observance all year, when Yom Kippur approaches, the way back to the synagogue and back to G-d to ask forgiveness, is remembered. The broken Jews of the ghetto wanted to seek G-d's forgiveness and beg G-d to remove the German scourge, salvage the surviving Jews of Lithuania and prevent their murder.

The Jews of the ghetto arranged places for public prayer as they had for Rosh Hashanah.

Dr. Zakharin, a non-observant Jew who was a director of the ghetto hospital, made room in the hospital for public prayer on Rosh Hashanah and on Yom Kippur. On the day before Yom Kippur 5702, the 30th of September 1941, he presented me with a set of serious problems.

A large number of the patients in the hospital wanted to fast on Yom Kippur. In Dr. Zakharin's medical opinion, it would be life-threatening for them to fast. He asked for my aid in convincing them to eat.

Despite the doctor's warning, these frail Jews insisted that they wished to join the rest of Jewry in fasting and praying that G-d show mercy on His people and redeem them from the German enemy. They did not doubt the danger fasting posed to their lives. They knew their weakened condition would surely worsen, since the food in the hospital, inadequate at all times, would certainly be insufficient to restore their strength after a fast. The 200 grams of bread and bit of horse-bone soup could not possibly provide for their recovery. Many would grow sicker.

Nevertheless, they insisted that G-d would help them survive the fast. The director wanted me, a rabbi, to explain that halachah did not allow a fast at such a time. He also told me that not only observant patients wanted to fast, but people who had never observed Judaism as well.

I was stunned. In my heart I said, "*Riboinoi-shel-olom*, (Ruler of the Universe) look down from Your Heavens and see Your Jewish people. Even at such a time of turmoil and anguish, Your spirit moves them and they believe firmly that the Eternal One of Jewry will never fail them, that the light of Jewry will never be put out. Even in the face of death they are ready to sacrifice their lives to sanctify You. They want to participate as much as they can in the continuity of the Jewish people by keeping Your commandments with all their heart, with all their soul, and with all their being."

I told Dr. Zakharin that I would first clarify to my own satisfaction that halachah did in fact require them not to fast, and then do everything in my power to influence them not to endanger their lives by an unnecessary fast.

I studied the matter and found that since it was the doctor's opinion that if the patients fasted on Yom Kippur they would be endangering their lives, halachah is incontrovertible: they were forbidden to fast.

I spoke to the patients about the great danger involved if they fasted and the seriousness of the ban they would be transgressing. Not only was there no act of righteousness involved but, on the contrary, it was a very great sin to transgress the Torah's commandment which said, "And he shall live by them," meaning that one should *not* die as a result of fulfilling the commandments. The patients listened and promised to heed the doctor's instructions.

One patient, however, who had always been non-religious, stubbornly insisted on fasting that year and refused to accept my explanation that in his weak condition it was imperative to eat. Regrettably, the man died the night after Yom Kippur. The other patients told me that he had wept throughout the entire day, apparently confessing the sins of his life in order to die a repentant Jew.

On Yom Kippur morning the Germans showed up earlier than usual to make sure the Jewish work brigades went to their slave labor. Fortunately, Jewish policemen who had been chosen by the Jewish Council had already gone everywhere prayer services were being held and warned that the men would immediately have to leave for the airport to work. "If not, Jordan threatens an *Akzion*." Fritz Jordan was the commandant of the Kovno ghetto; an *Akzion* ("Action") was the German word that meant a roundup and usually murder of Jews.

The Jews quickly put together the daily quota of 1,000 men, who were marched off under guard to the airport. In an *Akzion* just five days after Rosh Hashanah, a thousand Jews from the ghetto had been rounded up and led to the Ninth Fort where they were killed. Among them were Rav Nisson Mah-Yofiss, the rabbi of Panemun, a suburb of Kovno, and Rav Shlomo Mantzer, kashrus supervisor.

The German soldiers bombarded the laborers with insults and barbs. Some even killed a few Jews. Sweating, bloodied and weary from the difficult work, they were weakened further by their fasting and could barely remain on their feet. Silently many prayed, "*Riboinoi-shel-olom*, take pity and punish these evildoers! Rescue us from their hands!"

The Germans also entered the places of prayer and dragged people out, tearing at their *talleisim* and viciously beating the men as they herded them to the ghetto gate to join the labor brigades. These brokenhearted Jews were denied the solace of Yom Kippur prayers.

As soon as the Germans were gone, Jews who had hidden returned to their places of prayer and continued to pray to G-d for atonement and redemption.

· 10 ·

THE LIQUIDATION OF THE
LITTLE GHETTO

One of the most heart-rending chapters in the history of the destruction of the Jews of Lithuania is the German war against sick and hospitalized Jews.

What kind of war was this? How could the ill defend themselves?

However outrageous and incredible it may seem, the Germans— together with their Lithuanian helpers—did in fact wage such a war. They both seemed occupied by a simple concern: to make the Jews suffer more. Pleasure in the suffering of their victims was the goal of many of the pogroms and *Akzionen* against the Jews. The Germans toyed with the Jews: arresting them at will, freeing them at will, torturing them at will, even healing them at will—perhaps so that they could torture them further.

◆ ◆ ◆

Right after construction of the two ghettos was completed, the Germans issued an order to build a Jewish hospital in the ghetto. It was divided into two sections: one for patients with ordinary illnesses and one for those with contagious diseases such as typhus.

On October 4, 1941, the Shabbos after Yom Kippur, the Germans boarded up the doors to the hospital for contagious diseases. They forced Jews to pour gasoline over the building, then set it on fire with the patients inside. Approximately 60 Jews were incinerated, including many of the nurses and one physician, Dr. Davidovich. The cries that issued from that building must have rent the heavens. No one was allowed to enter. The fire burned throughout the day and the smoke could be seen everywhere in the two ghettos.

The Jews they had forced to douse the building and set it on fire were shot to death.

Standing outside were Germans and Lithuanians who made sure that not one of the suffering Jews inside escaped prevented the help-less ghetto Jews from entering the building.

◆ ◆ ◆ ◆

On that same day, the Jews of the Kovno ghetto discovered that the division of the ghetto into two sections had been part of a German plan to liquidate the Little Ghetto before the big one.

October 4th was a Shabbos. Early that morning some 50 German soldiers along with around 100 Lithuanian collaborators—far more than we usually saw, which we found terrifying—piled into the Little Ghetto and drove the people, without exception, out of their houses.

They chased people out of bed without even giving them the opportunity to dress. Into the streets they drove the old and weak, the children and women and men. Using their rifle butts as clubs, they struck people left and right. Blood gushed like water.

The Jews were chased into Sajungos Square, which had once been the horse market of Slobodka. There the Germans began to divide the Jews, similar to the way one sorts sheep for slaughter: "Right! Left!" Death! Life! Children were torn from their parents, parents from their children, husbands from wives, grooms from brides, brothers from sisters.

During the sorting, many of the victims produced a *Jordan Schein*, a certificate that had been issued on September 15th by Fritz Jordan, the commandant of the ghetto, which certified that a person was a skilled worker. Only 5,000 of these white cards were issued. The Jewish Council had had the terrible job of distributing these cards. Whoever had one was temporarily allowed to live. Nevertheless, if a German took a dislike to someone, he could send him to the "bad" side regardless. "Whatever the Germans felt like," is what the Jews said. Life or death was a matter of a German's whim. Naturally, people had fought ferociously for the *Jordan Scheins*, knowing that without one, his family's fate was sealed.

Most tragic was the fate of the 180 orphans of the Little Ghetto. These were the children of those who had been murdered during the first month of the German occupation, before the Jews had been rounded up and shut into the ghettos. These children had survived because the rest of the community, no matter how impoverished, had managed to feed and shelter them. The Jews feared that these orphans would be the first to be killed by the Germans, who valued only those who could labor for them. When the Jews in the Square saw those children "sorted" by themselves, a terrible wailing broke out, for they knew how those children's lives would end.

But no one begged for the children's lives. Because everyone knew there was no one to cry to, no one who would listen to our pleas. The Germans would pay no attention. They would only terrorize the Jews even more.

Nearly 1,500 Jews were taken to the Ninth Fort that day and shot to death. The 180 orphans were killed along with some of the nurses, teachers, and other adults who had protected and raised them.

The Jews left alive were driven across the wooden bridge into the Big Ghetto. They were not allowed to take even their paltry possessions with them.

The liquidation of the Little Ghetto was complete.

· 11 ·

HOW WE BUILT A *SUKKAH*

The Days of Awe were indeed awesome in the ghetto. And they were fearsome, too, because of the Germans. But the Jews are a stiff-necked people, and they continued to perform whatever *mitzvos* they could. In the Little Ghetto, immediately after Yom Kippur, a *sukkah*—a temporary home built to fulfill Leviticus 23:42—was built next to the residence of my Rebbi, the *gaon*, Rav Avrohom Grodzensky, spiritual dean of the Slobodka Yeshiva. But this *sukkah* was the exception, not the rule.

The problem of putting up a *sukkah* was a complex one that began to occupy our minds immediately after Rosh Hashanah. Where could we find room to build one? Where could we obtain the boards or the branches or poles used to roof a *sukkah*? And how could we build one unobtrusively so as not to run afoul of laws that forbade just about everything?

The Russians, during their occupation of Lithuania in 1940, had put up blocks of buildings outside the Kovno suburb of Slobodka to house laborers. When the Germans conquered Lithuania, they turned those buildings, many still incomplete, into ghetto housing. With the approach of the Sukkos holiday (Festival of Booths), ghetto prisoners set up a *sukkah* in the alleyway between two large buildings in Block C so that even in captivity they could fulfill this *mitzvah*. Hidden from passersby, there was some hope that the Germans would not notice it.

The boards that were used to build the *sukkah* had been taken from nearby workshops where Jews worked as slave laborers. In order to get a proper fit, it was necessary to shorten a number of the boards. Needless to say, the Jews did not have permission from the Germans to take those boards, and certainly not to trim them. Had they been caught, the people taking them would surely have been killed. But to fulfill this great *mitzvah* according to halachah, Jews risked their lives. The question was raised, "Is it permissible to fulfill the *mitzvah* of *sukkah* with raw materials stolen from the Germans?"

I replied that the Germans had not brought in their own lumber from Germany. All the wood in their possession had been stolen. In fact, Jews had been involved in every phase of the lumber business in Lithuania. Jews used to buy whole forests, and owned lumber mills that trimmed the logs into boards for export to all parts of the world. When the Germans invaded Lithuania they looted the lumber from either the local Jews or non-Jews. When the Germans looted the lumber, the owners no doubt gave up hope of it ever being returned. The Jewish owners certainly had given up after it became clear that the Germans were intent on killing them. Consequently, whoever took the lumber from the Germans to make the *sukkah*, took it after it had left the possession of the original owner who had no doubt forgotten that the lumber ever existed.

I therefore ruled that it was perfectly permissible to take the lumber in the first place. Thank G-d, many Jews fulfilled the *mitzvah* of *sukkah* according to halachah.

The Germans never did realize what we were up to. While they carried out their *Estland Akzion*—a roundup of Jews to be sent to Estonia—80-year-old Reb Zalman der Blinder (the blind Reb Zalman), hid in this communal *sukkah* and was saved. The Germans looked through the barracks, but did not look for Jews inside the *sukkah*.

◆ ◆ ◆ ◆

Two years later in 5703 (1943) as Sukkos, the Yom Tov of rejoicing, drew near, we were growing ever more despondent. We cried out to G-d, "How will we be able to fulfill the commandments of these holidays in the ghetto? Will the Germans allow us to put up a *sukkah*? Will a miracle take place and will we find an *esrog* (citron) and a *lulav* (palm branch) to fulfill the *mitzvah* of taking the four species as commanded by the Torah?"

When the holiday of Sukkos arrived, our faces carried solemn, pained expressions instead of joy. We were especially disheartened because we did not know if we would ever again get the chance to fulfill the beautiful *mitzvah* of the four species.

Suddenly a rumor spread through the ghetto that a Jew had just arrived from Vilna with a perfect set of the four species. Impossible! But true. When the Germans took over the factories in Vilna and in Kovno, they needed Jews who were experts on the machines and appointed them supervisors. From time to time there were mechanical breakdowns, and the Germans would send these experts from Vilna to Kovno or from Kovno to Vilna. These experts were guarded by Germans, whom it was sometimes possible to bribe to look aside and ignore what they might be carrying with them. More than once these specialists carried out vital missions for the underground in Kovno or Vilna.

A Jewish machine expert had just arrived from Vilna and had brought with him a rare *esrog* so that the Jews in the ghetto could fulfill the *mitzvah* of the four species. Needless to say, our joy was great. But there was a catch; that year the first day of Sukkos was Shabbos—the one day on which it is forbidden to take the four species in hand. By German order, this machine expert had to return to Vilna immediately after the Sabbath. When the Jews realized that despite the danger and sacrifice that went into getting the *esrog* into the ghetto, it would still be impossible for them to fulfill the *mitzvah*, their anguish was very great at having the *mitzvah* stolen from underneath their noses. Their joy disappeared and left gloom in its wake.

And then the question was raised, "Might there not be some way to permit taking the *lulav* and the *esrog* on the first day of Sukkos even though it was Shabbos?"

I analyzed the situation and studied why the Sages had forbidden taking a *lulav* in hand on Shabbos. I considered that for the ghetto prisoners this Shabbos might be their last opportunity to fulfill the *mitzvah*, for who knew if he would remain alive to fulfill that *mitzvah* again. It seemed that we could rely on the opinion of some of the earliest Sages, who said that if one had taken a *lulav* on Shabbos he *did* fulfill the *mitzvah*. In our circumstances, I could not say that a person who took the *lulav* was acting against the wishes of those Sages who originally forbade it.

I was not inclined to rule that one should or should not take the *lulav* and *esrog* on that Shabbos. But because I did not specify the contrary, the Jews understood that the decision was up to them. As a result, many people rushed over to where the machine expert was staying and fulfilled the *mitzvah* of *lulav* and recited the *shehecheyonu*[3] blessing. Their eyes gushed with bittersweet tears at this opportunity to fulfill the *mitzvah*—bitter because they were afraid that this might

---

[3] A blessing said when experiencing new things. It thanks G-d for "granting us life and sustenance, and allowing us to reach this occasion."

be the last time that they would hold a *lulav* in their hands, yet sweet because they were able to fulfill the *mitzvah*.

Happiest were the yeshiva students and other *bnei* Torah (students of the Torah). A *chosid* of Lubavitch, Reb Feivel Zusman—may G-d avenge him—said to me, "I am fulfilling this *mitzvah* without asking any questions. I am ready to suffer in *gehinnom* (hell) for fulfilling this *mitzvah*. All my life I spent large sums of money in order to purchase a perfect *esrog*, and now I am confident that this *mitzvah* that I perform before my death will stand me in merit when I come before the heavenly court."

Rav Avrohom Kahana-Shapiro, the rabbi of Kovno, was very ill at that time. Not only was he unable to fulfill the *mitzvah*, but because of his illness it was impossible even to discuss the dilemma with him. When he improved, I visited him and told him what had happened, discussing various aspects of the problem. He asked me how I had ruled. I said that I had left the question open. He responded without reservation it had been permissible for the ghetto dwellers to recite the blessing on the *esrog* because the decree of the Sages forbidding taking the four species was not applicable to our situation.

Some time later, while learning with my students at the Tiferes Bachurim group, I told them what Rav Shapiro had ruled, and they were thrilled to learn that they had truly fulfilled the *mitzvah* of *lulav*.

Aussiedlungsakzion (Resettlement Operation): Jews about to be deported from the Kovno Ghetto. In two such Akzionen in 1942, Jews were transferred from the Kovno Ghetto to concentration camps in Estonia.

· 12 ·

A DAY OF REST

I am often asked, "Was there no day in the ghetto—in Kovno or any-where else—not even a single day when the Germans didn't shoot, oppress, and murder? Is there no time when even murderers take a break?"

It seems that the Germans considered oppressing and murdering Jews work, and that they, just like any other worker, felt entitled to a day off. Sunday was their day off. Besides, they considered them-selves good Christians, even though cold-blooded murder did not seem to disturb their conscience.

Because the overseers were at rest, the slave laborers, too, had Sunday off. That is why on Sundays the ghetto synagogues and hous-es of study were packed with people. Jews prayed, studied, recited Psalms, and cried their hearts out. The rest of the week afforded most of them no such opportunity for prayer, nor even for crying. We spent the rest of the week surrounded by oppressors. We used the Sunday hours of respite to serve G-d. We never gave up our faith in G-d.

But not every Sunday was peaceful. On the 19th of October, 1941, German soldiers demanded 15 Jews who they said were needed for light work. The men weren't even required to be young and strong, but could be old and weak. Fifteen elderly men quickly volunteered, happy to be easing the load of the 1,000 men who did back-breaking labor at the airfield every day.

But as soon as the men stepped outside the ghetto walls, the

Germans forced them to run, beating them if they slowed down. The work for that day was to clean Gestapo toilets—without any equipment at all. Locked in the latrines all day without food or water, they were required to clean the German toilets with their bare hands.

I remember another Sunday when the rest the slave laborers looked forward to was disrupted. That was a Sunday after Sukkos in late October of 1941, when the first autumn rains fell on Kovno.

The rain poured down furiously, but that did not deter the Jews from gathering in synagogues and study chambers. It seemed to us that even the skies were bewailing our bitter situation. How could they not cry when so much innocent blood was being shed day in and day out?

That Sunday I went to pray in the Halvoyas Hameis kloiz. As I was standing and praying, pouring out my heart to my Creator expressing my anguish and the misery of Jewry as a whole, pandemonium broke out in the kloiz. There I was, standing with my *tefillin* wrapped around my arm and head, when shots rang out and Jews began to run.

To me it seemed insignificant. We knew that no *Akzionen* took place on Sunday. So I continued to pray. Perhaps it was simply that some of us had become inured to the shooting.

As many of the Jews in the synagogue ran away, they paused to try and convince me to run, too. But I wasn't afraid—I don't know why. Perhaps it was the merit of the *mitzvos* I was performing. I was in the middle of reciting *Shema* and did not wish to be interrupted. I wanted to complete the prayers this morning, at least through *Shemoneh Esray* (silent prayer of 19 blessings recited three times every day). But the confusion and noise grew greater, and I heard shouts in German from the next house. "Get out of here!" They must be rounding up Jews!

I swiftly removed my *tefillin* and hid them inside my clothing. By then it was too late for me to escape. I was arrested together with many other Jews.

The arrestees were lined up four abreast and led in the direction of the ghetto gate. In the same row with me were Rabbi Moshe Skaruta, one of the Rabbis of Slobodka, Avrohom Baron the teacher of the *cheder* (yeshiva for younger boys) until he was killed later that month, and Hirschel Cohen. We were some of the last surviving former students of the Slobodka Yeshiva in the ghetto.

At the ghetto gate we joined other Jews who had been arrested, some 200 in all, then we were ordered to march out of the ghetto.

The fear that fell upon us was overwhelming. We knew what

rounding up Jews and leading them out of the ghetto meant. No Jew was allowed to step out of the ghetto unless he was being led. And when Jews were led, it was either to work or to death.

We realized that we were not being led to work. Where could they be taking us if not to the Ninth Fort or somewhere else in order to murder us?

Many of the Jews, fearing that this was our final march, our last few minutes of life, began reciting *Viduy*.

Nevertheless, others still had hope. They prayed that since it was Sunday, these "devout" Christians would not execute us. Perhaps they were only playing some kind of game to frighten us out of our wits. Perhaps the Germans imagined that we had been enjoying our rest too much this Sunday?

As they were leading us to Yurborg Street, the way to the Ninth Fort, I became convinced that they were taking us to the Ninth Fort where they shoot Jews.

But we crossed Yurborg Street, and they led us not to the Ninth Fort, but in a different direction, toward Red Yard Street in Slobodka and the Petrikos furniture factory. There we discovered that the Germans had devised a new game.

The first Jews to arrive at the factory yard came out with chairs on their heads. Each man carried two chairs. The chairs were sort of worn on each man's head, with the legs of the chair held with his hands.

The new arrivals wondered what this signified.

Peretzka, a Slobodka porter, called out, "I can carry chairs under my arms. I've already carried heavier loads. Why should I carry them on my head?"

The German in charge yelled back angrily, "That is the order! Carry the chairs on your head! Whoever does it any other way will be shot!"

So, with the chairs on our heads, we were driven toward Kovno. We crossed the bridge that connects Slobodka to Kovno. As we walked through Laisvas Allée, one of Kovno's main thoroughfare, passersby looked at us as if we were escapees from a madhouse. At first they did not catch on that we were Jews. But after they saw the yellow stars on the front and back of our jackets, and when we heard people say, "They are only Jews!" they seemed pleased.

When we arrived at Kovno's main post office, high-ranking German officers awaited. They were accompanied by civilians with cameras who photographed us with the chairs capping our heads.

After our photography session we were paraded through Kovno

this way, until we arrived at the military barracks in Shantz, a suburb of Kovno. Then we were ordered to set down the chairs without clatter. The Germans beat anyone who did not carry out the order. Then we were marched through Kovno's side streets and then back over the bridge to the ghetto. Whoever did not march quickly enough was beaten. By the gates of the ghetto they counted us once more. Thank G-d, no one was missing!

This was a day of "rest," a day on which Jews were neither butchered nor murdered. We suffered only insults, denigration, beating, and fear of death. But we were still alive. And as long as there is life there is hope of salvation.

That's what a day of rest was like in the Kovno ghetto.

· 13 ·

"BLACK DAY"

Our life in the Kovno ghetto was an existence of the living dead. Every one knew that we could not last long, not without a few miracles. If the forced labor or oppression or hunger didn't kill us, then it was certain that we would be shot to death.

None of us imagined we could survive these troubles and anguish. In the ghetto there was a morbid way of expressing this sentiment: "We are all dead men on furlough."

When speaking about someone who had gone to where people do not return from, the morbid extension of the above remark was, "I suppose his furlough expired."

Morbid humor was rife. In the very worst of times, Jews told each other "jokes" that pithily expressed the horrible situation they were in, living with the expectation of death, yet juggling hope with it. No one knew when his turn would come. People never knew if they would see each other again, so every day we said farewell with "*Auf Wiedersehn in yenner velt* (See you in the next world)."

For one man, there was not much hope. A much respected member of the community, he came to me one night to say he felt he couldn't bear to see his wife, children, and grandchildren put to death before his eyes. He felt certain it would kill him to witness their horrible suffering, and asked if he might be allowed to commit suicide first. In this way, he would also be able to be buried with dignity in the Jewish cemetery instead of being thrown into some pit.

Although I appreciated his suffering, I could not permit his suicide. Doing so meant surrendering to the enemy. Germans often asked Jews why they didn't kill themselves. We replied that no matter what, we trusted that G-d would save us. I am proud that in the three years of the Kovno ghetto, there were only three cases of suicide.

◆ ◆ ◆ ◆

Every evening I would meet with a group to study Talmud at the home of the tailor Yaakov Gapanovitch on 7 Vitenu Street. The men who usually attended usually included Leiba Inteligatter, Mordechai Yoffe, Naftoli Weintraub, Wolfovitz, Gutman, Eliasha, Alperovitz, Garfinkel, Ozinsky, and Mehlman. (I can't remember everyone's full name.) Before our actual learning began, we generally discussed the news of the day: How many people were shot and buried alive today at the Ninth Fort? How much longer was the ghetto going to last?

From time to time we would recall our relatives overseas and discuss what they might be doing to help us. I remember old Wolfovitz of Gorztd saying, "Listen, Rebbi, I'm sure help is on its way. My son in America, together with other Jews, has left his home and is now protesting in Washington near the White House. Day and night they are protesting and demanding that the government save their parents and brothers and sisters."

Naftoli Weintraub challenged his assumptions, and Wolfovitz became angry, "How could it be otherwise? I am certain that all the Jews of America are in Washington." He said this with absolute trust, as if he had seen it with his own eyes. He was so sure that help was on its way.

Wolfovitz and many like him were certain that the American *landsmannschaften* (organizations of people from the same cities and locales) discussed only one subject at their meetings—how to save their relatives in Europe. No doubt national Jewish American organizations with their connections in the American government were pulling every string to save them. Every evening before our study the same theme would be repeated. And with that hope, Wolfovitz and uncounted others went to their deaths. May G-d avenge them.

◆ ◆ ◆ ◆

We felt that it would not be long before a mass *Akzion* would take place. In September and October of 1941 alone the people in the Little Ghetto had been murdered, another thousand people had been rounded up and killed, and the hospital—with patients inside—had been burned down. The feeling—more accurately, the premonition—that the Germans would soon begin a mass murder of Jews in Kovno, as we heard they had done in so many other places, turned out to be a correct one.

The terrible, fearsome day of mass murder finally arrived. Those Kovno Jews who survived that day will never forget it.

On October 27, 1941 the Gestapo issued a new order: All of us living in the Kovno ghetto had to present ourselves at Democracy Plaza on the morning of October 28th. We were warned that whoever remained at home would be shot.

The day before, Sunday, October 26th, at about 11 p.m., the members of the Jewish Council, who received the order first, went to Rav Avrohom DovBer Kahana-Shapiro, the chief rabbi of Kovno. They had decided to ask him whether they were permitted by Jewish law to post the notice ordering the Jews to assemble at Democracy Plaza on October 28th. They sensed the great danger that lurked behind the notice and felt that by posting it they would share responsibility for the killings that were almost sure to follow.

The rabbi grasped the situation. Although he was broken by his suffering and physically ill, he spent all night researching the issue, poring over his *seforim*. When the men of the Jewish Council returned in the early hours of the 27th, the rabbi kept them waiting several hours until he had completed formulating his response.

That morning I happened to come in to visit the Rav rather early and found him sitting up, absorbed in section 157 of *Yoreh Deiah*, which deals with forbidden and permitted things in halachah, the table piled high with reference works. His whole body was trembling, and his wife had brought drops of valerian for him.

The rabbi directed me to the great 12th-century scholar Maimonides and his ruling on martyrdom, and remarked, "I am asked such a question once in a lifetime." He showed me discussions of several similar situations in halachic literature. But he patiently kept on looking through the sources, citations, and responsa, despite the fact that his own life might be at stake if he displeased the Germans, for the Gestapo had tried to ensnare him more than once. In fact, during the major *Akzion* that followed, he was saved only by a miracle.

Finally at 11 a.m. he spoke to the anxious leaders. He said he had found similar dilemmas that had faced the Jewish people before. "If a decree is issued that a Jewish community be destroyed, and a possibility exists to save some part of this community, the leaders are obligated to take every possible measure to save as many as can be saved." He directed them to post the notice.

The "Black Day" for Kovno Jewry—as the survivors still call it—was October 28, 1941. On the Jewish calendar it was 7 Cheshvan 5702.

The Gestapo order required everyone to show up at Democracy Plaza—young and old, sick and well, children, men, and women. We were instructed to leave our doors unlocked so that the Germans could search for people who hadn't gone to the square. Before day-break, the 26,500 ghetto dwellers began to walk to Democracy Plaza.

It was a harsh autumn day, cold and damp with a sprinkling of snow on the streets. The weather reflected our mood. We felt that an end was near for everything. We felt like saying to the sky, "Cloud over more. Get blacker and darker. Cast darkness upon the world, because day is gone from us. Let there be darkness!"

It seemed that nature around us was mourning and weeping with us.

This movement of the entire ghetto population looked like a procession of shadows. Most of the ghetto inhabitants no longer resembled living humans, but rather looked like shadows of humans.

Each time we saw a Jewish child in a carriage, every time we saw a sick person being carried to the square, our terror increased. We knew how quickly the Germans murdered those not strong enough to work on their behalf. We prayed, "Ruler of the world, *Riboinoi-shel-Olom*, save at least these innocents who have never sinned!"

When we arrived at the square, it was still pitch-dark, and we had to stand in suspense a few hours.

At exactly 8 a.m., when the nearly 26,500 Jews were assembled, Helmut Rauca, commandant of the Gestapo security police in Kovno, went to work. He was accompanied by his gang of German soldiers and many Lithuanian Nazis.

On the hills surrounding the ghetto, on both banks of the Viliya River, an enormous crowd of Lithuanians had gathered to watch the spectacle.

Rauca personally began selecting Jews, ordering people to the right and to the left, which meant to death or to life. We weren't immediately sure which side was which, but we knew one side mean immediate death and the other meant we would be allowed to work a while longer.

Rauca did his work calmly, systematically, and cold-bloodedly. He was unaffected by the heart-rending cries as he split up families. At times he walked over to individuals or to families. At times they filed past and he sorted them.

The Jews had been told to gather in family groups according to their work units. Each man had his wife and children with him. Rauca relentlessly went on sorting: "Right" and "Left."

This time "Right" meant to death, and "Left" meant to remain alive temporarily. A tragic illustration of this was the instance of Mrs. Doba Kissinsky, the daughter of Reb Chonon Gurevitch, a wealthy *talmid chochom* (Torah scholar). When she and her child passed by Rauca, he asked her where her husband was. She replied, "At the Seventh Fort," meaning that he had been killed. Rauca pointed his finger to the right. She, thinking that "Right" surely meant life, thanked him and headed toward the right, where the Lithuanians drove her to her death with the others.

As Rauca went about his business, sorting people the way one sorts animals for the slaughter, after a while he even paused to eat. The famished children looked on as he wolfed down buttered rolls.

The work went on. With food still in his mouth, he indicated "Right" and "Left," separating wives from husbands, mothers from children, fathers from sons, brothers from sisters.

After his breakfast, Rauca lit up a cigar and continued his morbid sorting.

We stood there all day as the selections dragged on. It took so long and we were all so frightened and exhausted waiting for our sentence that some older people couldn't take the wait and died. When Rauca finished that evening, the Jews who had been designated to the left side were allowed to remain in the Big Ghetto. They were to continue as laborers. Those who had been designated to die were driven into the area where the Little Ghetto had been.

We walked back to our homes bereft. We knew what would happen to those who had been selected. And everyone had someone, a friend or relative, who had been selected.

Not everyone understood which was the "good" side, and which the "bad" side. In the confusion many Jews ran over from the "good" side to the "bad" one.

Early next morning, as the Jews in the Little Ghetto were being marched toward the Ninth Fort and certain death, Dr. Elchonon Elkes, the chairman of the Jewish Council, arrived with a permit from the Germans to remove 100 people. As soon as Jews heard what he was there for, he was surrounded. "Dr. Elkes, save my child!" "My mother!" "My father!" they begged, grabbing at him. The noise grew so loud that a Lithuanian guard clubbed Dr. Elkes over the head with his rifle butt, and the doctor fell to the ground unconscious. The Jewish policemen standing by managed to carry Dr. Elkes back into the Big Ghetto.

Jews being herded to the Ninth Fort on the morning after the "Black Day."

Afterwards, the Germans continued marching the condemned Jews from the Little Ghetto to the Ninth Fort. They walked down Poneru Street. Whoever was too weary to march was shot on the spot. People were also brutally beaten to keep them moving.

Many Jews stood and watched for hours as these Jews were driven to their deaths, but we were powerless to do anything.

While they were being marched, one mother made a valiant effort to save her baby. She tried to toss her child over the barbed-wire fence into the Big Ghetto. But she didn't have enough strength, and the baby got caught on the barbed wire and began to cry. A German soldier heard the infant and immediately pulled out his gun and shot it to death.

Ten thousand Jews were selected to be murdered on Black Day, including Rav Mordechai Krimer, rabbi of Sosei Barg. That morning 26,500 people had gathered at Democracy Square, and only 16,500 returned to the ghetto that night.

From all those led to the Ninth Fort, only one little boy managed to escape, and he reported what had been done to the Jews there.

He told us that at the Ninth Fort, the 10,000 Jews were ordered to strip naked. Any jewelry they wore was confiscated. They were pushed into ditches that had been specially dug, then soldiers aimed their machine guns and shot at them.

When they were lying in the ditches—whether still alive or not—the Germans and their Lithuanian helpers covered them with lime and earth. The corpses were later exhumed and burned.

The day after this terrifying *Akzion*, Bertshik the glazier came to me with the complaint, "Rebbi, is there no obligation to study Torah

*Abba Yechezkel's Kloiz, where Rabbi Oshry organized his Tiferes Bachurim shiurim.
It was used as a prison for ghetto Jews after the infamous "Black Day" Akzion.*

before one dies? All along we have been studying, and now—no more?" I assured him that we would continue our studies in the Halvoyas Hameis kloiz. Unfortunately in only a few weeks the boundaries of the ghetto were changed and the ghetto was made smaller. This kloiz and the Katzovisha kloiz and Poel Tzedek were all designated as outside the ghetto while the Abba Yechezkel kloiz was turned into a jail.

I was very deeply impressed by Bertshik's "complaint," and I began studying *Ein Yaakov* (a collection of legends from the Talmud, published in the 16th century) with the people; Talmud study required more concentration than the people could manage, for their minds were preoccupied with their daily travails and their constant fear of death. Some weeks after the terrible *Akzion*, when those terrifying incidents had assumed the character of normal living, Rav Moshe Skaruta, one of the chief rabbis of Slobodka and the son-in-law of Rabbi Moshe Mordechai Epstein, dean of the Slobodka yeshiva, began teaching a daily Talmud course.

◆ ◆ ◆

Helmut Rauca survived the war and moved to Toronto, Canada, where he was discovered in 1982. He was extradited to Germany where he died on October 29, 1983, 42 years after the Black Day of the Kovno ghetto.

· 14 ·

KOVNO—SLAUGHTERHOUSE
FOR GERMAN JEWS

Much has been written about Auschwitz, Maidanek, Treblinka, Dachau, and Buchenwald. Very few people know about the "Lithuanian Auschwitz," which was the Ninth Fort near Kovno, where the Germans systematically murdered Jews.

Not only were Lithuanian Jews murdered at the Ninth Fort—Jews from other lands as well were transported there to be killed. In particular, they were brought from Germany, Austria, and Czechoslovakia. Not far from Slobodka, and only a short distance from Kovno, they were martyred for being Jews.

The Ninth Fort was used for the murder of Jews until August 1944, when the Russian army liberated Kovno.

Typically when Jews arrived at the Ninth Fort, they were forced to undress. They then were told to run naked into trenches where the Germans mowed them down with machine guns.

Many were buried alive or put to death in even more savage ways. From the beginning of the German occupation, the Jews were taken to the Ninth Fort. When people were taken there, we knew it would be their end.

It was a Tuesday evening—I recall it as if it were yesterday. From the other side of the ghetto fence we suddenly heard people screaming and shouting in German, and soon after we heard moaning and groaning. Imprecations and curses, orders and shouts in the German language were no surprise to us; we had gotten used to hearing German around us. But victims screaming and moaning in German? Germans being beaten? This was very strange.

We went to the ghetto entrance, and looked through the fence. What we beheld was appalling. Men from the *Schutzstaffel*, or as it was known, the SS, were herding men, women, and children. Old and ill people were being transported in trucks. As the Jews were driven away, we could hear weeping, and in German, "Where is the Jewish ghetto?"

We immediately understood that these were German Jews.

That night when the Jewish ghetto policemen who had been outside the ghetto returned, they confirmed that Jews were being brought in from abroad to be killed at the Ninth Fort. The Jews we had seen, the policemen reported, were primarily German and Austrian Jews. The Jewish policemen had spoken with them, and were told that they were from Frankfurt, Vienna, Berlin, Hamburg, Breslau, Prague, and from a host of towns and villages in Austria, Germany, Czechoslovakia, and France.

Our policemen reported that these Jews had not originally known where they were being taken. The Germans had told them that they were being taken to the Baltic countries for resettlement; that in Lithuania, Latvia, and Estonia they would lack for nothing. The Germans described a veritable Garden of Eden. They told the Jews to take along their possessions, whatever household goods they desired, even holy and secular books. The works they brought with them included antique books with Baron Rothschild's seal, and books from Frankfurt's Old Synagogue. Some of these were in Hoizman's kloiz in Kovno after the war. "Take whatever you want," the SS men told them, "because you will need it there."

Only upon arrival at the train station in Kovno did the Jews begin to realize that they had been deceived.

At first they couldn't comprehend why they were being told to leave their property at the train station. The Germans explained that they couldn't take anything with them because they were going to the ghetto temporarily. And the official emphasized the word "temporarily."

The Jews then sensed that something was not quite right. Why was everything being taken away from them? If they were going to the ghetto, wouldn't they need their things there?

German officials had, meanwhile, ordered the Jewish Council to make room in the ghetto for more Jews.

That would not have been a problem for us. We would gladly have made room to save Jews. Every one of us was ready to share barracks bed, clothing, and crust of bread in order to save another Jew's life.

But these Jews were not taken into the ghetto. They were led past it to the Ninth Fort, where thousands of Jews had been murdered. As was later determined through witnesses and other evidence, these Jews staged a revolt. When the corpses of those buried at the Ninth Fort were eventually exhumed for cremation, the Jews from abroad were found dressed while the others were naked. We discovered that approximately 40,000 Jews from other countries were machine-gunned to death in the Ninth Fort.

After our liberation I saw an inscription on the wall of the fort dated July 16, 1941 written in French, evidently by someone in a group of French Jews who had been brought there to be killed.

The Gestapo and SS men who had brought these Jews to Kovno divided up the money and the property that remained after the Jews were murdered.

Ghetto Jews were employed at sorting this property. One of them brought me a small *siddur* (prayer book) that had belonged to a Jew from Vienna who was killed in the Ninth Fort. I managed to save that *siddur*, and still possess it. It is a treasure I never intend to part with. Yaakov Kerbel was the name inscribed in the *siddur*. In the United States I met Viennese Jews who had known Yaakov Kerbel as an Orthodox teacher in Vienna, a straightforward man. May the mention of this martyr be a blessing.

The only possessions of these foreign Jews that the Germans did not inherit were storerooms of Jewish books that I came across after our liberation. Somehow the Germans, busy as they were with robbery and murder, did not destroy these holy books. Among them I found rare works dating back to the fifteenth century. That is all that remained of these victims of genocide.

· 15 ·

THE FIRST CHANUKAH

After October 28, 1941, the Black Day when 10,000 men and women and children were massacred at the Ninth Fort, Jews put even more effort into strengthening their trust in G-d Who would not forsake Jewry. Their prayers were recited with increased intensity and they studied Torah ever more seriously. With so many people gone from the ghetto, many questions were put to me. A man came to me, broken and bitter that his family was starving. He had not so much as a crust of bread. But a family living in the same house had been wiped out. He wanted to know if he could sell their little bit of property in order to feed his family. I reassured him that that family of martyrs would certainly be pleased that some of their property had been put to the use of Jews rather than having fallen into the hands of their murderers.

People were likewise allowed to wear the clothes of murdered Jews that came from the Ninth Fort. The pockets of many of these garments still contained letters, photographs and other items that identified their previous owners. We could only assume that those martyred souls would derive spiritual satisfaction that their suffering loved ones could wear their warm clothes.

At the Tiferes Bachurim class that I taught, I was asked, "Chanukah will soon be here. Where will we obtain candles to light for Chanukah?" I replied, "*HaShem* (G-d) will help, and we will fulfill the *mitzvah* of kindling the Chanukah lights."

In the house of study at Gapanovich the tailor's, I brought up the subject of Chanukah lights, and one of the Jews present remarked that he might be able to help. The next morning a woman approached me during prayers and said that she wished to discuss a private matter. She told me, "I have heard that there is concern about fulfilling the *mitzvah* of kindling Chanukah lights. Since I lost my husband and three daughters and their children in the great *Akzion*, I am alone. My husband used to go to work in the city, and he would take wax with him to trade for bread. Now that he's gone, there is no one to do that. Besides, I need nothing for myself. How much longer will I live? So I'll make wax candles for Chanukah for the souls of my husband and daughters and grandchildren who died as martyrs. I don't have much wax. I'll be able to make a single candle for each person for all the days. I'll bring them to the Tiferes Bachurim, so that the youngsters can distribute them to the other Jews before Chanukah. All I beg of you, is that when I die you say a *kaddish* (Praise of G-d recited in memory of a dead person) for me."

That was how we had candles to light that Chanukah. We recited the appropriate blessings before kindling them. And in our *Shemoneh Esray* prayers we begged G-d to repeat the miracle of "handing the defiled ones into the hands of the undefiled ones."

· 16 ·

How Jews Risked Their Lives
for the Jewish Book

Much has been recounted concerning Jewish martyrdom during the German occupation in Europe.

One might think, "I already know the tragic bottom line—six million Jews were martyred." However, repeating this tragic number does not tell anyone how these Jews died or—what is perhaps more significant—how they lived until they died. Death in the ghetto was not always heroic. Ghetto life was always traumatic, tense, and bitter. But in the spiritual sense extremely heroic. Jews grew accustomed to the notion that every life was under constant threat. Nevertheless, as long as Jews could still draw a breath, they did not wish to live without at least a spark of sanctity. The sacrifices that I saw regarding the Jewish attachment to Torah—the risks taken for spirituality, for the Jewish Book—I will never forget.

Jews have been accused of too much optimism, of too much faith in the decency of man. But it was during those difficult and tragic days, weeks, months, and years that the sanctity of the Jewish people could be witnessed.

The more I look back, and the more I explore what I witnessed during those awful years, the more clearly and sharply do I perceive the great light in the darkness, the light of the Book. Jews were somehow able to part with everything that defined their place in life—home, business, job—but the one thing they could not part with was the

Book.

Where does one find the words to describe the great *kiddush HaShem* for Jewish books? Because I played a role in the campaign for the Book in the Kovno ghetto, this battle remains forever engraved in my memory.

Weary, famished Jews whose lives had been darkened, Jews who literally did not have a piece of bread for their children, made the Book their last handhold. Religious Jews saw significance in their holy books and perceived profound meaning in the Torah-scrolls. And they made every possible effort to hide them from the Germans. With their final energies they struggled to prevent their oppressors from robbing them of their Torah study.

They accepted having everything else taken from them, but not the Book. When it came to fighting for a Torah scroll, to hiding a Torah scroll, the weakest Jew demonstrated that he was a vigorous hero. Jews came up with the most extraordinary ideas when it came to saving sacred books.

The most touching scenes in this great drama were the sacrifices brought by small children. They were no longer mere children but heroes. Many knew very little, but they were guided by their unconscious attraction to the holy. The sacred spark within them was constantly afire.

Let me put this in chronological perspective: After the Germans had perpetrated a large number of murderous *Akzionen* against the unfortunate ghetto Jews, they proceeded on February 18th, 1942, to carry out a new kind of *Akzion*—this one against the Jewish spirit—by robbing the Jew of his Book. What could have been the purpose of this *Akzion?* What did they want? They intended, first of all, to deprive him of his spiritual support, thus turning him into a beast so he would be unable to withstand them.

In the purely physical aspects of the confrontation, the Germans did, sad to say, succeed in attaining their purpose. Physically we were not able to resist. But the Jewish spirit never broke.

The battle to save Jewish spirituality had begun back on July 10, 1941, when the Germans issued their decree ordering the Jews of Kovno to move into the ghetto in Slobodka.

We removed the sacred volumes from Kovno's synagogues. Every day coaches and wagons moved the belongings of the Jews of Kovno to Slobodka. Their belongings were accompanied by the sacred books. Torah-scrolls we transported separately. The books were well-hidden in the hope that the enemy would not notice them.

When we had succeeded in transferring those vital and valuable works to the ghetto—where we naively believed we would survive the difficult times ahead—we thought we had saved our spiritual heritage.

The holiest and most precious items we hid in four side rooms in the Christian School of Art which was inside the ghetto bounds. I was the custodian of the archive and I found it difficult to treat these holy works with proper deference since there just wasn't enough space for them. But there wasn't any more that we could do.

I recall the artist Esther Lourie (who survived and settled in Israel) visiting and photographing the book storage area—we could not refer to it as a library because the Germans didn't think we "sub-humans" were entitled to a library.

We imagined these holy objects to be living human beings in hiding from the German devils.

◆ ◆ ◆ ◆

Unfortunately, we were not able to keep our book storage area for very long. A new order was issued: Clear out the rooms for workshops.

So we moved everything to a building on Varenu Street.

The religious articles that we kept in our semi-secret book repository included *tefillin* and *talleisim* as well as *siddurim* and *machzorim*. These, as well as sacred books for study purposes, were made available upon request to young and old.

I was there when we were visited by one Dr. Benkers, a representative of Hitler's notorious theoretician of anti-Semitism, Alfred Rosenberg. He came to visit the book storage unit accompanied by the SS commandant of the ghetto, the notorious Fritz Jordan, and some members of the Jewish Council.

"Who are you?" Jordan asked me.

"I am the custodian."

Jordan apparently wanted to show off for his guest. He asked me to show him the oldest book in the collection.

I showed him Buxtorf's *Concordance*, which had been printed some 300 years earlier. Then I showed him some other antique books.

I understood that they had not come simply to look at a library. Every visit by prominent Germans meant, we knew, a new decree.

"What," I wondered, "will they order now?"

I did not have long to wait for the answer. It came later that very day.

As soon as the Germans left the storage area, they convened the

Jewish Council and instructed them, "The book collection must be sealed off immediately. That valuable property must be preserved. The Germans, you know, are a people of culture, and we do not want these valuable books to get lost. Every book must immediately be counted so that not a single one gets lost."

This, like so many German orders, contained a threat: They added that the Jewish ghetto police had been ordered to guard the books, and thus were responsible for making sure that no book got lost.

◆ ◆ ◆ ◆

We decided to protect our holy books with no less and perhaps with greater determination than we protected our lives. The enemy was tampering with the eternity of the Jew, and the Jew was determined to defend himself.

When I think of the attitude of the German murderers to Jewish books, I am unable to forget a peculiar detail—the fear that some of the Germans showed.

Some of the murderers displayed an instinctive fear of Jewish books. True, they were a minority, yet we noticed such men—men for whom it was easier to snuff out a human life that to destroy a Jewish book.

Extraordinary is the power of the holy Jewish Book. It has a soul of its own and encompasses the illumination of generations—a benign light for those who study it; a blinding light for those who would harm it.

Even when the Germans decided to destroy our books, many of their men were afraid to carry out the order. That is one reason why we managed to salvage Jewish works.

But the main reason we were able to salvage Jewish books was the great self-sacrifice of the Jews themselves. Jews of all classes and strata displayed great self-sacrifice on behalf of Jewish books, even risking martyrdom to hide Torah-scrolls. Workmen—shoemakers, tailors, carpenters—were elevated by this battle to the highest level of sanctity.

Jewish children stood no lower. They sensed in this battle a deeper aspect—that it was a battle over Jewish eternity. The ghetto-Jew was inspired and purified and elevated to the loftiest heights.

When the Germans issued an order that all Jewish books must be delivered to them by February 28, 1942, they added in that same order that if a Jewish book were found in the possession of a Jew after this date, he would be punished. The Jews understood that the battle for the Jewish Book had been engaged. And they understood that this battle had to be waged seriously and comprehensively. The most important books had to be saved.

The hiding of the Jewish books began in earnest. The most difficult task was hiding Torah-scrolls, which are large and bulky. We had collected about 300 Torah-scrolls from Kovno's synagogues when we had moved into the ghetto. Our decision was clear: Not a single one could fall into the hands of the Germans. We must protect them even if we have to pay with our lives.

But how to do it? We understood that self-sacrifice alone would not suffice. We might sacrifice lives, we might die as martyrs, and the Torah-scrolls could still fall into German hands.

So we deliberated. We realized that the only way to hide the Torah-scrolls was to wall them up. But where could we wall them up in a place and a way that would not be noticed?

We chose Hirshel Lapiansky's barn on Linkeva Street. We figured that we could place the Torah-scrolls on the storage platform, and nail boards in place over them so that no one would figure out that anything was hidden there.

I will never forget those days of dedication when the Torah-scrolls were hidden. Jews worked with great hardship and sacrifice and holiness out of the sight of the Gestapo in order to save those Torah scrolls.

The same was true for hiding the printed holy books.

Young men and old men dug pits and hid volumes of the Talmud, of Maimonides' codes, of responsa works, and many other *seforim*. These people as well as others hid on their premises single volumes of Talmud or the Torah for personal study. I recall how much self-sacrifice Bertshik Bricker, whom we called Bertshik the glazier, used in hiding volumes of Talmud and other works.

I recall how, after the decree was issued, I asked my youngsters in the Tiferes Bachurim, "Where will we get volumes of the Torah and Talmud to study?"

The youngsters stood up and declared, "Don't worry, Rebbi, each of us will hide a *chumash* (volume of Torah) or a *gemora* to study from!" Tears came to my eyes when I heard that. I thought, "Master of the world, what a holy people we are! For hiding a Jewish book the penalty is death. Nevertheless, each of these boys has undertaken to put his life on the line in order to have a *chumash* or a *gemora* to study in!"

I told them how dangerous it was to hide Jewish books. To this they responded, "Rebbi, if they shoot us together with our *gemoros*, at least we'll be sanctifying G-d."

In the process of rescuing these holy Jewish books, we also orga-

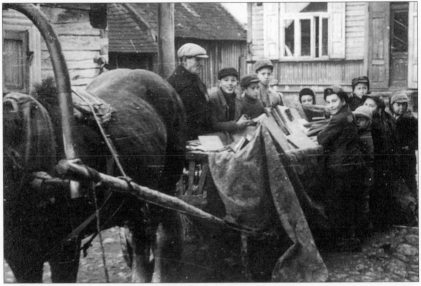

Germany's postwar plans included exhibits of Jewish books and ceremonial objects as "artifacts of the extinct Jewish race." To this end, the Germans ordered all Jewish books in the ghettos to be stored in warehouses. Here, ghetto children attempt to rescue books about to be carted off to the warehouse.

Rabbi Oshry holds his sefer Torah, the only Torah scroll to survive the Kovno Ghetto.

nized a special division whose function was to remove certain old books and antique objects. This was usually done while the books in the storage area were being loaded onto wagons or while they were being moved in wagons.

The holy Jewish books that the Germans received were transferred to their own library of anti-Semitism directed by Dr. Alfred Rosenberg, in Frankfurt, Germany. We also heard rumors that the books were made into paper.

The liquidation of the book storage unit was followed by the complete liquidation of Jewish spirituality. On August 26, 1942, they closed down the last schools, as the Jewish year was drawing to an end. We regarded the timing as deliberate, for the Germans were aware of the importance to us of Rosh Hashanah, of marking the new year on our calendar. Despite the decrees, the Jews prayed on that Rosh Hashanah and Yom Kippur with great passion—and in groups of 10 or more. We weak and oppressed Jews could not be robbed of our prayers.

◆ ◆ ◆ ◆

The walled-up Torah-scrolls were thus spared the indignity of becoming part of the Third Reich's proposed Museum of the Jews.

Later, when the ghetto was reduced, we had to move them once more. With great risk we moved them to Block C, where they were once more hidden. When the murderers liquidated the Kovno ghetto on July 13, 1944, they burned down the entire ghetto, including Block C where the scrolls were hidden.

Only one small Torah scroll, my personal one, survived, because I kept it with me wherever I went. This Torah scroll had been in my family for as long as I could remember. It is perhaps 150 years old. Whenever I thought it was in danger I would wrap it around my chest and it would be hidden beneath my clothing. That's how it survived all the years in the ghetto. I still have it today.

As to the holy books that were buried, a number of them were retrieved by survivors who were present when they were buried or who buried them themselves. Dug up after the liberation, these works were kept in Hoizman's kloiz in Kovno.

When I reopened Hoizman's kloiz after the liberation, only one Torah scroll was available—my own. Another was later brought from Vilna.

That is the story of the Battle for the Jewish book—for the Jewish spirit—as it was waged in the Kovno ghetto during the German occupation.

· 17 ·

PURIM

We managed to read *Megillas Esther* (the story of Esther) very early on Purim morning, before the ghetto Jews had to go off to their workplaces. The Germans came in some hours later to round up other Jews for slave labor. They beat them throughout the workday. One of the German taskmasters was a murderous sadist whom the Jews had nicknamed *"Die Oigele"* (The Eye) because he was always on the lookout for the slightest infraction of a rule and immediately beat the transgressor viciously.

Despite the best German efforts to make Purim joyless—including Germans shouting at Jews, "You will never have a Purim again!"—we sought ways to celebrate. After our *megillah* reading that morning, Gapanovich the tailor distributed some liquor, and we wished one another that we might live to see the downfall of our contemporary Haman and his Amalekites. At Chayim Shaffer's *minyan*, he handed out bits of sugar after *Shacharis*. Sugar was a rare commodity.

Jews even found a way to fulfill the *mitzvah* of *mishloach monos*, which is to give two portions of ready-to-eat food or drink to a friend on Purim day. We did this by swapping bread rations with one another, each giving his friend his portion of frozen bread. Some swapped their portions of the black horse bone soup with each other.

Many ghetto Jews even found a way to fulfill the *mitzvah* of *matonos loevyonim*, the obligation to give a gift of money to two paupers on Purim day. They took a piece of their bread ration and gave it to a fellow-Jew who was even hungrier than they were. And, under our breaths, as we worked, we sang *"Shoshanas Yaakov,"* a poem from the Purim liturgy set to music.

Jews who worked at digging pits at the airfield even managed to dance a Purim jig in the pits. One reminded others of the midrash that states that Purim will be fulfilled even when other Jewish holidays will not be kept. To this the others rejoined, "If only we could live to see that!"

· 18 ·

How We Baked Matzos

I have more than once related in previous chapters that, notwithstanding the horrible circumstances of ghetto life, the spark of Judaism was not extinguished; Jewish life continued.

When a Jewish holy day, a Yom Tov, arrived we invested our strength into creating a Yom Tov atmosphere, even though we knew that the German murderers would be reminding us of the Yom Tov through their special mistreatment of us, which they deliberately scheduled for the holidays in our calendar.

The murderers were as punctual as the calendar, particularly as Pesach (Passover) approached.

Our preparations for Pesach began immediately after Chanukah. That is when we began to make plans: seeking ways to obtain flour, searching for a place in which to bake the matzah, and trying to find where to obtain parts for the matzah making machine and how to bring them into the ghetto. We also had to hide the supplies and the equipment so that the Germans would not become aware of them. Then there was the matter of fuel. And all this we had to do while we were encaged behind barbed wire.

But a strong will overcomes everything. We put together a matzah-machine. At times we had not only one machine, but two, with two areas for baking matzah. The main problem was obtaining flour. We spoke with Jews who were in the "good" work brigades and asked them to try to smuggle flour into the ghetto.

In 1942 and 1943 there was flour for Pesach, and there was more or less matzah for everyone. The two baking areas turned out enough matzah between Rosh Chodesh (the beginning of the Hebrew month) of Nisan and Pesach to supply the ghetto Jews with matzah. The flour was, naturally, not all wheat flour but included unhusked grain. A *maos chitim* committee was established, which deducted a bit of flour from every person who baked matzah in order to provide a small amount of matzah for almost every Jew. *Maos chitim* means, literally, "money for wheat." This was customarily collected from residents of medieval Jewish communities. The flour acquired with that money was distributed to the needy so they could bake their own matzah for Pesach. In the Kovno ghetto, the contribution took the form of ready-baked matzah.

◆ ◆ ◆ ◆

Two weeks before Purim, a Lithuanian brought 30 pounds of flour for me and handed it over to Feivel Margoliyos at the ghetto entrance. Margoliyos gave me the flour. I found a note inside the flour that said it had been sent by Franas, a non-Jewish man who used to put out the lights in Abba Yechezkel's kloiz and who also used to light the heating ovens for the Jews in Slobodka during the winter. He asked me to share it for Passover with the rabbis and yeshiva students whom he knew from over the years when he used to come on Simchas Torah to enjoy good liquor with us. With this flour we baked matzah which we distributed among rabbis and yeshiva students.

While studying in Gapanovitch's *beis hamidrosh* on 15 Vitena Street, I was asked by some of the ghetto dwellers how they should deal with selling the *chometz* (leavened food forbidden on Pesach) that they, with great sacrifice, had managed to hide to still the hunger of their children. The problems were two:

One: Because there were almost no non-Jews within the ghetto walls, there was simply no one to sell the *chometz* to. Even if a gentile were to be found within the ghetto, it would be impossible to sell the *chometz* to him because of the dangers involved. Jews were forbidden to speak to non-Jews or to have any dealings with them. If we managed to find a gentile we risked that he could betray us and report the food to the Germans who would then exact blood for the great "sin" of owning food.

Two: If the *chometz* were not sold, was there a way of permitting it to be eaten after Pesach without transgressing the prohibition against eating *chometz* that was owned by a Jew during Pesach?

I ruled that the Sages' ban on *chometz* that remained unsold did not apply to the ghetto circumstances where selling was impossible. I told them that whoever owned any *chometz* should come before a *beis din* (Jewish court) of three men and, in accord with Jewish law, declare his *chometz* ownerless. The ex-owner would then put the *chometz* in a hidden place for the duration of the holiday. After Pesach, it would be permissible to eat this *chometz*.

Studying the laws of Pesach with my Tiferes Bachurim students in the period prior to Pesach, I was asked by them if there was some substitute or equivalent way to fulfill the rabbinical commandment to drink the four cups of wine required during the Pesach *seder*, the festive meal held on the first and second nights of Pesach (only on the first night in the Holy Land)—since no wine was available.

The famine was growing worse from day to day, and the only common drink available was tea sweetened with saccharin. And even that could be obtained only with great difficulty. Could one fulfill the commandment by drinking four cups of this saccharin-sweetened tea?

Since in the ghetto sweetened tea was considered a popular drink, I ruled it was permissible to use it for the four cups. Although the blessing to be recited would be different—*Shehakol*, it was to be recited only over the first and third cups.

In order to inspire Jews with hope that the redemption was not far off, and also to fulfill the halachic requirement, my students made the tea available to as many people as possible. Those who could not get this tea were obligated to recite *kiddush* on matzah, if available. Since they had to recite the blessing of *Hamotzi* over the matzah as part of their *kiddush*, they did not have to say the blessing of *Borey Pri HaAdama* when they ate their *karpas* vegetable, which in the ghetto was either potato or onion. Since both were normally eaten as part of the meal, there was no need to recite a separate blessing for them once one had said the blessing of *Hamotzi*.

At the approach of Pesach many problems arose concerning *chometz* at a time when hunger was growing from day to day and one could not even find an olive's-bulk of matzah to eat for the *mitzvah* on the first night of Pesach. Two of the problems that came up were:

1. Might one eat the black beans that were part of the ghetto food ration? This was a concern because Ashkenazic Jews are prohibited from eating beans and lentils on Passover.

2. Some people had managed to find dirty potato peels at their places of work. They wanted to pulverize these potato peels and to mix that powder with the little bit of flour that was available to them,

and thus bake matzos for Pesach. This combination is normally permissible because vegetable and fruit juices are not leavening agents. But here it was imperative to scrub the filth from these peels before grinding them. Yet washing them with water in order to cleanse them would introduce water, a leavening agent, into the mixture. Was there any way to allow the use of these potato peels?

In the horrifying circumstances under which the Jews were compelled to live, there was no question that they were allowed to eat the beans on Pesach provided they put them directly into boiling water. When it was impossible to put them into boiling water and cook them, they could be eaten anyhow.

As to the filthy potato peels, the great sage Rav Avrohom DovBer Kahana-Shapiro ruled that the filth had to be wiped off with a cloth or a rag. Under no circumstances were they to be cleansed with water, because the water would act as a leavening agent on the flour. After cleansing the peels with a garment or a rag, the peels could be pulverized and mixed with some flour and baked—even on Pesach proper. Before baking the raw matzah cakes were to be punctured with a fork so that they would not bubble up. Rabbi Avrohom DovBer Kahanna-Shapiro, may he rest in peace, gave instructions that the details of this procedure be publicized so that no one would misunderstand it.

◆ ◆ ◆ ◆

Matzah baking was risky. The machines were noisy, and the Germans patrolled the ghetto; everything we were doing was "illegal," from the machine to the finished matzah. Even the location where we baked was dangerous, for the Germans would wonder how the Jews came to have empty rooms for baking matzah. And where did the flour come from? And white flour at that?

Most difficult was Pesach of 1944. The *Akzion* against the children and the old people had taken place on the third and fourth days of Nisan. Our matzah-baking plans were interrupted because everyone was so frightened. It seemed certain that not a single Jew was going to survive. So who had a mind clear enough to focus on matzah-baking? Who was sure he'd even still be alive on Pesach?

Days passed. Pesach drew closer. Where would we find even an olive-sized piece of matzah? Despite the troubles we were suffering, we began to bake matzah. This entailed risk to life, because Kittel, the Gestapo official, visited the camp frequently.

The rabbis—Rav Yehoshua Levinson, director of the Radun Yeshiva and a grandson of the Chofetz Chayim; Rav Zalman Permut, director of the Kovno Kollel; Rav Binyomin Ozinsky; and Rav Shimon Dubiansky—went with great joy to draw water (called *mayim shelonu*) for baking the matzah. I recall Rav Levinson saying to me, "You may be wondering why I am doing this with such joy? It may be that this is the last *mitzvah* of my life."

Erev Pesach, the day before Passover 1944, arrived and there was still not a crumb of matzah available. Late that afternoon, I was standing together with other Jews who were baking matzah, when we suddenly heard a noise outside. Kittel the murderer had stopped his Gestapo car right in front of where we were baking matzah in Block C.

Hiding was out of the question; before I could even think, the butcher was at the door. "Too bad," I thought, "if I'm going to die, let it at least be for the *mitzvah* of baking matzah." I began to recite *Viduy*, but Kittel interrupted me, "Who are you?" Before I could respond, he had picked up two parcels of matzah and walked out. I stood there dumbfounded, unable to understand what I had seen.

Then I noticed Efraim Bunim, the manager of the small workshops, being arrested. The matzah baking was not resumed, and many Jews did not have even an olive-sized piece of matzah for the *seder*.

This disrupted Pesach was, in fact, our final Pesach in the Kovno ghetto. I shall always remember how I divided the little matzah we had into olive-sized pieces that Pesach so that the *mitzvah* of eating matzah could be fulfilled by as many people as possible.

How can I ever forget how Jews from the work camps around Kovno—Alexot, Shantz, Faleman, and Rotenhauf—requested the minimum-sized piece of matzah; how one Jew called out, "All my years I kept the *mitzvah* of matzah, and now, before I die, I can't! Beloved G-d, forgive me!" His words still ring in my ears today.

· 19 ·

SPIRITUAL LIFE

A whole book could be written about the spiritual life in the Kovno ghetto. A long string of pearls was woven into the fabric of that awesome period in which, despite everything, a life full of beauty and wealth was revealed. It is my duty to record several events so that future generations will be able to learn what spiritual life was like during the Jews' time of suffering and isolation.

Even during the bitter and dark ghetto years, when murder was the order of the day, when the majority of Torah leaders and the yeshiva students were martyred, when death threatened every Jew every minute—still Kovno's Jews continued to go to houses of worship to study and to pray, to recite Psalms, and to pour out our hearts to the world's Creator. This recharged our energies, enabling us to continue living until the One Above would take pity on Jewry and rescue us from our horrifying situation.

The Sounds of Torah Study

Throughout history, even during times of terrible persecution, the sounds of Torah study could be heard emanating from the homes and synagogues of the Jewish People. Our ghetto joined in this sacred tradition. One outstanding place of study was the home of my revered teacher, Rav Avrohom Grodzensky, the spiritual dean of the Slobodka Yeshiva. In his home, Torah study never ceased. People studied in groups and sometimes individually. Rav Grodzensky would lecture in *mussar* for all who were present. Rav Yechezkel Bernstein, one of the deans of Yeshiva Or Yisroel, one of Slobodka's preparatory *yeshiv-os*, had a study group in Talmud tractate *Nedorim*. The *tzaddik* Rav Yisroel Y. Lubchansky, son-in-law of Rav Yozel Hurvitz of Novhorodok, lectured there on *Shaarey Teshuva*, the classic *mussar* book by Rabbi Yonah of Gerondi, first published in 1500. In fact, as mentioned previously, the great *gaon* Rav Elchonon Wasserman had been lecturing on tractate *Nidah* when he was seized and taken to the Ninth Fort and killed.

Every day brought new travails, new decrees, terrifying news about rabbis and leaders of other towns in Lithuania who were murdered along with their entire communities. Parents looked on as their children were taken to be killed, and yeshiva deans as their students were massacred. As tragedy mounted upon tragedy, my holy master, Rav Avrohom Grodzensky, stood firm and discoursed on the topic of martyrdom; extraordinary lectures that would have enriched the world had they been written, had someone taken notes. Unfortunately, no one did, and they were lost along with their originator. But I am a living witness to everything that went on in that house.

My Rebbi's loftiness of spirit was comparable to that of Rabbi Akiva. In the second century, Rabbi Akiva smiled and prayed while the Romans tore his flesh with steel combs. His disciples asked, "To this point you are happy to recite the *Shema*?" And he replied, "All my life I have been waiting for the opportunity to fulfill the command-ment in *Devarim* (Deuteronomy) 6:5, to love G-d with one's entire self." Rav Grodzensky too, it seems, had waited his entire life for the opportunity to offer himself in sanctification of G-d, to be able to ful-fill the commandment to love G-d with his whole self.

In the synagogues and private homes the melodies of Torah study continued to be sung. In the Abba Yechezkel kloiz, where I was the rabbi, I prayed and taught groups of adults. Prayer and study went on every day until the 7th of Cheshvan, October 28, 1941, the day of the great *Akzion*, when 10,000 Jews were taken away and massacred, and the house of study was turned into a jail for Jews.

Every evening I taught *Ein Yaakov* and *Chayey Odom* to a group that met at 7 Vitena Street in the home of Gapanovitch the tailor. He con-tributed the little room—where he and his wife and daughter lived—for study and prayer. I also taught the men who met to pray in Chayim Shaffer's wood storage chamber.

In the ghetto everyone knew that the way to survive was to work.

As long as the Germans needed our labor we believed they would not kill us. Youngsters knew this as well, but were not allowed to leave the ghetto to work unless they measured up to a bar near the ghetto gate: Whoever reached the bar was considered old enough to work, whoever could not reach the bar was considered too young. Many youngsters stuck pebbles or rags in their shoes in order to raise their height enough to join a work brigade.

The youngsters who couldn't work I gathered together. We studied Talmud, *Chayey Odom*, and *chumash* (Bible). I tried to encourage them to retain their Divine image. Our major difficulty was the lack of sufficient space for study and prayer.

The remaining Slobodka Yeshiva students and the married men of the *kollel* used to study a leaf of Talmud in depth every night at the Halvoyas Hameis kloiz, with as much involvement as in the "old days." The driving force in that group was Rav Zalman Permut, who had been the dean of the Slobodka *kollel*.

Among the yeshiva students, Yitzchok Danziger hid in the attic of the kloiz and studied there alone for three months. In mid-winter his uninsulated attic hideout was freezing. Yet Danziger ignored the discomfort and absorbed in his studying, lived in another world. Another yeshiva student, Leib Orlinksy from Yanova, spent all winter in hiding, studying Torah without interruption.

On Shavuos, which celebrates the giving of the Torah, yeshiva students followed the tradition of staying awake all night to study Torah. They did this with extraordinary enthusiasm and devotion. It seemed as if they were trying to arouse their souls in order to compensate for the strenuous physical labor they endured under the German whip. These men and their dedication to the Torah made a strong impression on the other Jews, helping to raise their spirits.

Tiferes Bachurim

From August 15, 1941 until liberation, I studied with youngsters for three to four hours every day. Even in the worst of times we met to study the Talmud, *Nach* (the Prophets), *Kitzur Shulchan Oruch* (the Concise Code of Jewish Law put together in the 19th century by Rav Shlomo Ganzfried), and other works. Even after the great *Akzion*— when 10,000 of Kovno's Jews were killed—the survivors did not stop studying Torah. Although exhausted by the hard labor forced upon them by the Germans and chilled by the cold weather, they nevertheless continued to study. Rav Shmuel Marak—may G-d avenge him— who was one of the deans of Yeshiva Ohel Moshe, also studied with the older students in the Tiferes Bachurim, an organization whose purpose was to spread Torah and awe of G-d among young working-men. Groups met nightly to study Talmud, *chumash*, and Jewish law. The Tiferes Bachurim branches in 110 Lithuanian towns had had some 3,000 members, and the organization had even published a monthly journal, *Tzum Yugnt* (To Youth).

The Tiferes Bachurim in our ghetto desperately needed space for studying and praying. Thanks to the Singer family at 8 Kolka Street we found the space we were looking for. Mr. Singer had an unfinished basement without windows or doors or even a floor. One of my students, Shimon Segal (now a well-known rabbi and executive director of the Kamenitz Yeshiva in Brooklyn, N.Y.) and I had the idea to move into that basement. This was not easy to do, since the basement was piled high with waste and debris. But with energy and determination, the youngsters of the Tiferes Bachurim girded themselves for the task of cleaning the place. Within a few days the job was done, and we moved in and started studying there.

Thanks to Berel Friedman (who survived and later settled in Israel) we acquired glass for windows as well as lumber to construct a floor and doors, and whitewash to coat the walls. The electrical work was done by Efrayim Gutman, whose father was a *dayan* in Kovno (he also later settled in Israel). Benches, tables, and an *aron kodesh* (Holy Ark) were constructed. All the work was done with great effort on the part of the youngsters. In one wall, near the Ark, we constructed a hiding place in case, as expected, we were surprised by the Germans while we studied or prayed.

On July 28, 1942, we celebrated the dedication of the Tiferes Bachurim chapter of the Kovno ghetto. In the middle of our suffering and anguish, a group of youngsters could finally sanctify G-d. All the factions in the ghetto recognized and praised this achievement. And everyone participated in the dedication ceremony.

The Chief of the Second District Jewish Police, Ika Greenberg, undertook to guard the area during our celebration in case of a sudden German visit. He also provided police escorts to accompany the people home safely after the celebration ended late that night, since curfew was 10 p.m.

The speakers at the dedication were Rav Moshe Skaruta, myself, and representatives of the Jewish Council. The dedication celebration was joyful and was, fortunately, not disturbed.

The survivors of the Kovno ghetto Tiferes Bachurim include Rabbi Shimon Segal, of Kamenitz Yeshiva in Brooklyn; Rav Gibraltar in Bnei

Brak, Israel; and the brothers Dov Ber and Leibel Zusman of Brooklyn, New York.

What about the younger children? Avrohom Baron—who was killed in an *Akzion* in October 1941, may G-d avenge him—had organized a *cheder* for young children in the Halvoyas Hameis kloiz. He sought out children, and gave them slices of bread with sugar or saccharin. When his *cheder* grew so large that he could not teach so many children, Rabbi Mordechai Suckerman, who was then in his thirties and had learned in the yeshiva in Radun (he survived and settled in Israel), assisted Avrohom Baron in learning with the children.

The Jewish Council also organized schools for children, with Dr. Nachman Shapiro (chief Rabbi Shapiro's son) as director. But they were immediately closed down by the Germans. Although the Germans forbade praying and studying, the secret study and prayer groups continued to meet. The *cheder* for the children also found a way to keep functioning.

Strict Adherence to Halacha

The spiritual heroism displayed by many people in the ghetto as well as their strict and unbreakable adherence to halacha are things that I feel must be described.

One assimilated Kovno family in the ghetto had been so estranged from Judaism that they didn't even circumcise their son. And yet after being forced, just like all the other Jews, to move into the ghetto and after sharing the suffering of his fellow-Jews, the son decided he wanted to rejoin his people. He said that "if in death I will not be separated from my people, why should I be separated from them in life?" In accordance with the covenant of Abraham, he therefore had a circumcision performed.

Shabbos observance in the ghetto was especially problematic. Because everyone was compelled to work on Shabbos and holidays, we were afraid that Shabbos would be forgotten altogether. So we founded a group called *Mazhirey* Shabbos (Shabbos warners) whose task was to keep an eye on the ghetto families in every area that related to Shabbos observance. A special assembly was convened on behalf of Shabbos observance, at which the speakers were Rav Shag, myself, and Rav Shmuel Marak, one of the deans of Slobodka's Yeshiva Ohel Moshe. I also gave a sermon every Shabbos to encourage the people and strengthen their faith.

Many people did continue to be very strict in their observance of Shabbos. Many questions regarding proper observance were posed to me by people who wanted to be sure they were adhering properly to halachah. On one occasion I was asked whether Jewish law permitted the fulfillment of the *mitzvah* of lighting Shabbos candles by using electric lights and whether the blessing could be recited on those lights. Under the circumstances I ruled that it was permissible since candles were impossible to find.

Others felt obliged to put up *mezuzzos* (scrolls with special prayers that are attached to the doorposts of Jewish homes). I determined that a *mezuzzah* was not required, for the law is that *mezuzzos* are required only on the doorposts of permanent dwellings. As our homes in the ghetto were by no means permanent, for we would leave them at once if at all possible, a *mezuzzah* was unneccessary.

Despite great concern and effort, we were never able to construct a *mikveh*. But *kashrus* was carefully maintained. The Jews who worked at the airport made every effort not to eat from the communal pot of food provided by the Germans.

Most of the time when the Jews were force-marched in autumn and winter mornings to their slave labor at the airport it was totally dark. When they were marched home to the ghetto it was already night. This posed a problem for the men and their donning of *tefillin*, for *tefillin* may be put on by day but not at night.

Although in my responsa[4] I found authority for allowing—in those unique circumstances—the men to put on their *tefillin* before leaving for work, the pious among the workers could not bring themselves to put them on at night. One man wore small *tefillin*, despite the great risk if the Germans caught him. But this way he could pray at work while wearing them. After praying, he would remove the *tefillin* and cautiously pass them to a fellow-laborer. In that manner the pious had the chance to wear *tefillin* by day. Even in the greatest cold they did this and thus fulfilled the law stringently.

Meir Abelow of my Tiferes Bachurim class—may G-d avenge him—sought ways to make it possible to fulfill the *mitzvah* of *tzitzis*.[5] His mother Rebetzin Abelow spun the *tzitzis* for all the boys as well as for other Jews.

Later, in November 1943, when the Big Ghetto was liquidated and proclaimed a concentration camp, it was impossible to designate a formal place for prayer. Nevertheless, prayer sessions as well as daily study sessions were organized in a room in Block C that served as our house of prayer and study. We even maintained our branch of Tiferes Bachurim.

---

[4] *Responsa From the Holocaust* (Judaica Press), p. 31.
[5] Fringes attached to four-cornered garments worn by Jews in fulfillment of Numbers 15:37-41.

Noteworthy, too, are the *Mincha* (afternoon prayers) and *Maariv* (evening prayers), tearfully and entreatingly recited on the airfield of tragedy, in the pits where Jews were laboring.

Friday nights quietly—in a blend of pain and trust in G-d—each of us sang *Lechah Dodi* (a poem recited to greet the Shabbos) at *Kabbolas Shabbos* (the prayers that welcome Shabbos). After our Friday night prayers we would wish one another *"Gut* Shabbos." I recall once being one of a group of Jews pressed into service and loaded into a truck to be taken somewhere to unload cement. Shimon Segal, then around 14 years old, who studied with me in my Tiferes Bachurim group, was one of the group. As the truck rode along we managed to *daven Mincha* with a *minyan.* The leader of that *Mincha* was a man named Kovalsky (whose first name I don't recall).

Every day after *Shacharis* and *Mincha* prayers, we recited Psalms 130 and 142, which are commonly recited in times of crisis, as well as the special prayers "Our brethren, the entire House of Israel, who are in trouble and captivity" and "Our Father, our King!" The weeping during the recitation of these psalms and prayers was heartrending. From time to time fast days were organized on which collectively we prayed for the nullification of the decrees against us. At about midnight we would gather to recite Psalms and arouse ourselves to repentance.

◆ ◆ ◆

That is how the light of Torah and Judaism was spread in those deep, dark days, the most abysmal period in Jewish history.

· 20 ·

THE SECRET *BRIS*

On 24 July 1942, the Germans issued a decree forbidding the women of the Kovno ghetto to bear children. Any child born would be shot along with its mother. The director of the hospital, Dr. Zakharin, was ordered not to allow any pregnant women into the hospital.

Imagine the terror of pregnant women. Their primary concern became hiding a newborn child. They lived in dread of the Germans' regular inspections of ghetto apartments. The very day of the edict, a pregnant woman passed by the ghetto hospital. A German soldier noticed her condition and shot her for violating the order. His bullet penetrated her heart and she fell dead on the spot. Passersby immediately carried her into the hospital, thinking that since she was clearly in her final weeks of pregnancy, there might be a chance to save the fetus. A Jewish obstetrician was rushed over, who said that if surgery was performed immediately the baby could be saved. The operation was a success, but the Germans soon came into the hospital to write down the name of the murdered woman in their records. When the baby was found alive, a German soldier grabbed the infant and cracked its skull against the wall in the hospital room.

If you think any Jews surrendered to the decree against pregnancy, you are mistaken. "Even though we are not the masters of our lives," we told ourselves, "we will not be the murderers of Jewish children." However, many women did begin to use contraceptives, and abortion was considered acceptable if it meant saving a woman's life.

Women began to have their babies in secret. Not only were children born in secret, they were also circumcised in secret. And I note that, thank G-d, many of those children born and circumcised in secret are still alive. They were born miraculously and survived miraculously.

I can never forget the *bris* (ritual circumcision) that took place for the son of Yitzchok Bloch and his wife, the daughter of the rabbi of Remigala, Rav Zissel Steinfeld. They had been married five years and had had no children. Suddenly, after the German decree, G-d granted them a child.

They lived near me in Block C, which was a large building, four stories high and some 65 yards long.

Block C housed many ghetto institutions including a Tiferes Bachurim, two synagogues, the kitchen, secret food shops, underground apartments for hiding Jews and weapons, and a trade school that made small items for the German war effort.

How were we able to arrange all that under the Germans' noses?

When the area to be the ghetto was assigned to the Jews, that particular building was incomplete. The Jews were ordered to complete it. And we completed it in a manner that made it possible to provide for all sorts of communal needs.

The *bris* took place in Block C. It was a Sunday morning. As the *mohel* (person trained in circumcisions) picked up the circumcision scalpel, a car suddenly stopped in front of the building, and out stepped a number of Gestapo men. We were terrified. The *mohel*'s hands began to tremble.

The scene is as vivid to me as if it were happening today. What could we do next? What could we do with the mother? The baby? Mrs. Bloch, the mother, was the only person there who had her wits about her.

"Quickly, circumcise the baby," she said. "If they're going to shoot us all, let my son die a Jew!" We obeyed, and in the shadow of death, the child was circumcised. Though we expected the soldiers to enter the room any moment, somehow they left us alone. The only price we paid was our terror.

◆ ◆ ◆ ◆

Block C also contained the bathhouse known as the Delousing Institute, which I was in charge of. Because people had no undergarments and usually never more than a single shirt, their clothes were always filthy. In addition, they had no soap to bathe or to launder clothes. However, the Germans did officially allow people to take turns to delouse. Bathers received enough liquid soap to wash their bodies, while they placed their clothing in the delousing chamber. There, intense heat killed the lice in the clothing. I made every effort to get enough wood to keep the delousing chamber functioning well. I knew people's suffering was made more bearable when their bodies were somewhat free of filth and stench.

There were three showers and we were open in the morning and in the afternoon. A doctor came twice a week. There were separate times for men and women. I was there when the men came. While we put the clothes in the ovens in order to delouse them, the men took showers. Many of the homes in Slobodka had no running water, so this was the ghetto's bathhouse as well as delousing institute.

· 21 ·

HANGED

After the bloody mass-*Akzionen* of October 28, 1941, and after the book-*Akzionen*, a period of relative calm commenced in the ghetto, although there was never a complete respite from Nazi brutality. The shooting of individual Jews for a variety of "crimes" never came to a halt. When measured against the mass murder of Jews during the first four months of the German occupation, however, this period could be called a breathing spell. Underground ties were created with the ghettos in Vilna and Shavl, and we discovered that their situation was similar to ours. A ray of hope stole its way into our hearts that the worst might be over.

At that time a number of religious and secular movements began to organize. The economic situation also improved slightly. The number of ghetto workshops also increased, all of the workers laboring to produce goods for the German armed forces.

The idea of increasing the number of work stations originated with the Jews themselves. In order to free themselves from the heavy outdoor labor at the airport, under the supervision of the abusive Germans, the Jews proposed that they might make themselves "productively useful" in other ways and in that manner save as many lives as possible.

That is, in fact, what happened. Those ghetto workshops, in a very large measure, helped sustain Jewish lives, and so they played a major role in ghetto life. There were workshops where tailors, carpenters,

The public hanging of Mek on November 18, 1942, sketched by Joseph Schlesinger,
an artist who sketched many scenes from the Kovno Ghetto.
From the personal collection of Avraham Tory.

Mek's grave.

shoemakers, and leather workers worked. There were also workshops where machinery was repaired, clothes mended, posters were made and laundry was done. Besides this there was a brush workshop, candlemaking workshop, a children's toys workshop and a saddler's workshop. These large and small workshops supplied both the Germans and the ghetto.

The Jews of the Kovno ghetto were getting used to their "peaceful" existence, and it seemed that some of our wounds were beginning to heal, when suddenly the ghetto was shaken by an unexpected incident.

On Sunday afternoon, November 15, 1942, several revolver shots were heard, followed by running and shouting. Soon everyone learned that a man named Mek, the former owner of a jewelry store in Kovno, had tried to leave and had become caught on the barbed wire. When a German watchman named Fleischmann ran over to arrest him, Mek either grabbed the watchman's revolver or drew his own and fired a few shots which hit no one. Another Jewish man, who was about to follow Mek out through the barbed wire, turned and disappeared into the ghetto. The Germans, assuming that Mek was acting on behalf of the ghetto Jews, arrested all the members of the Jewish Council except for its head, Dr. Elkes, who was ill at the time. The Jewish ghetto police were ordered to detain 20 additional hostages pending the arrest of Mek's accomplice. Fearing that the hostages might be killed, the ghetto police chose as many certifiably insane and hopelessly ill people as they could, so that healthy people and heads of families would not be harmed.

Tension mounted unbearably. People expected the worst. On Monday morning, the members of the Jewish Council were released, but not the 20 hostages, and the Gestapo's decision was announced: Mek would be hanged publicly at 12 noon on Tuesday, November 17th; every Jew who was not out at labor was obliged to attend.

Although the ghetto Jews had survived many *Akzionen*, a public hanging was new. They were unhappy with the Gestapo "invitation" to Mek's execution. Besides, they mistrusted the relative mildness of the German reaction; they expected a much harsher punishment. Who could tell what the Germans had up their sleeves?

Tuesday, November 17th, the Gestapo and SS arrived exactly at noon and forced the Jews to set up a gallows in the empty yard across from the Jewish Council. The SS man Müller, "liaison for Jewish affairs," ran into nearby buildings forcing Jews out to witness Mek's execution. Most of Jews took the risk of not showing up to see Mek hanged. Many sought work in the brigades outside the ghetto that day so they would not have to witness a fellow-Jew's execution. And despite the risk, others sneaked back into buildings for the same reason.

Half-dead from his interrogation, an apparently calm Mek was led with his hands tied behind his back toward the gallows. He asked the Jewish policemen about his mother and sister. They told him his loved ones were fine, but in fact the Gestapo had already killed both his mother and sister at the Ninth Fort.

Mek's body was left hanging for 24 hours to remind the ghetto Jews what they might expect if they tried to escape.

The day after the execution, the Gestapo released the 20 hostages and allowed the ghetto Jews to cut Mek off the gallows. He was buried in the ghetto cemetery, but off to one side so as not to antagonize the Germans. A board with the name Mek was put up to mark his grave.

· 22 ·

THE EFFECT OF THE BATTLEFRONTS

It is worthwhile to relate how the events at the front lines of the war affected the Germans and Lithuanians in Kovno. Even more interesting were the feelings of the Jews as the war news reached them.

While we Jews were in the ghettos and extermination camps, every one of us believed that the world outside the ghetto was simply unaware of what was happening to us. That was the only reason we could conceive of and accept the world's silence. Today we know how baseless were our hopes. But how could we have believed that the world was so insensitive to our suffering?

The Germans and their allies regularly spread rumors that the entire war was being fought because of the Jews; that other nations fought Germany only on account of the Jews; and that the Jews were responsible for whatever tragedies befell the German people.

The Germans made sure, after every setback, to shout, "The Jews are doing this!"

When Berlin was bombed, the Germans announced, "The Jews and the Jews' allies are destroying Berlin!"

Frequently they would announce, "The Jews are killing our wives and children!" It was, as incredible as it seemed, the poor Germans and not the Jews who were the victims.

But as the German war effort began to suffer setbacks, both the Germans and their Lithuanian allies grew more and more nervous.

As long as the German armies were advancing and their soldiers marching from military victory to victory, so too did they continue to torture and murder Jews. They were not concerned with "why"—they simply continued their butchering.

But when they began to grow upset about the progress of the war, however, they changed and began to oppress and kill *with* "explanations."

The first time I noticed the Germans and their cohorts agitated was after the battle of Stalingrad. At the beginning of 1943, the situation on the Eastern front grew worse for the Germans. They were forced to retreat from much of occupied Soviet territory as the Red army continually drove them back, until the historical turning point was finally reached—the dramatic German defeat at Stalingrad.

That defeat, on February 12, 1943, drove the Germans berserk, and they vented their fury on the Jews. At the gates to the ghetto, workers were searched thoroughly; the Germans' rage grew even greater when they caught a Jew trying to bring a loaf of bread or a newspaper into the ghetto, or send off a letter. These Jews and their entire families were arrested and taken to the Ninth Fort to be killed.

The Germans were so upset that they neglected their system and order. Normally they primarily killed Jews they considered useless. Now they wantonly grabbed whoever came to hand. Among those caught that day was the blacksmith known as "Cherna's husband," a man employed at a job that was important to the Germans. But in the heat of their anger they killed him anyway.

By the 14th of February, the German defeat at Stalingrad was avenged by the Germans in Kovno by killing more than 44 ghetto Jews.

On the other hand, the Jews drew courage and encouragement from the German defeats. We believed that the world would finally avenge the Jews. During the most difficult times, there was always the hope that "if we survive, we will be avenged."

The situation on the Eastern front grew increasingly worse for the Germans. The young people responded by planning partisan groups that would fight a disruptive war at the enemy's rear.

In the spring of 1943, Soviet airplanes began bombarding Kovno. Our youths were on fire to join the partisans. Since there were no partisan groups in or near Kovno at that time, small groups of youngsters set out into the forests to seek partisans. Some of these groups were captured and fell into the hands of the Gestapo.

But that did not deter them. A committee was organized to establish contact with the nearest band of partisans.

During the fall of 1943, when the German situation on the Soviet front was catastrophic, the Jews in the Kovno ghetto discovered that the ghettos in Vilna and Riga were beginning to be liquidated by the Germans. The mood became sad and tense.

Around September it became evident that the Kovno ghetto was being put under the aegis of an even more murderous group than the Gestapo—the SS. It became clear to us that they were planning to treat the Kovno ghetto the way they had treated the ghettos in Vilna and Warsaw. About Warsaw we knew no details, only that the ghetto had been liquidated and that some Jews had fought back. How that affected us, I will relate in the next chapter.

· 23 ·

THE EFFECT OF THE WARSAW UPRISING

I t took a very long time for the Jews in the Kovno ghetto to become convinced that the Germans were planning to kill all the Jews without exception, that every Jew was in fact under a death sentence unless a miracle took place and the German regime was destroyed.

By the time we grew convinced of this, it was so late that we had little energy for fighting. We were weak and worn out. The slave labor, the *Akzionen*, our permanent state of famine and anxiety had so weakened us that we looked like skeletons.

But we still had some resources left. Eternal Jewish faith, our trust in G-d, sustained us and kept us alive.

In April of 1943, we received the news of the destruction of the Vilna and Warsaw ghettos. Vilna was a sister city to Kovno. On April 5th, 5,000 Jews from Vilna and several small towns near Vilna had been loaded into 80 railway cars, and taken two or three miles to Ponar. There they were all murdered. But we were encouraged when we heard a rumor that a number of Jews had resisted, and some had even managed to escape.

Warsaw, largest of the ghettos, was the vestige of the greatest concentration of Jews in Europe, once half a million strong. They rose up only two weeks after the 5,000 Jews of the Vilna ghetto had been murdered. We were electrified by the news of the resistance and heroic stand of the last survivors, which we received through the underground, through the Jewish Council's secret connections with Lithuanians in Kovno, and through a secret radio built by Tzodok Bleiman, son of the rabbi of Aran. (Tzodok survived and settled in Israel.)

The destruction of these ghettos meant that we had to believe that the Germans intended to kill us all, too. Even the most optimistic felt that our fate was sealed. Only a miracle could save us.

At first this created deep despondency. We were stunned that one of the largest Jewish communities in Europe had been totally wiped out. Slowly, however, that feeling turned into new resolve. We regarded the news from Warsaw as a call to a holy war, a call to make a last stand against these modern-day Amalekites. Jews said to one another, "We have nothing to lose. Let us at least fight!"

Organizing a resistance movement became a priority. People began talking more often and more seriously about joining the partisan groups hiding in the forests. Boys and girls by the dozens escaped from the ghetto into the forests to the partisans. The smuggling of weapons into the ghetto began in earnest.

The revolutionary movement grew so strong that representatives of the partisan groups showed up in the ghetto openly. All the Jews knew them. It was hardly an easy matter to enter the ghetto from the forest, nor was the reverse any easier, since the ghetto was surrounded by barbed wire and armed Germans.

Some Jews were killed enroute, some after shooting it out with the German guards. But that did not deter others from trying to join the partisans.

Two problems had to be dealt with: the problem of the elderly members of families and the problem posed by small children—neither of whom could escape to the forests. For them bunkers and hiding places were built, sealed-off underground apartments to which one could gain entry only through a variety of clever ways. Every day new twists were invented to wipe away any trace of an entrance to such a bunker.

There were bunkers whose entrance was through an oven, and others were entered through toilets—all planned so that no one would imagine there was an entrance to living quarters nearby.

When the Germans entered such a place and didn't find the Jews they were seeking for their *Akzion*, it never occurred to them that behind the oven there was a hideout for human beings; that Jews would or could make an escape route behind or under a flaming oven.

The people who built the bunkers planned living areas carefully, so that people could survive in them: there had to be enough air for breathing and enough space for survival. The most important aspect was keeping suspicion away from the hidden entrances.

Every night upon our return from hard labor, we worked on these hideouts. Regular meetings were held where preparations were made for the time when the hideouts would have to be used.

This atmosphere of preparing to wage battle, to revolt, strengthened the spirits of the Jews. A new attitude was born. The terror—a result of the long years of German control—disappeared as if waved away by a magic wand. We suddenly felt freer. The decision to fight had turned us into different people. We even stopped fearing death. The smuggling out of people to join the partisans became better organized and entailed less risk.

◆ ◆ ◆ ◆

There were about 16,000 Jews left in the ghetto at that time, and the Germans did not yet guess what might be going on. Optimistic Jews once again began to believe that the Germans might let the survivors live.

In the middle of these preparations and these reports, a new decree was issued. In July 1943, we became aware that the ghetto, run by the Gestapo, was being turned into a concentration camp to be run by the SS. We also heard that the ghetto was to be put under the supervision of a new commandant.

On September 15th, 1943, the notorious liquidator of Jewish towns, SS *Obersturmbahnführer* Wilhelm Göcke, arrived in Kovno. The Germans announced that the Gestapo would now manage the ghetto and that the ghetto was to be liquidated and would be replaced by the Kovno concentration camp. The Jews would be transferred to the camp, with the women separated from the men.

In October we discovered that camps were being established near the Kovno suburbs of Alexot and Shantz, as well as near Ezernai, some 12 miles from Kovno. The Rosh Hashanah and Yom Kippur of 1943 were unforgettable. We *davened* in different *minyanim* throughout the ghetto. We Kovno-Slobodka Jews understood that our turn had come. We had heard that the Vilna ghetto had already been liquidated in September. And now they were getting ready to murder us all. Seas of Jewish tears poured forth. Jews banged their chests while reciting "*Al Chait*" (confession of sins), not in the usual prayerful manner but as a preparation for death.

Many people even taught their children to recite the *Viduy*, because we sensed that this would be our last Yom Kippur.

On October 26, 1943, the first *Aussiedlungsakzion* took place. Into the ghetto came SS men, Gestapo members, and Vlasovtzes (Russians who supported the Germans). They began hunting down and seizing men, women, and children in the streets and the houses, leading them into the waiting wagons.

Knowing what to expect, the Jews looked for hiding places. The hunt took all day. 2,700 people were taken away that day. The adults were sent to Estonia, the children and the old people to Auschwitz.

That awful day was the beginning of the end. Those of us hiding in bunkers were ready to fight if the Germans discovered us. If a German entered we were ready to shoot rather than allow ourselves to be shot.

I was hiding in a bunker together with 87 others. The Jews there revealed to me that there were weapons in our hideout and that if discovered we would mount an offense. "Rebbi," they said, pointing to a sack, "there are weapons hidden in there. We think you have to learn how to shoot. We will no longer let ourselves be slaughtered like sheep."

As the end of Lithuanian Jewry approached, as the end approached for the last surviving Jews in the Kovno ghetto, Jews were prepared to fight. Although many Jews went off into the forests to fight and many hid in bunkers, unfortunately, the Germans managed to kill most of them.

· 24 ·

THE MARTYRDOM OF
BEN MOSHE YEDABER

L et me now recount the tale of the extraordinary sanctification of G-d displayed by Rav Gavriel Shusterman, a preacher in his thirties renowned in Lithuania by his pen-name, Ben Moshe Yedaber.

This Torah scholar and holy man was arrested and taken to the Ninth Fort for having committed a terrible "crime" according the German anti-human decrees.

What had he done?

In Koshedar, a town not far from Kovno, there was a slave-labor camp for Jews. Several hundred Jews had been brought there from the Kovno ghetto, among them Rav Shusterman.

The Germans had forbidden prayer, particularly public prayer, in the camp. Additionally, the Germans particularly sought to kill rabbis, so as to deprive the Jews of their spiritual leadership.

As far as Rav Shusterman was concerned, the German decrees did not exist. He did not merely refuse to submit to them, he ignored them. When it came to serving G-d, he was ready with all his heart and all his body as required by G-d, and nothing else mattered. German punishment was not going to stand in his way.

Didn't the fear of death deter him? On the contrary "If the penalty for this is death," said Rav Shusterman, "then it is a very meritorious act, for which one must sanctify G-d publicly."

In the Koshedar labor camp, Rav Shusterman decided not to obey the German laws against Jewish observance. Decrees that restricted Jews physically, Rav Shusterman accepted as a punishment from Heaven for Jewish sins. But where the Germans' decrees impinged on his faith, where they touched upon his soul, there Rav Shusterman balked.

A man who was with Rav Shusterman in the camp later related to me a statement Rav Shusterman made when the decree forbidding Jews to pray was issued. He said: "They can get a lot out of Ben Moshe Yedaber. They can force me to slave for them, they can do whatever they will to weaken me physically, to harm my health. My body is not my concern in the sense that I need not suffer martyrdom on account of it. It was decreed so from Heaven; we are probably sinful. But when they want to put their filthy hands on my soul and keep me from praying, studying Torah, and performing G-d's service, then I will fight. I will not allow it!"

To this Rav Shusterman added, "I will not merely pray by myself, but will see to it that others pray and study Torah. A Jew has not fulfilled his duty if he prays alone, if he studies Torah by himself, and leaves others to lead a spiritually irresponsible life."

And that is exactly what Rav Shusterman did.

Despite the edict, despite the threatened death penalty, Rav Shusterman organized a *minyan* in the camp, and Jews prayed there.

Rav Shusterman even convinced his German commandant to allow him to remain in the camp and not work on Shabbos. He was known as the rabbi of Koshedar camp.

That was not enough for him. Despite the difficult circumstances, every Shabbos he led gatherings for *sholosh seudos*. He recited Torah thoughts for the Jews who joined him, preaching wonderful sermons that uplifted their spirits and healed the wounds of their souls.

Most remarkable is the story of how Rav Shusterman obtained a Torah scroll for his *minyan*. There was none in the camp; the town of Koshedar's Torah scrolls had been buried by the Germans. One Torah scroll—so claimed a Lithuanian gentile—was in his house. He had hidden it. When Rav Shusterman heard that the farmer had hidden a Torah scroll, he decided to retrieve it for his *minyan*.

Many of his friends tried to dissuade him. They told him, "At such a time we can satisfy the requirement by reading from an ordinary *chumash*. We don't really need a Torah scroll."

"Rebbi," they cautioned, "this is a very risky business. A Torah scroll cannot be hidden as easily as a *chumash*. Leave the *sefer* Torah where it is. We'll read from a *chumash*."

For Rav Shusterman, however, these rationales were unacceptable. "We cannot allow a *sefer* Torah to remain in the possession of a gentile farmer. Do you really expect us to fulfill our obligation by reading from a printed *chumash*?"

He circulated in the camp and collected money from Jews who had it hidden, in order to redeem the Torah scroll from the farmer. Then he went to the farm and negotiated the acquisition of the scroll, which he brought into the camp with great joy.

◆ ◆ ◆ ◆

Not long after, two Jews slipped out of the camp to join the partisans. When the Gestapo discovered that they were missing, they arrested Rav Shusterman, the camp rabbi, as hostage for the missing Jews. As they led him off they brutally beat him, tearing his clothes and his flesh with their clubs. As his *tzitzis* trailed, the murderers decided to have some "fun." They wound his *tzitzis* around his bloodied feet and let the wounds dry for a short time. Then they pulled off the *tzitzis* with the scabs and the skin, crying out, "May G-d help you!"

Rav Shusterman coolly retorted, "If G-d wishes it, you won't be shooting me."

Miraculously, in fact, the Germans did not shoot him. He was taken to the Ninth Fort, where the Germans were keeping the two young men who had been caught trying to escape to the forest.

At that time Jews who were taken to the Ninth Fort were assigned the task of cremating the corpses of the Jews who had been murdered. After the Jews were shot in the pits, they were dug out of their graves and burnt on pyres. This was done because the Germans had decided to remove every trace of the mass murders.

The Jews at the Ninth Fort were "adorned" with the classic decoration of the slave ships of old—leg irons. Not only Jews were assigned to this task; Russian prisoners also were compelled to work cremating the corpses.

Some time later a heroic breakout from the Ninth Fort took place. Among the escapees was Rav Shusterman.

On January 3, 1944, Feivel Margoliyos came and told me that Rav Shusterman had escaped from the Ninth Fort and was now hiding in the ghetto. We needed to continue hiding him until he could move on into the forest.

When he was brought into my Delousing Institute to be cleansed, his body exuded the odor of burnt flesh. During the period of his labor at the Ninth Fort, his feet had become frostbitten. After his escape he had hidden in the forest and lived under the open sky during the coldest part of the harsh Lithuanian winter.

Dr. Zakharin, the surgeon at the ghetto hospital, determined that Rav Shusterman was critically ill. Further escape was impossible. All we could do was keep him hidden, let him rest, and feed him as best we could. But the end was inevitable. He passed away on February 16, 1944.

Before he died he told me, "When I was working for Jewish observance, many Jews told me that the Germans would catch me and shoot me. But the Germans did not shoot me. If G-d wants it, the Germans don't shoot. I'm dying normally, on a bed and will be buried in a Jewish cemetery."

Thus departed the soul of the preacher, Ben Moshe Yedaber. He was buried in the ghetto cemetery, and a board was put up as a marker, bearing a text etched in my memory:

Here Lies
The Warrior of G-d's Battles
Rav Gavriel Shusterman, Ben Moshe Yedaber
Died 22 Shevat 5704
תנצב"ה
May his memory be sacred.

· 25 ·

WHEN THE JEWS ESCAPED
FROM THE NINTH FORT

When the Germans began to sense that they were losing the war, they were overcome by panic. They decided—in order to prevent ultimate vengeance—to eliminate the few remaining Jews, the witnesses to their heinous crimes. They made every effort to wipe away every trace of their genocide, their murder of innocent victims. I heard the details of how the Germans tried to cover up their tracks after liberation from Pinka Krakinovsky, one of the brigade survivors.

◆ ◆ ◆ ◆

The Germans began by eliminating every trace of the mass graves of the Jews who had been murdered in the Ninth Fort. "Graves" is the wrong word since they were really gigantic pits—300 to 400 yards long, three yards wide, and two yards deep—into which Jews had been thrown or had been forced to enter while still alive then shot while lying on an earlier layer of corpses. The Germans and Lithuanians were determined that none of these remains be found, for the bones would be evidence against them.

The orders from Berlin that fall of 1943 were that by February 1944, all traces of genocidal activity must be removed. The victims must be exhumed and incinerated. In the Ninth Fort a brigade of 72 people was assigned to this task: 34 Soviet prisoners of war, 14 Jewish partisans, three local Russian saboteurs, four women—three Jewish and one Polish—and 17 Jews from the Kovno ghetto. The ghetto Jews assigned to this task were young men who had fled the ghetto in the hope of joining the partisans in the forests. Unfortunately, they had been intercepted by Lithuanian policemen, who handed them over to the Gestapo.

Because the Germans were aware that these Jews expected nothing but death and that they had already attempted to escape once, they put leg irons on them to guarantee that they would not escape.

In Lithuania, the victims' corpses were not consumed in modern crematoria. The Germans in Lithuania were not as efficient as their colleagues in Poland. They ordered rows of wood laid out and the corpses stacked on the wood, a layer of wood then a layer of corpses, several rows high. Then fuel was poured over the pyre and it was set on fire.

Piles of murdered Jews placed on gasoline-soaked stacks of wood for cremation at the Ninth Fort. (Russian forces arrived in Kovno before the Germans could finish.)

Master of the world! Who can fathom, yet who can forget this Hell-image? Who can erase from his memory the shocking scenes of Jewish children and old people, men and women alike, burning on wooden pyres?

The slave workers were divided into work units called *kommandos*. Each unit had a clearly defined task: One unit had to lay out the wood for the pyres. Another had to dig out the corpses from the pits. A third unit was assigned to the actual burning of the corpses.

Imagine how the Jews who were doing this horrible work felt when they recognized corpses they were unearthing and stacking! One recognized his wife, a second his child, another his father, a fourth his beloved fiancée or friend. Every one of them discovered the body of a relative or friend.

The cremating was done at the same place in the Ninth Fort where the people had been murdered not too long before. But there was a slight difference. The murders had been done openly, in broad daylight. The Germans had been sure of themselves then, certain they would win the war and thus would not have to give any accounting for their actions.

When the Germans sensed the end of the war drawing near, they began murdering secretly to ensure there would be no witnesses.

The area where they had perpetrated their murders was closed up. They kept their slave laborers in chains to do their dirty work to ensure that no one would escape. The Germans calculated that they would later eliminate them, too, and they therefore let no one out of the Ninth Fort.

When the ghetto residents first saw the great fires on the hill at night, we had no idea what they were. Slowly, however, by the stench from the burning pits that blew for miles in every direction, we discovered the grisly secret.

◆ ◆ ◆ ◆

The people working unearthing and burning bodies grew so despondent and broken that they were disgusted by their own selves. Yet they were chained by their legs and could do nothing about their situation.

Remarkably, their sense of revulsion at being alive was quickly supplanted by a desire to save themselves from this hell and start life anew. They were determined to become witnesses for the prosecution on behalf of their martyred people. They realized their days were numbered. If the Germans did not want the corpses of the martyrs to exist, they surely would not want living witnesses to exist.

As if to emphasize this, when one of the ghetto Jews in the brigade fell seriously ill, he was shot on November 5, 1943. Seven prisoners of war, considered too old or crippled, were shot on November 13, reducing the brigade to 64 people.

The Jews in the camps and ghettos still believed that the world knew nothing of the suffering and murder of the Jews. We were certain that if any of us escaped and informed the outside world what was going on, there was no question that the German nation would have to account for its bestial oppression and genocide. This belief gave us the strength to hope and to live. This is what motivated the Jews who had been forced to do this dreadful work into imagining ways to save themselves, ways to escape from their hell.

On first thought, the whole idea seems inconceivable. How can people fettered in leg-irons escape? Their awareness that the murderers would never let any of them remain alive, coupled with their desire to inform the world of what the Germans had done to the Jewish people, kindled their wish and their readiness to plan an escape.

So there began, among the corpse cremators in the Ninth Fort, a movement for escape. To this day I find it nearly impossible to understand how it came about.

Their first concern was to find a skilled locksmith. Fortunately, Pinka Krakinovsky was one.

Pinka was ready to strain every muscle in the effort to cut through the leg-irons and iron bars. But that was mere talk: How do you saw through bars and chains without tools? For the Jews of the Ninth Fort, this was akin to splitting the sea. Yet they proceeded to make their plans—and to carry them out.

One of the brigade members was a Jewish doctor, Dr. Portnoy, who had been arrested for violating some German "law." He was the brigade doctor.

Pinka Krakinovsky made himself mildly ill, so that the doctor could recommend that he be given sick leave for a while. In his cell, Pinka began making lock-picks and other tools from pocketknives that brigade members found in the clothing of corpses. Pinka's primary task was to fashion saws that could cut through the cell bars and also through the iron door that led to an escape tunnel.

Pinka did his work precisely, cautiously sawing the screws at the end of one of the bars on his cell. He left the bar in place so that none of the guards would notice that anything was different. Even then, with a cell bar removable, even with the locked doors picked, even with their leg-irons removed, they would not yet be free. They would have to pass through a corridor and then drill through an iron wall in order to get out of the fort. There they would have to unlock or break through an iron door that led into a tunnel.

One of the Russian prisoners of war was a Jewish officer who had been held in the Ninth Fort for a long time, during which he had learned its every nook and cranny. He had discovered a tunnel that led out of the fort to a steep incline which was out of the visual range of the tower guards. It was this wondrous discovery upon which the escape plans were focused.

The leaders of the group decided that Christmas Eve would be the ideal time for this escape since they could count on the German guards drinking themselves unconscious, certain that the Jews were secured by their leg-irons.

On December 24th, the Germans stopped the work earlier than usual, gave the Jews their food rations plus some cigarettes and whiskey, which the brigade leaders made sure went to the guards for their celebration that night. While the Jews were presumed to be sleeping, the guards celebrated and got themselves drunk.

In groups of 10 the Jews tiptoed out of their cells and passed down the corridor through the steel door opened by the lockpicks into the tunnel. All 64 walked out that night. Free! But now where to go?

They divided up into four groups, two of which—the majority of the escapees—decided to head for the forests to join the partisans. Another group fled into the Lithuanian villages, hoping to find hiding places there. The fourth group decided to seek a way into the ghetto in order to inform the surviving Jews and then to organize an escape from there.

It was not easy to bypass the armed Germans, but they managed to make their way into the ghetto.

When the Germans realized that every one of the 64 members of the brigade were gone, that 64 living witnesses to the horrors they had worked so hard to keep secret had escaped, they mounted a search that bordered on the insane in its zeal and excess. Many of the escapees were caught and killed by the Gestapo. Those who made it into the ghetto remained in hiding. Eventually they obtained weapons and slipped out of the ghetto to join the partisans.

◆ ◆ ◆ ◆

Inside the ghetto the news of the courageous escape spread immediately. In the middle of the night, Chayim, a member of the underground movement, suddenly appeared at my side. "Rebbi, may I have a word with you, please. Do you know about the escape from the Ninth Fort?"

"I know."

"We have some of them here." I knew exactly what that entailed as I was in charge of the Delousing Institute, the bathhouse. These people needed to be thoroughly bathed to get the stink of the cadavers out of their skin and hair. Otherwise, if the Germans came searching with bloodhounds, they—and we—would be lost.

Chayim said to me, "Rebbi, are you aware of the risk?"

"I know, but to die while saving Jews does not disturb me."

I immediately heated up the water myself so that no one else would know about it. The escapees—including a Russian officer—all came in, washed, and donned fresh garments.

The Gestapo organized a new brigade of Jews from the ghetto and nearby camps. They completed the dreadful task of cremating the massacred Jews. The new brigade was kept under very strict guard, and when they completed their task, they too were shot and cremated.

Many of the escapees survived the war among the partisans. I only know about some of them: Pinka Krakinovsky settled in Kovno. Berel Gimpel settled in Montreal, Canada. Michoel Gelbtrunk settled in Israel and changed his family name to Yitzchaki.

After liberation I met Pinka in Kovno and heard from him many of the details of the heroic escape from the Ninth Fort. A group of us went to visit the Ninth Fort, and Pinka and Gimpel gave us a detailed tour.

· 26 ·

THE DEATH OF
RABBI AVROHOM SHAPIRO

The Chief Rabbi of Kovno, Rav Avrohom DovBer Kahana-Shapiro has been mentioned earlier. The last years of this esteemed and beloved man's life were spent in the ghetto witnessing the beginning of the annihilation of Lithuanian Jewry.

This great genius was one of Lithuanian Jewry's major personalities. He was born the night following Yom Kippur 1870 in Kobrin. His father was Rav Zalman Sender Kahana-Shapiro, best known as the rabbi of Maltsh, a town near Brisk (Brest-Litovsk), where he also headed a yeshiva.

In his youth, Rav Avrohom studied in the Volozhin Yeshiva where he was known as the *iluy* of Kobrin. He married the daughter of Rav Yeruchom Leib Pearlman who was then rabbi of Minsk. When he was 25 years old he became the rabbi of Smolovitch near Minsk. In 1913 he became Chief Rabbi of Kovno. He served as chairman of the Union of Lithuanian Rabbis. During his lifetime he published *Taharas Hamishpocha*, a book on family purity, and two volumes of responsa, *D'var Avrohom*. The third volume of his responsa and a work on homiletics were published in the United States after his death.

Perhaps the man who suffered most during the German occupation was Kovno's spiritual leader. In addition to his personal suffering, as the spiritual father of his community, he shared in the suffering of every Jew in Kovno. As Chief Rabbi of Lithuania, he felt responsible for all of Lithuanian Jewry, responsible for everything that happened to every member of his flock.

Besides communal problems, Rabbi Shapiro shared the problems of individual Jews. That was his occupation day after day, hour after hour, minute by minute, and unfortunately, he was bathed in a sea of Jewish suffering and pain. In addition, Rabbi Shapiro was himself unwell. For a long while he suffered from a stomach cancer for which he had undergone surgery in Switzerland. Nevertheless, he was unconcerned about his own physical pain. His sensitivity to the pain of every Jew, his concern for the communal suffering, may well have made him ignore his own pain.

When the Gestapo ordered Rav Shapiro to create a Jewish Council (*Altestenrat*) to represent the Jews for the Germans, a meeting of Kovno's leading men convened at the rabbi's home. The majority of the Jewish Council members chosen were non-Orthodox Jews. When one of the Orthodox Jews, David Itzkovitch, secretary of the Agudas Harabonim asked the rabbi why, he replied, "This is not a matter for the Orthodox."

When the Jewish Council was formed, there were Jews who erroneously thought that the council had the power to help Jews. So when Jews were arrested in the early days of the German occupation, or if a Jew was dragged to the Seventh Fort or to the Ninth Fort, people ran to the rabbi to help free the arrestee.

Kovno Jews were not the only ones who came to Rav Shapiro for help during the occupation. One day the rabbi of Yanova, Rav Nachum Boruch Ginsburg, was dragged by the Lithuanians into Rav Shapiro's study. They expected Kovno's rabbi to raise the ransom that they had imposed on the Jews of Yanova, which the latter were too poor to pay.

The rabbi of Yanova looked like a wreck. His beard had been plucked and his face showed signs of a brutal beating.

Although Rav Shapiro was unable to help the rabbi of Yanova, he wept and commiserated with him. It was the same with any Jew whom the rabbi could not help; he wept and commiserated. I went to see him every day. One time he confided, "The troubles of the community make me forget my own troubles." He always spoke with a smile, in a friendly manner, despite the fact that he was often lying in his bed wracked with pain.

Since I was in daily contact with the ghetto Jews during their slave labor, I used to relate to the rabbi the *sheilos*, the problems and questions that had been brought to me, and I would recount how I had ruled. I recall telling him once about the following problem: The Jews at slave labor were issued daily a liter of "soup" made of water that had been cooked with horsemeat. Many of the Jews refused to contaminate themselves with non-kosher food and, as a result, grew weaker. When I was informed of this I ruled that they were allowed to eat the soup, because their life was at risk. "It's true," I said, "that the danger to your life will become apparent only later when you become even weaker. You will be compelled to eat the soup then. Now you are healthy enough to eat, so do not commit suicide."

Rav Avrohom DovBer Kahana-Shapiro, Chief Rabbi of Kovno and Lithuania, 1913-1943.

The rabbi agreed with my ruling. Similar questions arose. About them he told me, "The time has come to understand these *halachos* on a deeper level, particularly when they entail danger to life. At every step now, life is at risk. And you know, Reb Efroyim, it would not be out of line for you to put together a compendium of these risk-to-life cases. It is important that such a document survive." I wrote down a number of the queries and my responses, which I have published in my responsa work, *Sheilos Ut'shuvos Mima'amakim* (Questions and Answers from the Depths), which was distilled in *Responsa from the Holocaust*.

Rav Shapiro also encouraged me in my daily Talmud study group, and my directing and teaching in the Tiferes Bachurim. "You must give Jews faith and trust in G-d," he used to say. "That is immeasurably important."

Although near death, he asked me to write up the third volume of his responsa *D'var Avrohom*, which has since been published in the United States by his son, Leib Shapiro.

Lying there in his anguish, the rabbi kept everything in his mind. He even wrote his memoirs. They were fascinating—but unfortunately they were lost.

I visited him one day only a few weeks before he died, and found a number of Kovno's older men there, among them Reb Leib Intelligatter, Reb Mordechai Yoffe, and Naftoli Weintraub, a merchant who had owned two large women's clothing stores on Kovno's main street. The rabbi remarked, "You know, my dear Kovno men, I have to beg the Jews of Kovno for forgiveness because they have paid my salary these long years, and I have surely not done enough to give the Kovno Jews full value."

During the same conversation, the talk turned to *Eretz Yisroel* (the land of Israel), and he groaned and remarked, "I wish I could merit burial in *Eretz Yisroel.*"

His courage and trust in G-d were absolutely incomparable. Until the last moment of his life, his brilliant mind was at work and his heart ached. On the Friday before he died, he discussed the issue of freeing *agunos*—women whose husbands had disappeared and were presumed dead—to marry again. He also gave me his guidelines for dealing with the *agunos* issue after liberation.

On Shabbos 22 Adar I, February 27, 1943, at 3 a.m., Rav Avrohom DovBer Kahana-Shapiro died. His funeral took place the following day. Kovno's great love for its rabbi was evidenced by the decision to organize a public funeral, despite the risks. The Jewish Council decided to "officially" make a public funeral.

The rabbis and the yeshiva students decided that only they would carry the rabbi's coffin. All those who were going to come in contact with the body went to wash themselves with nine *kabim* (approximately three gallons) of water in a ritual manner, which I arranged at the Delousing Institute.

The frosty February Sunday morning witnessed an outpouring of every person in the ghetto, escorting their beloved rabbi. The ghetto police maintained exemplary order. No eulogies were held in the street since that would have been provocatively dangerous. Two eulogies were delivered in his house, one by Rav Yaakov Moshe Shmuckler of Shantz, and the other by the *maggid* of Kovno, Rav Chayim Most.

Among the crowd who attended the funeral there were many who remarked,

Rav Chayim Most, the maggid of Kovno.

"The Rav was a great *tzaddik*. That is why he merits being buried in a Jewish cemetery." Others were more personal: "I wish I were where the Rav is. I wonder if I'll be buried in a Jewish cemetery."

The Jews of the ghetto considered this funeral a victory over the German government. They went through with it even though such "manifestations" were strictly forbidden. The Jews risked their lives in order to pay their beloved rabbi their last respects.

Unlike the majority of the Jews in Kovno who had died in the last two years, butchered like animals and then flung into a pit, the rabbi's burial took place in full accord with halachic practice. A wooden tablet was placed on his grave:

> Here lies our master and teacher,
> the master of all Diaspora Jews,
> Rav Avrohom DovBer Kahana-Shapiro
> son of the great genius,
> Rav Zalman Sender HaKohen
> —may his mention be a blessing—
> The great *kohen* who was a loyal shepherd
> to our community for nearly 30 years
> died in the ghetto captivity on
> Shabbos 22 Adar I 5703
>
> תנצב״ה

Thus was Kovno's rabbi brought to his eternal rest.

◆ ◆ ◆ ◆

Later in 1943 the Gestapo arrested the Rav's wife Rebetzin Rochel Shapiro along with her son, Dr. Nachman Shapiro, and his wife and only son. They were taken to the Ninth Fort, where they were shot and cremated while still alive. Eyewitnesses who escaped were able to salvage only Dr. Shapiro's teeth for a proper burial.

· 27 ·

THE SLAUGHTER OF
THE JEWISH CHILDREN

In the bleak life of the ghetto where people flitted by like shadows in anguish over their todays and in dread of their tomorrows, we referred to ourselves as "dead men on furlough." We were the living dead.

There was a single area of illumination in our lives: our children. They were beautiful—shining like luminous suns. Their little faces radiated so much goodness, so much love, that our hearts melted with joy and fear—with joy that we had such a beautiful young generation, full of devotion and faith in G-d and in His people. But we also felt fearful lest, G-d forbid, the German angel of death stretch out his talons to harm our precious future.

Try to imagine the sheer joy and faith the children's faces expressed when they came to study Torah at the Tiferes Bachurim after their daily slave labor. Their suffering and constant hunger were forgotten for the moment. How does one forget Menachem Shereshevsky (son of Reb Zeidel Shereshevsky, who survived and settled in Worcester, Massachusetts), the brilliant 12-year-old who used to explain the Talmud with the commentaries of *Tosofos* (commentaries on *Rashi*, the famed twelfth century french scholar) so lucidly? How does one forget the *Maariv* the children prayed after learning? How they prayed! How earnestly and vigorously they entreated G-d on behalf of the survivors in their families and on behalf of the rest of Jewry! Who can forget how they recited Psalms every night, the tears rolling down their faces? Their high-pitched voices still ring in my ears, the sad chant with the psalmist's words (142:7), "Save me from my pursuers for they are overwhelming me!"

Who can forget the joy of the celebration at the inauguration of their own branch of Tiferes Bachurim at 8 Koklu Street? They had built it with their own hands.

Who can forget their *sholosh seudos* meals every Shabbos accompanied by their singing? And their holiday celebrations? Their Simchas Torah?

I will never forget the little Jewish boys at the *cheder* in the Halvoyas Hameis kloiz reciting *Modeh Ani* (prayer recited in the morning) and *Shema* prayers. Looking at them, we used to forget where we were; our souls would be lifted beyond the barbed wire surrounding the ghetto to another world, a world of beauty and purity, of nobility and soulfulness. How much courage, how much hope did we teachers derive from those children!

I shall forever remember the day the ghastly deeds began. The Germans' name for collective murder was *Akzion*. *Kinderakzion* meant child-roundup and child murder!

On the evening of March 26, 1944, the Jewish ghetto police received an order to appear before the German command in pressed clothing and polished boots for an air raid inspection. The next morning, March 27th, 3 Nisan 5704, the Jews left the ghetto to their labor and the police left to go inspection, dressed as if for a show.

At 8 a.m, with many of the able-bodied adults out of the ghetto, pandemonium broke loose. The ghetto had been surrounded, and dozens of buses entered the ghetto. Every bus had its windows painted over with white paint. German soldiers with dogs charged out of the buses, as did members of the White Guard and Ukrainians (defectors from the Russian army to the Germans).

A car drove through the streets of the camp, and over its loudspeaker a fearsome voice declared, "Attention! Attention! Whoever does not remain at home will be shot!" The announcement was repeated constantly and the atmosphere became fraught with the fear of death. The Germans also played music hoping to attract children—and they carried candy.

Like beasts the murderers ran from house to house, dragging struggling and wailing children out. Mothers ran after their children, screaming hysterically. The children were shoved into the buses. An unfortunate mother tried to push her way onto a bus and was clubbed over the head with the butt of a rifle. She collapsed but soon rose. A shouting match ensued, and she was clubbed over the head again.

Wild screeching and cries could be heard. And wild laughter, too; a mother had gone insane.

Mothers made desperate efforts to hide their children wherever they could: in a prepared hideaway, in a closet, in a cellar, in a pit. But hiding a child is a complicated matter: some children cry, others scream. And how do you take a child through the streets without being noticed? If you didn't prepare a hideaway, where do you suddenly find one?

In the Delousing Institute where I worked, there was a hideaway. Some mothers managed to bring their children in sacks and baskets to hide them there. The entire Block C was turned into a hideout for children.

To insure that children did not give themselves away by crying or screaming while being carried through the streets, they were given sedatives. While the poor little lambs were fast asleep, their mothers slipped them into sacks and pillowcases and carried them to safety.

One mother, wishing to hide her little boy who was screaming in panic, injected him with a sedative to knock him out quickly. Her hands trembled because she was not sure how much to inject. The child calmed down, fell into a coma, and died. In her fear and hurry, his mother had given him an overdose.

Then there was the mother who hid her only child in a bed. She covered him carefully with pillows, and she was "lucky." The Ukrainian who searched her quarters noticed nothing and walked out empty-handed. The mother's joy was indescribable. She ran to the bed, pulled off the pillows, and picked up her darling to kiss him. But the baby was limp. He had suffocated under the pillows.

Dr. Zalman Greenberg (who survived and moved to Israel) wanted to save his two-year-old son, Emanuel. He injected him with a sedative, and placed the sleeping tot into a barrel in the yard, which he covered with straw. The child slept through the entire day of the *Akzion*.

Horrifying scenes took place when children were grabbed off the streets of the ghetto. One mother fought for her child, refusing to let go of her little daughter. A bullet was fired into her head, and her hands released the child as she fell to the ground.

One of the mothers begged the killers, "Take me along too. I want to go with my child!" The murderers roughly pushed her away and remarked sadistically, "Your turn will come!"

Not only children were taken away that day, but elderly people as well. They took away the *maggid* of Kovno, Rav Chayim Most, his *tallis* and *tefillin* under his arm; they led away Reb Mordechai Yoffe and Reb Leib Intelligatter, the last of the older prominent citizens of Kovno. They were thrown into the buses with the children.

Mothers who grabbed hold of the buses were driven off by bayonets. Dogs tore at the women's clothing and flesh. One mother who held on to a bus firmly and refused to be frightened off, was shot through the heart. Her wailing child witnessed his mother's murder. Every bus had the radio inside turned up loud in order to drown out the children's screams. Full buses were driven off, and empty ones replaced them to take on new loads.

A number of buses pulled up in front of the ghetto hospital and took away the children there. A few were hidden in the beds of adult patients.

The murderers continued their hunt until nightfall. This was when we were informed that all the Jewish policemen had been arrested and taken to the Ninth Fort. They were accused of having helped young people leave the ghetto to join the partisans and of knowing the locations of hideaways and bunkers where children were hidden. A few days later the Jewish Chief of Police and his immediate assistants, a total of 40 men, were shot to death. Approximately 70 ordinary policemen were released back into the camp.

On March 28th, early in the morning after the *Akzion*, the ghetto was on its feet. That night had not been calm. The anguished mood was still in the air. The murderers were not sated. Too many children had eluded them. The Gestapo knew how many children there were from the many censuses they took and now they knew how many they had captured.

The streets were still full of people. No one had left to work yet. Suddenly buses with SS men and Ukrainians came driving up to the ghetto. Panic rose.

This time the murderers came prepared to seek out the children's hideaways. They had bloodhounds, axes and picks with them. Soon they were smashing walls and cracking floors. The Germans threw grenades inside anything that resembled a possible hiding place and blew to pieces anyone who was inside.

The murderers soon approached the Delousing Institute, where Rav Avrohom Grodzensky was hidden. I feared they might discover him and take him away. I prayed to G-d that I would not have to witness that. Sadly, though, I heard an explosion from the area of the hideaway, and my whole body shook with shock and fear. What happened to my Rebbi! Was he still alive? I could barely wait for the murderers to move along, so that I could go into the hideaway and see what had happened. When they finally left, I went and discovered that my Rebbi had only suffered fright. He was alive, spared death in the Ninth Fort.

But the murderers were relentless. They inspected a second area in the building and discovered a hideaway in the kitchen from which 11 children were led away. Then I witnessed a scene where little Aharon was taken away from his mother's sister. His mother was in Siberia, and had entrusted her son to her sister. The aunt kept screaming and repeating, "Let me go with the child!" But this was denied the unfortunate woman.

The aunt survived and moved to the United States, while the child's mother survived in Siberia. But the child is gone.

Then I saw SS men leading away a group of children and parents. Among them was someone I knew, Reb Feivel Zusman, a former businessman in Kovno who was also a *Chabad chosid*. Away he went with dignity—one of the few Jews who bravely kept his beard—he walked tall accompanying one of his children. They had been found in a hideaway.

Until darkness fell, the murderers went on searching for and grabbing children and the elderly. The toll for the two days was a total of 2,000 children and elderly people who were taken to the extermination camps at Auschwitz and Maidanek. Those very same days, *Kinderakzionen* also took place in the camps around Kovno—Shantz, Alexot, Koshedar, and Keidan. There the *Akzionen* were so thorough that not one child survived. The *Kinderakzion* in the ghetto of Shavl took place before the one in Kovno.

Thus were most of Lithuanian Jewry's children murdered.

Only a few children remained well hidden to anxiously await the redemption along with the rest of the Jews.

From the soil of sinful, bloody Europe the blood of our children cries up to G-d, "Our Father, our King, act on behalf of the innocent children! Our Father, our King, avenge, before our very eyes, the blood of Your butchered children!"

· 28 ·

THE MARTYRDOM OF
RAV AVROHOM GRODZENSKY

One great leader of the Slobodka Yeshiva—its righteous and sagacious dean, Rav Avrohom Grodzensky, managed, with G-d's help, to elude the Germans for three years despite their *Akzionen*. Astonishingly, my holy master survived despite a handicapped leg, and perhaps because of it.

Throughout the ghetto years, he studied constantly. He occupied his mind and heart with Torah. In the ghetto he studied Torah with his surviving students—emphasizing the Torah's perspective on martyrdom and the halachic guidelines pertaining to martyrdom. The surviving yeshiva students gathered late every Shabbos afternoon in his narrow, little room at 8 Furman Street near the Slobodka Yeshiva. There, despite the Gestapo, my Rebbi would discourse on ethical and moral matters in his deep, extraordinarily exciting manner. He spoke often about *kiddush HaShem*, martyrdom, instilling courage and soul-vigor into the downtrodden survivors of Lithuanian Torah-Jewry.

My holy Rebbi used to remind us that a person who accepts martyrdom intending to sanctify G-d does not feel the pain inflicted upon him. One need only recall the Talmud's description of Rabbi Akiva's martyrdom to learn that even the most excruciating pain is not felt during true martyrdom. For three years we were privileged to have my Rebbi's encouragement and soul-support for the handful of surviving Torah students. But even this giant of his generation was ulti-

mately lost to us in a tragic manner.

On Shabbos, July 8, 1944,
while the Kovno ghetto was
being liquidated, Rav Grodzensky was hidden, but his hideaway was discovered. As he ran
for his life, he broke his bad leg,
and had to be carried to the
ghetto hospital. There were a
number of ill patients in the hospital, including children. There
were also people there who had
tried to flee the camp and had
been shot and wounded and
were now hovering in great pain
between life and death.

The Germans were preparing

Rav Avrohom Grodzensky,
spiritual dean of the Slobodka Yeshiva.

to burn down the hospital with all the Jews in it, along with the entire
ghetto.

Rav Grodzensky's pain from his broken leg was excruciating.
When Shimon Segal—who survived and settled in Brooklyn, New
York—visited him shortly before his death, my Rebbi told him, "Try
to help the little girl in the next bed. She is a child. Calm her down.
Why is she responsible? Why should she be burned alive?" He knew
what was being planned; the ghetto was already on fire.

A yeshiva student was the last to report a visit with the great and
righteous sage. He reported Rav Grodzensky's last words to him, "I
do not care what happens to me. My pain will not cause me anguish.
I will suffer from hearing the groans of my brothers and sisters and
the little children as they are asphyxiated by the fire."

The next day, July 13, 1944 (22 Tamuz 5704), my holy Rebbi was
burned to death along with all the other Jews in the hospital when the
Germans set the building on fire. This was how the great *gaon* and
tzaddik, Rav Avrohom Grodzensky, perished *al kiddush HaShem*.

◆ ◆ ◆ ◆

Rav Avrohom Grodzensky was born in Warsaw in 1883. His father,
Rav Yitzchok, was a *tzaddik* and the head of a yeshiva in Warsaw. Rav
Avrohom studied in other *yeshivos*, and under Rav Nosson Tzvi
Finkel—known as "Der Alter"—in the Slobodka Yeshiva. Rav
Avrohom married the daughter of Rav Dov Tzvi Heller, the spiritual
dean of the Slobodka Yeshiva. When the Chofetz Chayim met Rav

Avrohom, he excitedly remarked, "I compose literature, and Rav Nosson Tzvi composes people."

In 1919, Rav Avrohom joined the staff of the Slobodka Yeshiva. In 1926, when "Der Alter" founded the Hebron Yeshiva in the land of Israel with a number of his disciples, Rav Avrohom became the spiritual director of the Yeshiva in Slobodka. His work, *Toras Avrohom*, part of which he had sent out of Lithuania before the war, was published in Israel after the war.

Avraham Golub (Tory), a secular writer and survivor of the ghetto who settled in Israel, accompanied me to one of my Rebbi's Friday night *shmuessen* (lectures). Here are Golub's own words from his well-written diary, *Ghetto Yom Yom* (recently translated into English, retitled *Surviving the Holocaust* and published by Harvard University Press).

5 June 1943

Oshry is my good friend and I am his fan on account of his uprightness and his faith. When he visited me in connection with his concerns I asked him, as usual, "How are the yeshiva students doing?"

He replied with a smile, "They're doing fine. The daily *daf* (page) is a daily *daf*. The yeshiva students are studying Torah. And the same is true for the Tiferes Bachurim."

"Tell me, now that Rav Shapiro is gone and Rav Shmukler [Rabbi of Shantz who died on April 20th, 1943—the first day of Pesach] in the ghetto is gone, who is the rabbi?"

Oshry is now dealing with the religious matters. He told me about the problems that currently occupy the religious community. One of them is the problem of the *agunos* (women whose husbands are missing and who may therefore not remarry). There are several thousand *agunos* in the ghetto, and after the war one can expect that number to swell. In many of the cases it is still possible to obtain positive identification from witnesses. There are dozens of men who survived the Seventh Fort, where some 400 men were killed. Many of the survivors can declare that before their very eyes men they knew were shot, men whom they can identify by name. The right thing to do, Oshry tells me, is to immediately convene a special *beis din* to collect the testimony of those men, and free as many women as possible from their *agunah* state. He sees this as one of the primary tasks of the surviving rabbis. Since the passing of Rabbis Shapira and Shmukler there is no single rabbi with the authority to decide these matters.

That is why a special *beis din* is needed for this issue.

Today is Shabbos. At 6 p.m., between *Mincha* and *Maariv*, Oshry and I will go to visit the *mussar* master, Rav Avrohom Grodzensky. He lives in the old city, Slobodka, in a narrow alley, in a two-story building near the Slobodka Yeshiva building.

The work-brigades have just returned, and the alley is full of people...whose faces are darkened, sad, and whose garments are torn and baggy. Weighed down by backpacks, they are returning from a hard day's labor.

Here and there one sees yeshiva students wearing Shabbos garments. Shabbos and weekday are intermingled here. At a nearby house a concert will be given by the police band in honor of Liptzer. The members of his division and his near ones are hurrying to present him their hypocritical smiles and cheap words of praise.

...We approach a wooden house. Oshry leads the way up narrow wooden stairs, and I follow him. We walk through two small rooms crowded with beds and armoires, and enter a third room that is also full of furniture and assorted objects. In the middle of the room stands a round table covered with a red velvet tablecloth reminiscent of synagogue reading-table covers. On the table is a pile of volumes of Talmud and *chumashim*.

At the table sits Rav Avrohom Grodzensky, an old man with a hoary, white beard and a pale, sickly face. He is wearing Shabbos attire with a yarmulka covering his head. At his hand is a black-bound *chumash*. Rav Avrohom is speaking, expressing Torah thoughts. Young yeshiva students as well as older men are standing around him in this room and the next one. All eyes are upon the seated old rabbi. They swallow every word he utters. The room is crowded and stifling. It is hot outside, too. The men wipe the sweat from their faces and from under their hats.

When we entered the room, Rav Grodzensky was in middle of speaking. He extended his hand to me, the guest. I sat down and was ready to listen to Rav Avrohom's words of *mussar*. Rav Grodzensky went on, "There exists only one greatness in the world, and that is the greatness of the Torah that the Holy One, blessed is He, gave to the Jewish people through Mosheh Rabeinu at Mount Sinai. (The Shavuos holy days were approaching, and the rabbi was discoursing on the Torah that was given then.) The Jews accepted the Torah, and even before they knew what it contained, they hastened to declare: 'We will fulfill it and we will heed it.' This was an extraordinary event. The Jews trusted G-d and that is why they were sure that His Torah was good for Jewry...

"The nations of the world see greatness and glory in literature and in art. This estimation of theirs comes from the fact that they do not recognize the significance of Torah. Many Jews, as well, are mistaken in their priorities—because they do not understand that true greatness is embodied in the Torah. The Torah does not demand from a Jew things that are beyond his capability; it demands of him to be what he truly is, to act in accord with the character traits with which he is gifted, not to escape from himself, not to deny his nature. He must become what G-d had created him to be.

"Man is good by nature, and he must take care not to be misled from the path of uprightness. He should not yield to his evil inclination. The Jewish people was chosen by the Creator of the world to be His nation. That is why we must suffer more than other nations. The Holy One, blessed is He, gave us the Torah so that we should know how to behave.

"The Jewish people have three fundamental character traits: [Shame or] fear of G-d, mercifulness, and generosity. Fear does not mean simply being afraid of G-d in heaven. Fear—awe—results from awareness of the Creator's loftiness. Analogously, shame does not mean simply to be ashamed. It signifies humility; aware of the Creator's greatness, man regards himself as so small as to be ashamed. The trait of mercifulness, Jewish mercy is boundless. All Jews are the merciful children of merciful parents. As to generosity—that is the relationship of man to man. All these traits gave the Jewish people to bear the troubles that beset it over many generations. The tribulations that the Jews are now suffering are familiar from the past. The Torah states explicitly why one punishment or another is given—why the first *beis hamikdosh* (Holy Temple) was destroyed, why the second one was destroyed.

"People of faith, people of good character, may be certain that they will overcome their tribulations. Jewry as a whole will overcome the troubles of our times." With that Rav Grodzensky ended his *mussar* discourse.

We thanked Rav Avrohom for his instructive lecture, and left.

This is how a secular Jew was impressed by my holy *Rebbi* and recorded what he understood of his words.

· 29 ·

THE HIDDEN PRODIGY—
RAV MORDECHAI POGRAMANSKY

One the of Torah world's best-known *iluyim*, Rav Mordechai (Mottel) Pogramansky from the town of Tavrig, spent the war years in the Kovno ghetto. He used to visit Kovno frequently, and that was where he happened to be when the Germans occupied the city. Yet if you had asked ghetto Jews if they were aware of Rav Pogramansky, the answer would have been, "No." Amazingly his name never appeared in any of the many lists compiled by the Germans or by the Jewish Council. It did not appear in the work registry, nor in the apartment registry, nor in any statistical compilation. He was present but officially non-existent.

Rav Eliyohu Lopian, the great *mussar* teacher, once told me how he discovered Rav Mottel Pogramansky. After World War I, Rav Lopian traveled from town to town in Lithuania encouraging Jews to remain loyal to Judaism, to study Torah, and to educate their children in the Torah way. He would spend two or three days in a community and lecture from two to three hours each day. His powerful voice and his stirring tones won the hearts of the masses. Simultaneously, he sought former students and other boys in each town who might wish to renew or begin their Torah studies in his preparatory yeshiva in Kelm.

After an inspiring lecture during a visit to the town of Tavrig, Rav Lopian was approached by a boy who told him that he was very interested in visiting his yeshiva. The boy, Mordechai Pogramansky, was 14 years old and had never studied Talmud. Although his grandfather, Rav Chayim Yanover, had been renowned throughout Lithuania as a genius, Mordechai's parents were modern and he had attended a high school.

Rav Lopian, impressed by Mordechai's obvious brightness coupled with his sincere interest in Torah-study, agreed to take him along to Kelm. But the boy added a further stipulation. He was already such a successful merchant that he had even obtained an import permit from the Germans and was wholesaling paint, so he could not afford to remain in Kelm very long.

Rav Lopian agreed to this and took Mordehcai back to Kelm with him. He introduced Mordechai to a number of older students and arranged to have them help him prepare for attending the first level lectures in Talmud. Each of the students prepared a few lines of Talmud with him. With his brilliant mind, he easily grasped everything he was taught and, within a few days, was pushing forward on his own. Despite the pressure to return home to his waiting customers, he was so fascinated by the Talmud and the yeshiva that he remained in Kelm for several weeks. Then he returned home to Tavrig and lost contact with Rav Lopian.

Rav Lopian did not give up, but traveled to Tavrig to bring him back. This time he succeeded in convincing the boy to give up his business and he brought him back to the yeshiva to stay. Young Pogramansky put his brilliance into his study of Torah, and developed a reputation as the *iluy* of Tavrig. Within two years he had mastered what Kelm could offer him, and moved on to the yeshiva at Telz. There he grew in knowledge of Torah and in service of G-d, and achieved renown as a holy genius.

In the ghetto, Rav Pogramansky did not appreciate visitors, since he feared discovery. He lived with a family named Lopiansky who were able to provide him little more than bread and water. On my few visits to him, I found him deep in thought, studying Torah without any texts. He would tell me some of his thoughts on *mussar* subjects—called *da'as* in the Telz Yeshiva—which he had developed with his own sharp perspective.

I've always been amazed that he managed to stay hidden in the ghetto when everyone else was required to be registered or listed in some way; he had remained hidden even during the great *Akzion* of October 28, 1941, on Kovno's Black Day, when even the sick had to be carried out on their beds, and even the chief rabbi of Kovno—old and sick as he was—had to appear in the main square. Even my Rebbi, Rav Avrohom Grodzensky, old and limping, could not avoid appearing despite the risk of his being selected for death.

Yet Rav Pogramansky was not seen. He managed to spend all his days and nights in study. I don't know how he did it. But he must have had some Divine protection, for he survived. Day and night, I was told, he studied without texts, was always absorbed, never engaged in conversation. He too survived hidden in block C, and was liberated by the Russians. He too was a member of the newly founded Kovno community. At Hoizman's kloiz, he spoke every Shabbos at *sholosh seudos*.

After liberation I noticed that he was always dressed in tatters, that he had no decent clothing. When rescue parcels arrived via Teheran containing pairs of shoes and overcoats, I made sure that Rav Pogramansky got some immediately. When I met him some weeks later, I noticed that he was still wearing his tattered clothing. So I asked him, "Why aren't you wearing the new items?"

He replied, "I have a question for you. Is it possible that the clothing that was sent to us was bought with money that came from Shabbos desecrators?"

This is how scrupulous he was in his service of G-d.

After Lithuania became a Soviet republic, Rav Pogramansky smuggled himself into Poland. As a fugitive from the USSR in Poland without Polish identification papers, he was in serious danger. The famous rescue heroine, Mrs. Recha Sternbuch of Switzerland, arranged to have him smuggled out of Poland through Czechoslovakia into France. He settled in Bailly near Paris where other refugee Torah scholars set up a yeshiva.

The Sternbuch family took a personal interest in Rav Pogramansky's health and brought him to Aix-les-Bains in southern France where they had established children's homes. He became the spiritual mentor of those homes and of the nucleus of what became a cluster of Jewish educational institutions.

He married and moved to Versailles where he headed a yeshiva. When he fell ill soon thereafter, the Sternbuchs arranged for medical care for him in Switzerland for over a year. He died in 1949 and was buried in Bnei Brak, Israel.

· 30 ·

HOW WE BUILT OUR BUNKER

One more day, one more minute of life! With incomprehensible vigor and stubbornness people clamored to keep their unpromising lives. They knew their fate. Their future was as clear to them as it had been for the Jews who now lay over Lithuania devoured by dogs, or rocked in the wind as they hung from trees, or decaying in mass graves. They knew the manhunting SS men were more dogged than bloodhounds, and that all over Europe German allies would ruthlessly turn in Jews in their attempt to curry the Germans' favor. The Jews had heard about what happened to Jewish communities throughout Lithuania and Poland. And as the news reached us about the continuing losses of the German Army and the Russian advance, we knew that our liberation was in sight.

But a few days, a few hours, even a few scattered minutes, did allow hope to operate. The fantasy was always "Perhaps I'll be one of the lucky ones they won't find!"

None of us completely understood why we desired life so much. What could life offer? Everyone was convinced that we were dead, not only from the Germans' point of view but from our own as well. We each bade our near ones farewell, and regarded every hour of life as unexpected, a gift from Heaven.

Where did people hide? The question should be: Where didn't they hide? In walls, under houses, in chimneys, in the depths of the sewage system. Wherever imagination suggested that one's body would not be visible, that is where people hid. People sought places where no one would ever imagine that a person could hide.

Other ways to survive were found. Information about partisans became available, and people began escaping into the forests. Initially, however, people thought themselves too big: "If I were smaller, I'd fit into this hole." People walked around shrunken, afraid of their own shadows. Their hands were too long, their legs too thick.

People developed skills. It made no difference whether they were gifted or not. Everyone became adept in order to save the bit of life that still fluttered inside them.

Very few survived. Nevertheless, despite the daily toll of people being dragged out of their hideouts and shot on the spot, hope was not diminished by a hairsbreadth, and people kept hiding wherever they could. One of the methods for hiding, especially as the war dragged on, was to build a bunker.

Each bunker was constructed secretly, so that only one's nearest friends or family were aware of it. This was understandable, because we feared that if word got out, too many people would want access to the bunker and everyone would be discovered.

How do you build a bunker? I know only how our bunker was built.

Back at the beginning of 1941, the Russians had completed construction of a number of four-story, identical apartment buildings for workers. These blocks of apartments stood in a row outside of Kovno. When the Russo-German war broke out, they had not yet completed the very last building. Four exterior walls were standing, covered by a roof, but there were no internal fixtures. The walls stood high and bare with many dividers for the hundreds of apartments that were planned for that building. Many were the people who found the building useful. People would hide there, in any of its hundreds of niches, to avoid the *Akzionen*. Later, a goodly part of Jewish ghetto life was concentrated in that building, which was called Block C. Workshops for small handicrafters were set up there.

The German authorities had allowed carpenters to build workshops for themselves and for other crafts. Since the German authorities needed the Jewish crafters, they had electricity drawn into the building. The Tiferes Bachurim *beis hamidrosh* found its home there, too. The Zionists used to meet there and the partisans used it, too, for secret meetings. In the cellar was the Delousing Institute, where I worked, which comprised a bath and a disinfection chamber for clothing and other objects.

Beneath the bath is where we decided to build our bunker.

Why there? First of all, no one would have imagined it possible to build underneath the cellar. Secondly, down there we were able to dispose of the large clods of earth. From the carpentry workshop we were able to obtain much of the material that we needed for the construction— primarily lumber, which was available nowhere else except in the workshops. Without the consent of the carpenters we would not have been able to get even a single piece of wood.

The next requirement was good workers who could hold their tongues so that we would not be discovered or suddenly find ourselves buried alive. We needed someone who was, if not an engineer, well-grounded in construction matters. The smallest error could cause the deaths of its tenants.

The supervisor of construction materials in the small workshops was Feivel Goldschmidt, an engineer who survived and settled in Israel. He knew construction and had access to the necessary materials. We told him what we were planning and he concurred both with the plan and with the location.

I was not informed about the original plans for the bunker, because the people involved feared that if the Germans discovered what was afoot they would kill me first because I was a rabbi. Nevertheless, they had to let me in on the secret because I was in charge of the Delousing Institute/bathhouse and they could do nothing there without me.

The Lipman family, who worked in the bathhouse, originated the plan to build the bunker. They made an agreement with Feivel Goldschmidt and Engineer Indursky. All together, including the bathhouse workers, their partners and their families, we were 34 men, women, and children. The bunker would have to be fairly large.

Work began in strict secrecy. The bunker was to be five yards high and 10 yards square. An enormous quantity of earth had to be dumped somewhere that would draw no attention, not even from other Jews. We also needed some way to move the earth out of the building unnoticed. We had to always be aware of the German patrols watching our every step. For the least, most unsuspecting move, we would be shot or sent to a place from which we would never return.

We finally discovered an appropriate place for the earth. This cellar shared one wall with a small workshop. We broke through that wall, and put the earth in the workshop. The workshop workers threw the earth into a lime pit that they had dug next to the outer wall. At the end of their day's work they would put out the fire in the lime pit, and during the night they dumped our earth into the pit. If the supervisor or a German noticed earth in the pit, the assumption would be that the earth from the side of the pit had fallen in.

The religious members of the group saw G-d's hand in this, as we saw it in our every movement. It was G-d's will that we should be saved. In what merit? Who can fathom G-d's mysterious ways? Everything happened at its time and in its place.

◆ ◆ ◆ ◆

Next to the Delousing Institute there was a storeroom for lumber. We removed the lumber and began to deepen the cellar by a full five yards.

We built up walls around our new "cellar" with lumber supplied by Feivel Goldschmidt and his workers in their workshop. We built a soffit-roof of beams which we covered with two yards of earth to absorb the effects of a direct hit by a bomb. We put down a floor of boards and thus completed our wooden ark.

Our bunker had two entrances, one for entering and exiting when necessary, and the other as an emergency exit in case of discovery.

The entrance was made in the following manner: A toilet stood right next to the wall of the bathhouse. We made our main entrance in there, through a removable wooden panel that opened into a two-yard-long tunnel through which you had to crawl on all fours into the bunker. But before crawling one had to push soil up against the panel so that if someone tapped on it, it would not sound hollow.

At the other end of the bunker was our emergency exit, which led into a workshop. From this exit one had to crawl on all fours through a yard-long tunnel toward a wooden chute built to look like a drain for water.

We drew electric lighting into the bunker and installed a radio. Air was a problem. How could such a chamber be ventilated? This was one of the most challenging problems we had to deal with. The failures of others had taught us that no pipes or chimneys could protrude aboveground, for the Germans had learnt to recognize these signs immediately.

Our first solution was to install two electric fans to draw in air and blow it out through a chimney. Looking like a thin stick standing over the center of the building, the chimney reached down into the cellar to serve the bathhouse. We made a hole and installed the fans, one of which blew the stale air out of our bunker while the other drew fresh air in. Unfortunately we realized that we were at the mercy of the electrical power source. If a bomb struck the electric plant or even an electric line, we could suffocate within several hours. We saw no alternative until Engineer Indursky thought of a way to provide us with another source of air. To the water and toilet pipes that lay outside the building, he added another pipe that seemed to be part of the plumbing. This let in a small amount of air.

Since our bunker was so deep that its floor was only a yard above water level, we took advantage of that to dig a well inside the bunker. Considering that the construction of our bunker had taken us only two weeks, you can imagine how hard we worked to accomplish so much in such a short time. The people working on the bunker worked nonstop.

The work had to be done so silently that the people doing the digging should not be able to hear the sounds of their own shovels digging into the ground. No stone could fall. The workers had to quickly grasp what was required of them without being able to ask again what was needed. Despite the frightening cavernousness, despite constant fear of death, despite hunger, and despite the hopelessness around them, these people had to dig within themselves to discover enough willpower for the work to turn out exactly according to plan.

When the bunker was ready, we were leery of entering our ark until we were sure that the Germans were about to liquidate the ghetto. Meanwhile we carried in what food we could obtain, and a supply of bedding. Some families soon decided to move in there; some of the elderly and women and children also moved in; and others stayed out for a while longer.

What the least error in our plans would have meant, we had ample proof of all the time. The Gestapo, the SS, would rip a hideway apart with grenades or simply take the people that they had found hiding and shoot them on the spot.

· 31 ·

HIDDEN

The Russians drew closer and closer to Vilna. The speed of the Russian advance told the Germans that they would have to give up not only Kovno but all of Lithuania as well. Their defeat was now so obvious that even a small child couldn't miss it. But the Germans still had work left to do. Their bloody days, however numbered, were not over yet.

The Jewish ghetto in Kovno—to be exact, the remains of the ghetto—still had to be liquidated. Since time was short, the Germans took themselves to the task energetically. Some 14,000 Jews remained alive in the Kovno ghetto/concentration camp and in the other camps near Kovno. On July 8, 1944, 17 Tamuz 5704, the liquidation of the last Jews in Lithuania began and the Jews of Kovno sensed it. In insane confusion they ran from death in every direction. Jews even tried to save themselves by hiding in the Christian cemetery that bordered the ghetto, and many were shot.

We knew that it was only a matter of days; liberation was imminent. But so was death. And the drive to survive was stronger than ever. Russian airplanes and the bombs they dropped on Kovno announced the future. It was horrible to imagine that, after all this time, in these final days having survived *Akzion* after *Akzion* we might yet be killed by the Germans.

On July 18th we went into the bunker. Hiding in our bunker were 34 men, women, and children—34 human lives locked into a Noah's ark of our own, trembling every moment with the fear of death. However Noah was outside on the water, while we were underground. In addition, no one hunted Noah, while we were the objects of an increasingly thorough search. We thirty four sought the privilege of continuing to live, of continuing to breathe G-d's air—the same right granted to the tiny worm crawling along the moist earth before our very eyes. We asked for nothing but to remain alive.

We died a thousand deaths in that stuffy bunker. The worst problem we had was our air supply. There never was enough air, even when the ventilators worked well. G-d, where does a person get the strength and the clarity of mind to think? All that mattered was that we were alive!

For the first several days we lay there like mutes, afraid to say a word lest our voices carry upwards. We could and did hear the Germans: "Get out, Jews!" "I'll shoot!" Their shouts were followed by shots, as the work of the murderers proceeded furiously. We could imagine the hell broken loose outside above us, but we could do nothing.

Suddenly, an explosion! A powerful blast shook our bunker and the electric light went out. The radio was silent. We shivered in the darkness. Worst, our ventilator fans stopped working when the electricity died. The air flow from the chimney was reduced by about half. We could overlook this if only—as the brilliant, hopeful thought illuminated our darkness— the Russians were truly approaching. To be more exact, it was our lives we saw drawing closer. The front had already come closer to us, perhaps Kovno was already the front. Or perhaps we were only a few hours or a day or two away from this.

One tremulous moment of happy expectation was followed by a minute filled with despondent trepidation and fear of death. One minute we heard footsteps overhead, screams, the banging of rifle butts on the roof of our bunker—and a flashing in the mind, "They've discovered us!" And a minute later a loud explosion shook the ground beneath and around us. And suddenly silence.

The impressions changed from minute to minute. For the most part, however, we suffered. We knew the Germans did not want to leave a single living Jew behind. They scoured every corner, searching the smallest hole, dragging people out and shooting them on the spot. Hope departed as we continued to hear the cadences of the German language above us. The Russians had not yet taken the city.

Ten thousand Jews had been taken away from Kovno by the Germans, as the butcher of the Kovno ghetto, Captain Wilhelm Göcke, phrased it, "to keep them from falling into the hands of the enemy."

They knew they were still missing 4,000 Jews. They sought them out, flushed them out, and shot as many of them down as they could while we held our breath in our bunker. Across the ghetto in Block A, Rav

Moshe Skaruta of Slobodka and Rav Dovid Perelman of Alexot were killed in their bunkers.

Explosion followed powerful explosion as the Germans rampaged through the ghetto blowing up buildings. Wall after wall crumbled as the Germans systematically blew the ghetto apart. We heard the sound of trucks approaching our building. Then came a deafening explosion. The ground under and above us trembled. We felt everything around us shaking, cracking, and crumbling. The boards of the bunker groaned under a heavy load, and we wondered what would happen if the beams in our ceiling collapsed. And the air supply seemed to have been cut off. The ceiling began to sag and we worried that we were about to be buried alive. There was nowhere to escape to. A hellish fire was burning the entire building. The heat grew unbearable. For the thousandth-millionth-time we prepared to die.

"Come here, Moishe. Come here my child, Noachka," said Ida Shalansky one of the women in the bunker. "Let us be buried alive together."

"*Rebbi,*" Yosha the butcher had moved his face, distorted from pain and lack of air, close to mine, "say *Viduy* with me, *Rebbi.*" I said *Viduy* with Yosha. As he repeated each word after me, he looked ahead and surely saw what he was leaving behind—life!

"Why aren't you saying *Viduy* for yourself?" Yosha asked me. I responded with words I didn't quite understand myself: "I still want to live!"

I just didn't feel death in me yet. The life I had all along been so far from, suddenly grew closer to me and I felt it pulsating within me so strongly that I felt I could not have answered otherwise.

We lay down on the floor and waited for the ceiling to collapse; we waited to be buried alive. Everyone quietly prayed. What it was they were praying I could not hear except for the prayer of six-year-old Itala Garber, which I noted in my memory.

"Oh, G-d," begged the little girl with the burning eyes and the sunken cheeks, "let us die gently. Don't make us suffer. Not me, not my father and mother." This was Itala's prayer.

· 32 ·

BUNKER HELL

The fact that we were suffocating for lack of air demonstrated that we were alive. Those last days our bunker was reminiscent of Yechezkel's (Ezekiel) valley of dry bones. We were skeletons on the floor who did not know what was happening outside. Even our little lamp had gone out.

In the thick darkness we would, every so often, hear a choked-up cry, "Oh, people, save me! Give me air, I'm dying!" Or the frequent cry of children when their mother or sister had fainted. We poured water over those who fainted and let them lie in their places. What else could we do? A terrible vapor rose from the water and increased the heat in the bunker. The vapor had nowhere to exit; the chimney hole was too small. The temperature in our bunker must have been well over 110 degrees. It was a real hell. And we stayed in that suffocating atmosphere for ten days.

Can you imagine ten days and nights in such heat? Every day comprises 24 hours, every hour 60 minutes, and every minute 60 seconds. You need to breathe every second and you can't. You inhale fire and you exhale fire. *Gehinnom.*

Little Itala said, "G-d is bringing a flood of fire upon us!"

On the eleventh day an explosion broke our ceiling beams. The two yards of earth above the ceiling were pressing on the broken beams and the whole ceiling looked like it was about to cave in. At any moment we might be buried alive.

Nevertheless, people didn't move. They could barely breathe. Moreover, during the last several days a terrible sickness had manifested itself in the bunker. Almost everyone developed countless body sores which not only festered terribly but hurt as well. People could not move because of them. The steady heat in the bunker irritated the festering making people suffer terribly. I was the only one who did not suffer those sores. I have no idea why that was so.

When I stood up and saw the condition of our ceiling, I asked the engineer if he knew why the ceiling was still up although it seemed to be completely broken.

"This question you must ask the Divine Engineer," he replied. "It is truly incomprehensible, a miracle. Meanwhile, let us put up some boards as supports, because we can be buried alive at any moment."

And so this is what we did. As we worked with the boards we felt that the boards in the bunker were burning hot. The chimney opening was emitting terribly hot air since, as we later discovered, the buildings around us—ours, too—were on fire. The heated air brought with it the odor of roasted human flesh. The greater the heat grew, the more painful grew the body sores. Berel Penkinsky begged in a plaintive voice which sounded like it was coming from a grave, "Jews, take pity! Shoot me! Kill me! The sores are devouring my head, my marrow is bursting out of me!"

Doniyel, the boxing champion of the Baltic States, was lying like a gigantic block of wood on the dirty floor, unable to move. We were frightened by that—if he, so strong and energetic, was in such straits, what could the rest of us expect? How much longer could we hold out?

The heat drove some people to say terrible words. The groaning and crying combined into a horrible yammer that made my skin crawl. The absolutely unbearable heat was coming at us from above and below. The putrid odor of burning, of decomposing human flesh, of the stinking sores on the bodies of the people in the bunker, and the malodor of excrement turned our bunker into a hell that grew worse from minute to minute.

I frequently wondered, "How will we bury a body? It can happen anytime. Where can we put the body?" The thought made me shudder. All around me lay people who in normal times could not have tolerated so much agony: Old Basya Lipman, who had had a heart condition for ten years and every so often seemed about to die; Mrs. Chodosh and the others whose lungs seemed about to burst because of the heat and who were lying on the floor, the dirt infecting their wounds, which were festering and excruciatingly painful—they should have died long ago. Indeed they wanted to die. At this point they would have thanked the person who took away their life.

"So, where will we bury them?" I kept worrying.

Yet these people lived on. They breathed fire and spit it out, and lived on.

*The Kovno Ghetto in flames: In July 1944, as Soviet forces approached Kovno, the Germans liqui-
dated the ghetto, using grenades and explosives to kill Jews hiding in the ghetto's bunkers. About
8,000 Jews were sent from the ghetto to concentration camps in Germany proper. 80 percent of them
died before the end of Hitler's Third Reich.*

· 33 ·

BUNKER HELL, CONTINUED

As I have noted earlier, I was the only person in the bunker who did not suffer from sores. The sad joke that went around was that my *tallis* that I wore for my thrice daily prayers protected me. But it was my strength that allowed me to assist the sick as much as possible.

We had reached the end, we thought. We could not hold out any longer. There was no air!

We could die easily. All we had to do was step out of the bunker into the sunshine. If the Germans were still there (we had been cut off from the outside world for ten days) they would shoot us on the spot, whereas inside we were dying slowly and painfully. We decided that no matter what the consequences we would open one entrance and see what was happening. In the meanwhile we would be letting in some fresh air.

Engineer Indursky said that we would get more air if we opened our second entrance, the one that led into the small workshops. There would also be less chance of discovery that way.

So we got to work. We had blocked the entryway from the inside with soil, and had to dig it away to make a clear passage to the workshops. We hoped for fresher air, but found ourselves inhaling smoke and the odor of roasted human flesh. Even that smoke and stench-filled air was fresher than what we were breathing inside our bunker. We set up a watch at the entrance to give us an opportunity to seal it up if discovery were imminent. A few men were put on watch at the entrance and they gladly took the opportunity since it afforded them a turn at somewhat less labored breathing.

Opening that entrance brought us, besides the bit of air, some disheartening news, "The Germans are still here!" And we had thought we had already suffered through their last days.

The bearer of this news was Hirshel Garber, who had been standing on guard duty. He suddenly came running and called over several men who began to whisper among themselves. We had no idea what was happening, but we grew frightened as we saw them push the soil back over the entrance. The order was given to lie still, not even to whisper or groan. So we lay there in indescribable terror for about four hours. Nothing happened.

When I asked Hirshel what had happened, he told me that while he was on guard duty he had suddenly heard a German yell, "Jew! You're going to be shot!" This was followed by the reverberation of several shots, a shout of *Shema Yisroel*, and the thud of a body falling onto the drain that led to our bunker. "I am certain," he concluded, "that they are now going to search for us. So we must be very quiet."

The rest of the day passed in silence, and at night we again decided to dig out and see whether we might still be able to save that Jew. But he was already dead. We closed the entrance and remained on duty to conserve air.

Suddenly.... My G-d! How many suddenlies there were when one's heart seemed to stop beating in terror of death! A human life does not contain enough minutes for that.

I heard whispering in the bunker. Chayim called to Doniyel and Hirshel, "Get your guns and let's defend ourselves. We will not give up our lives so easily." What was going on?

What's the difference? Death was again at our door. No one moved a limb. Their attitude was, "Let death come already. As long as it will soon be one minute after death." No one trembled, no one was anguished, no one was upset about what must ultimately happen. Merely silent apathy and a light flicker of anticipation.

But death did not come then.

We heard powerful bangs directly over our heads. We also heard something pouring down over us. We were once more certain that they had discovered us and were digging us out. We lay there in fright all night long, those of us who still cared recited *Viduy* from time to time. By morning we realized that a strong wind was blowing outside, and that it was blowing sheets of construction metal that the explosions had severed. It was the banging of these big sheets of metal that we had heard all night. The same wind was blowing clods of loose earth onto our bunker, the sounds of which we had mistaken for digging overhead. Through our chimney-air pipe we felt fresh air coming through, an indication that the air outside was turbulent.

As soon as the terror of death had passed, people began to pass out from the heat again. It was truly extraordinary: as soon as death knocked on our door, the ailments and illnesses took flight and fled. No one fainted, no one groaned; people found air to breathe—somehow. And as soon as the terror passed, the fainting began anew, wounds began again to burn and fester, and people again began to beg for death.

We again decided to try and open the other entrance to our bunker, and send the strongest and healthiest of us out to see what was going on. We dug away the soil that masked the entrance. We knew that what we were doing was extremely risky, for we needed shovels to dig the soil away, and any noise could give us away. For all we knew, the Germans could be standing directly overhead.

But we took the risk. We finished moving the soil, and removed the panel. Doniyel went into the toilet and from there slowly, on all fours, crawled out into the open. It was 2 a.m., and we sat or lay down below, tremblingly awaiting his return.

Doniyel did not tarry. He crept back in, frightened, and told us that as soon as he crawled out he bumped into someone and fell directly into his arms. He was ready to fight, but discovered that the man was dead and had been lying there with his arms outstretched. He also saw that the entire Block C, as well as what other buildings he could see with his lamp in the dark, had been blown up and the entire ghetto had been turned into heaps of bricks.

As day dawned, Doniyel, Chayim, and Hirshel went up to get a better look.

Above our bunker was another bunker that had been built before ours when the Delousing Institute was set up in the cellar of Block C. It had served as a hideout for Jews who wished to avoid round-ups when Germans quickly grabbed Jews off the street and did not thoroughly search the houses.

Once it became apparent that the Germans were determined to murder every Jew, that bunker was deemed too vulnerable in case of a serious search. That was the point at which the Lipman family—keeping the secret even from me—began to build "our" bunker. We ultimately provisioned the upper bunker so that when the Germans discovered it they would think its Jews had already been discovered and would not search any further. As it turned out, other people did hide there and were caught. Later we found their possessions, as well as their work cards, in the bunker. We also discovered the dead body of Meir Levy of Tavrig. Although his face was charred, we could establish his identity through his clothing and work card. He was buried right on the spot. We intended to bury him in a Jewish cemetery if we survived.

What we could see of the ruins of the ghetto—we were afraid to look beyond Block C because that would require standing up, and in daylight we were afraid to do that—was horrifying. In the wreckage of Block C alone we saw hundreds of corpses amid piles of bricks and other rubble. The corpses were burned and lacked limbs; and their putridity was overwhelming. Everything seemed to be sooty from smoke which rose from the smoldering houses around us.

It was clear to us that there were no Jews left, with the possible exception of people like us in some undiscovered bunker. But where were the Germans? Were they still around or were they gone?

We soon had an answer to our question. In the distance we could hear German-speaking voices. Swiftly, we scurried back down into the tunnel and crawled into the bunker, quickly covering the entrance once more with soil.

After burying ourselves again, we felt the oppressive heat of the bunker even more. Again people passed out and groaned in anguish. Having breathed the outside air for a while, we realized how horrible the air was where we were. Everything was covered or filled with sand and mold. A mighty layer of mold coated our food and also our well, our only source of water. My *tefillin* were covered with mold. If we removed the mold at night, it grew back again by the next morning. So we decided to open up and look out again.

This time it was Hillel who stood guard. We later found out how he saved our lives. Lying next to the panel he suddenly heard two Lithuanians talking. The Lithuanians were often worse than the Germans. Their hatred of Jews led them to search the ruins of the ghetto, to seek possible survivors even when they knew the Russians were about to enter Kovno.

Hillel heard their voices as they approached our bunker and came upon the drain. They searched it for further entrances. One of them banged on the boards to determine if there could be a hollow space behind them. Hillel put his hand on the boards so that when the fellow banged the sound was firm, not hollow. Believing the boards lay against solid earth, they went on their way.

· 34 ·

OUR LIBERATION

We understood from overhearing the Lithuanians that the Russians were already at the gates of Kovno, and so our liberation was just as close. But every second we waited was still intensely difficult.

We decided not to open either bunker entrance so as not to take any last-minute risks. But the dose of outside air we had breathed made it now unbearable for us to endure the air in the bunker, particularly when the temperature there reached 40 degrees centigrade. So once again we opened the "front" entrance.

Before going up we listened very cautiously. Who could know whether the Russians had finally arrived, or whether they had been delayed, G-d forbid?

We decided that only the men would go up to the bunker above ours, because the women had no strength to crawl and climb up. Besides, once the men had gone up, the women would have more air.

We again moved the soil with our hands, and the men crawled out and crept up. When I finally raised my head and looked outside, what I noticed amazed me.

"Green grass!"

Short shoots of fresh grass were pushing their way up in the cracks between the piles of ruins. How quickly nature "forgets"! Done with Kovno's Jews, nature continued her constant tasks.

Everything was cemetery still. It seemed incredible that a year ago there had still been vibrant Jewish life here, that a veritable anthill of people lived here, worked here, hoped and dreamed here. People with assorted faces and a variety of characters loved and hated, cried and laughed, studied, thought, and were silent. Each had a home and a past and hopes for a future. Now it was one gigantic cemetery. The city had died along with its population. Only the sky remained the same as before—clear, blue, and silent.

Heaven had decided that they should die and that we should live. As their deaths were incomprehensible so too was our survival incomprehensible.

Everything that dies in nature is recycled. But Jewish Kovno will never live again. Our home was destroyed forever. We, the sole survivors of tens of thousands, stood in a tiny circle and looked out at our razed past—and were absolutely silent.

But because we still couldn't tell if the Russians had come, we returned to the upper bunker and lay there for a day and a night, and greeted our first guests from the living world—flies! I have never seen so many and such large flies. They were as big as bees and there must have been literally millions of them. Buzzing around us, stuffed with human blood, they bit us mercilessly. We could not drive them away. Yet deep in everyone's heart was a sense of joy at being alive! The flies recognized us as human beings! They, at least, recognized us as creatures with equal rights.

Lying in the bunker in the evening, we again heard the voices of Lithuanians. They were discussing among themselves the imminent arrival of the Russians. Of course, we crept down into our lower bunker as quickly as we could, and covered the entrance with soil. We did that just in time. We heard the Lithuanians enter the bunker above and search it. It was not enough for them that they had robbed Jewish fortunes, that they had taken everything they wished from us, and that they had murdered tens of thousands of Jews. Even at the last minute they were still looking for Jews and their property.

Back in our bunker, the lack of air grew so serious that all of us lay faint and gasping for breath. We lay that way for five more days before once more deciding to open an entrance, this time on the side where the Lithuanians had discovered the drain.

After we managed to get it open, we heard shooting nearby. We figured that the Russians were probably fighting street battles. The shooting continued all night, and ceased in the morning.

To go out or not to go out? Who could say for sure? Nobody wanted to get killed at the very last minute. And so we lay low for *another* two days. Wednesday at 4 p.m., August 3, 1944, we concluded that one of us, no matter what, had to go out and see what was going on.

The first one out was Doniyel. As soon as he reached the open air, he heard someone loudly counting in Russian, *"Raz! Dva! Tri!"* "One! Two! Three!" This didn't prove that the Russian army had arrived; the man could have been a Russian prisoner-of-war being used to build a bridge. Doniyel stretched out on his stomach, and crawled toward the sound. It was a difficult route to crawl, and a horrifying one, for it was strewn with dead bodies, which he had to push aside or crawl over. Many of the bodies were disintegrating and filling the air with a disgusting odor. Doniyel kept inching along.

Another step, and another, and finally he lay there and raised his head to look around: Russians!

Were they in fact people? To Doniyel at that moment it seemed that they were non-human creatures, some kind of superhuman beings. Those creatures who were standing there and repeating, *"Raz! Dva! Tri!"* had brought freedom!

He tore himself up from his spot and ran over to them. He fell on their necks and kissed them, unaware of what he was doing, nor aware of himself. He wept and shouted in ecstasy, *"Ya Yevrei!* I am a Jew!"

For the first time in so many long years, a Jew dared to express that he was a Jew without fear, without whispering, but aloud and joyously, with happy eyes. Then suddenly he left the Russian soldiers standing in confusion and ran back to us. As quickly as he could, he raced back to our entrance hole and shouted with his remaining strength, "Brothers and sisters, we are freeeee!"

And how do you suppose we reacted? Do you suppose we fainted, screamed, laughed, cried, hugged and kissed each other? Did we crawl out of the bunker and lay like fish on land with wide open mouths gasping for air, air, and more air, full and pleasant and refreshing? Did we throw ourselves around and around, enjoying the space we had until now not had?

None of the above. In these initial minutes we were still afraid to speak loudly, afraid to stand up to our full height. Every stone intimidated us. A shadow, a human voice, a quivering ray of sunlight was enough to make us tremble. Our hands could not believe they were touching our own live bodies. Our eyes had to adjust to the bright light and to looking freely without fear at the blue horizon. Our feet trembled when we first placed them on the charred terrain.

Two Russian officers came right over to us. They were speechless when they looked into our bunker, where we had survived the 38 days. They stared at the bunker and then at us incredulously, as if we were part of a supernatural event, totally unable to accept the facts that were staring them in the face. They had seen much that was strange and frightening in their long years of battle. But our situation was one they were

The survivors of Rabbi Oshry's bunker, outside the bunker after their liberation.

In front of the ghetto bunker in which he survived, engineer Indursky (left, front), explains to Red Army Major Bulganov (in uniform, at right) how the bunker was built. Rabbi Oshry (beardless, in dark jacket) is standing between Indursky and Major Bulganov.

encountering for the first time. They gazed at us and silently shook their heads.

We had been in the bunker for 38 days. We had not been counting the days, probably the way one does not count the minutes of dying. But on that wonderful, miraculous day—14 Menachem Av 5704, the 3rd of August 1944—we tallied up the days.

Yes, yes, we had spent 38 days in Hell. The Russian officers told us that the Red Army had entered Kovno on the night of the first of August. In other words, we had spent two extra days in the bunker.

All we saw as we looked around was one vast ruin filled with corpses, one massive scream of anguish for the world of horrors.The ghetto was gone. Slobodka, the world-famous city of yeshivos, had been expunged from the world.

But the sun was the same. The sun that used to shine upon Jewish Slobodka and Kovno was now shining on their ruins.

· 35 ·

KOVNO AFTER LIBERATION

The situation on the battlefronts grew consistently worse for the Germans, and the hopes of the Jews rose ever higher that the day of total German defeat might soon arrive.

On August 1st, 1944, the Russian army liberated Kovno. But the Jews, in shock from their horrible experiences under the Germans—and still not aware of the Russian liberation—were afraid to show their faces and remained in their hideouts. Eventually, however, the Jews began to crawl out of their bunkers, attics, cellars, wells, and forests.

The partisans, too, soon began to stream into Kovno from the forests.

Three days later, on August 4th, 265 survivors gathered for the first time after liberation in the courtyard of the Choir-synagogue on Azeskiena Street in Kovno.

The gathering was dramatic and emotional. Friends recognized friends; brothers and sisters, parents and children, met again. There was much kissing and hugging, and the cries of joy surely rose heavenward. Each of us had believed that we were the only one who had survived or one of only a handful.

Slowly, slowly people came to themselves and a meeting was held. A committee of four was formed whose members were a lawyer named Dinner, Hillel Birger, (both of whom had been in the bunker with me) Avrohom Shapiro, and myself. The main purpose of the committee was to seek ways to provide food for the refugees. We immediately asked Professor Rebelsky who had been a doctor with the Russian army to intercede with the Red Cross, which provided us with barely enough food for a *hamotzi* blessing.

We opened a communal kitchen in Kovno at 20 Leisvas Street. It did not have the capacity to supply everyone with cooked food, because new survivors arrived every day. The numbers soon reached about 600 and the food problem became very serious.

The Red Army did not concern itself with feeding the civilian population since the battlefront was no more than six miles from the city. Bread was not available, not even for money. All the more was it unavailable for the impoverished, barefoot, starving, and frightened people who had just emerged from their hiding places.

In this situation, I proceeded on my own initiative—without the committee's approval—to approach the municipal Social Assistance organization to provide food for us, at least for the sick and for the children.

Accompanied by Mr. Lurya, who knew the director of the organization personally, I visited the Social Assistance office in Kovno to obtain food—not, G-d forbid, for free, but at their "reasonable" prices. Mr. Lurya introduced me to the director, Mr. Petraitis, and to his co-workers. The director pretended to be pleased that a rabbi had managed to survive and greeted me effusively. His co-workers also greeted me and maintained an official stance of friendliness. But it was hard to believe after what we had experienced, that any Lithuanian cared at all for a Jew.

I got right to the point. I asked for bread, nothing else. And not for everyone, only for the ill and for the children. The director smiled broadly and in the most refined tones refused my request. His official line was that he could only issue bread to citizens who possessed a card that affirmed their neediness. Since I could not produce these cards, our people were not entitled to bread.

His ironic smile and his false concern so upset me that I took courage and retorted, "Mr. Petraitis! I have regretfully deceived myself into believing that there are Lithuanians who commiserate with our suffering. But now I am convinced that you would prefer to watch with your own eyes as the survivors die of hunger!"

Without a farewell, I walked out and slammed the door behind me. He ran after me and apologized. Then he invited me back into his office to calm me down and gave me a certificate for 200 pounds of bread.

I walked away with the certificate, trying to figure out how far 200 pounds of bread might go to satisfy the appetites of nearly 600 people. But whatever I calculated turned out to be wrong because by the time I brought the news to the survivors, their numbers had been swelled by new arrivals from nearby towns and villages: Pilvishok, Shemlishok, Zhoslia, Vilkovishk, and Rasseyn.

◆ ◆ ◆ ◆

On the 10th of August, a number of the city's citizens requested that I become the rabbi of Kovno. Aware that the city's communal institutions had been destroyed and that my task would be to reestablish them, I was anxious about undertaking so responsible a position and so I turned down their request.

But they did not leave me alone. They argued that at this time a spiritual leader was essential, and they appealed to my religious conscience with an assortment of talmudic and midrashic citations. At last I accepted their proposal, and the Soviet authorities also recognized me as the official leader of Kovno Jewry.

My first step was to organize a community. This community was recognized by the Soviet authorities and received the status of a corporation authorized to deal with the remaining synagogues and cemeteries.

We immediately hired two *shochetim*, Reb Mordechai Zuckerman and Reb Yitzchok Ezros. We founded a chevrah kadishah (burial society). Nachum Levitan, a lawyer and former head of the Kovno community—was elected *gabbai* of the synagogue. Rebetzin C. M. Shulman was chosen community secretary.

Although we had elected a *gabbai* for a synagogue, we actually had no synagogue suitable for praying. Almost all the synagogues and houses of study in the center of Kovno had been destroyed, while those that were left standing had been turned into horse stables, automobile garages, or warehouses.

Only one synagogue was miraculously intact—the Choir-synagogue. But it was too far from the area where most of the Jews had settled to be designated the house of prayer. So Hoizman's kloiz at Mairana Street was designated the official synagogue.

When we first saw it, Hoizman's kloiz had no doors, no windowpanes, and no benches. It had been partitioned into a stable for horses. The broken ark was a lonely, muck-shamed orphan amid hay and straw. We fixed it up as best we could and on Shabbos, August 12, 1944, when we read *parshas Ekev* (the third portion of Deuteronomy), we blessed the new month of Elul in Hoizman's kloiz.

The first Rosh Hashanah and Yom Kippur after liberation, Hoizman's kloiz was packed with Jewish soldiers and officers of the Red Army, among them Professor Rebelsky from Odessa in the Ukraine. It had been many years, they told me, since they had last participated in synagogue prayer with fellow-Jews. The crying of some of them and the anguished silence of others were noticeable in the large crowd. We prayed in particular for our brothers and sisters who remained in the forests and in bunkers in the part of Lithuania still in German hands, and for those who were imprisoned in the German hell-camps. We prayed to G-d to take pity on them and redeem them from suffering and death.

Hoizman's kloiz was not limited to use as a place of prayer. It became the central address for communal matters, and for all dealings with the municipal offices.

The post office delivered letters whose addressees it could not locate to Hoizman's kloiz. This is also where letters arrived from overseas with inquiries about relatives and friends. In this kloiz the Jewish community council held its meetings, and in this kloiz we witnessed the heartrending scenes of relatives rediscovering one another.

As mentioned earlier, I had managed to save my small Torah scroll. I placed this *sefer* Torah in Hoizman's kloiz; it was the first of several *sifrei* Torahs we managed to gather.

The first sermon given by Rabbi Oshry after liberation at Hoizman's Kloiz.

Rabbi Oshry with Professor Rebelsky of the
Russian Army Medical Corp at the Choir-synagogue.

· 36 ·

A TREASUREHOUSE OF JEWISH BOOKS

After liberation we founded a Jewish school and 24 children were enrolled. We obtained the building of the former Jewish National Council at 36 Kestucia Street and appointed Mr. Refoel Levin and Mrs. Abramovitch as teachers.

The establishment of the school brought up a new problem, textbooks. Where could we obtain *chumashim* and other *seforim* for studying in the school and also in our new synagogue and *beis midrash*?

We obtained a permit from the Soviet authorities to seek Jewish works in the cellars and attics of buildings in which Jews had dwelt before the war. Our searches brought golden results.

In the customs house we found 12 boxes of holy books that bore the stamp, "*Beis Midrash Hayashan*, Hamburg." These works had been the property of German Jews who apparently had taken them along when the Germans "resettled" them, and were left behind, collected by the Germans after they murdered the Jews in the Ninth Fort. These works, many of which had been printed in the 16th century, were of great cultural and historical value, true Jewish treasures.

We also found holy books from the library of Baron Rothschild. In addition we put together an enormous library of holy books we found in houses that had been occupied by Jews before the war.

All of these works were ceremoniously carried into Hoizman's kloiz where they were set up properly. The vast number of *seforim* was testimony to the spiritual height of the Kovno Jewry that was. As we looked over these works, our hearts ached and we could not hold back our tears at the tragic deaths of all the martyrs who used to study these works. We asked each other, "Where are the people who studied from these sacred books? Where are their corpses, their skeletons? Almost none of them was buried in a Jewish cemetery."

That was the point at which we realized that the crushed and charred corpses and bones of several thousand martyrs were still lying in Slobodka, where the Kovno ghetto-camp had stood. We concurred that these bodies and bones needed to be buried in a Jewish manner.

German prisoners forced by the Soviets to help bury the Jewish dead in the ghetto cemetery.

The Ghetto cemetery.

· 37 ·

KOVNO BURIES ITS MARTYRS

There had been 14,000 men, women, and children in the Kovno concentration camp on July 8, 1944, 17 Tamuz 5704, when the Germans, having decided to liquidate the ghetto, began to transport the ghetto Jews to Germany. Nearly 10,000 Jews were transferred out of the ghetto, while the other 4,000 sought refuge in hideouts and bunkers.

When the Germans realized that so many of the Jews were missing, they blew the ghetto apart with dynamite. Those who were flushed out were either shot on the spot or transported to Germany. Of those who remained in their hideouts, many were burned or suffocated to death. Those who were killed during the liquidation of the ghetto numbered in the thousands and parts of their bodies were strewn all over the area. Only the dogs found visiting the area worth their while, as the Psalmist phrased it, "the flesh of Your pious ones for the beasts of the earth."

It was difficult to identify the corpses, mangled and bloated as they were. Nevertheless some individuals were able to identify their dear ones by their garments, their card numbers, or by the objects they had on or in their clothing. Chayim Weintraub identified his father and mother, his sister and his brother-in-law. Other

Rabbi Oshry assisting Chayim Weintraub with keriah after he recognized his parents' bodies.

Rabbi Oshry (in tallis), flanked by Jewish partisans, eulogizes the martyrs of the ghetto on the grounds of the Ninth For

A group of partisans and Jewish survivors at the Ninth Fort after liberation in August 1944.
Rabbi Oshry (wearing a hat) is in the center.

Jews envied him; I tore *keriah* (rending a mourner's garment) with him, done as part of mourning.

I poked around among the dead, hoping to recognize some trace of my former *Rebbi*, the *tzaddik* Rav Avrohom Grodzensky, dean of the Slobodka Yeshiva. I looked for his body among skeletons, amid bones, among torn-off hands and feet, among heads without bodies and bodies without heads. I discovered that he had been incinerated in the hospital when it was burned down on 22 Tamuz, July 13, 1944.

Suddenly I came across a shocking sight: The not-yet-decomposed body of a woman half-wrapped in a quilt. In each hand she tightly held one of her two dead children, their half-open eyes gazing emptily towards their mother's face. As I stared in shock at this heartrending tableau I felt as if my feet had been knocked out from under me. When I think of this even today, it nearly drives me crazy and arouses within me an overwhelming desire for revenge.

Considering the Torah's prohibition against letting dead bodies lie unburied, I discussed with the members of our burial society what needed to be done. They made it clear to me that burying those bodies and body parts was an enormous undertaking that required the labor of several hundred people. The few people we had in our burial society could not handle it themselves.

We turned to the Soviet authorities for assistance. After much effort, the Soviets put 100 German prisoners-of-war at our service. With their labor, we were able to dig out several hundred corpses that had been buried in their bunkers. We filled several dozen carts with bones. We also filled up some wagons with heads we were unable to match with bodies.

Those martyrs were buried together in the ghetto cemetery in very long, narrow graves, each skeleton separated from the next by the appropriate distance and separation as required by Jewish law.

G-d, avenge their blood!

We also collected the individual bones that were lying in the open field at the Ninth Fort—the cremated remains of the approximately 90,000 Jews of Lithuania, Germany, Austria, and France who the Germans murdered in the years from 1941 to 1944. The funeral pyres had left traces in the form of bones, charred and whole alike, which were finally buried in the Jewish ghetto cemetery outside of Slobodka.

After the burial of our martyrs, the community breathed more freely and began to think about finding the Jewish children who had been entrusted to Christian families or to children's homes run by priests, or had been hidden in churches and monasteries.

· 38 ·

LET MY CHILDREN GO!

To find the Jewish children who had been hidden throughout the terrible war years with Christian families and orphanages, I sought the aid of the highest Catholic spiritual authority in Lithuania, Bishop Adamovicius. He received me graciously and I appealed to him in the name of integrity, and in the name of the Heavenly Power before Whom all must ultimately render account. I asked him to utilize his personal influence on behalf of the return of Jewish children to their origins.

My appeal fell on deaf ears, however, and I left him in disappointment.

I then sent out circulars, in the name of the community, to all priests requesting that they announce in all the churches on the following Sunday that individuals and institutions that still harbored Jewish children should inform us. At the same time, I thanked them in the name of the survivors for what they had done for the children until now, and appealed to them to complete their good deed properly by returning the children. For this the survivors would remain eternally thankful.

These circulars, too, had little effect. Only a few priests were courteous enough to make the announcement in their churches. The majority ignored my request. In fact, not one Christian individual or institution informed the Jewish community about any Jewish children in their custody.

We did learn that many children were being kept in unsanitary conditions, and the community instructed two doctors, Dr. Abramovitz and Dr. Gurevitz, to visit the orphanages and determine the true facts.

At the Lafseles Orphanage, which stood a short distance from the old Slobodka cemetery the two doctors found children with sores who were tearing at their skin in anguish. They found children undernourished, thin, and pale. They immediately gave them medication and wrote a report to the Jewish community.

The community decided that it had to first establish an orphanage and then propose that the Christians—the very Christians who had first participated in murdering the parents and later had displayed "compassion" for their children—hand over our children to the Jewish orphanage.

With the assistance of Professor Rebelsky and others we established in the Jewish school building an orphanage that was recognized by the Soviet authorities. The four children with sores and four other ill children from the Lafseles Home were turned over to us. In the course of time, we managed to "beg" and receive 17 more children who were somewhat healthier. And that was how our orphanage retrieved 25 children from their Christian protectors.

In contrast with the number of infants and older children who remained among the Christians, this number is tragically minuscule. From the point of view of our Sages that "whoever saves a single Jewish life is considered as having saved a whole world" (Sanhedrin 4:5), our achievement was a major success.

The fact that we did not know exactly where the Jewish children were greatly hampered our rescue efforts. For example, we learnt that Brochala Shliapobersky, a granddaughter of Rav Eliyohu Meir Feivelson, Kupishok's rabbi from 1907 to 1926, was in the home of Keidan's chief of police. I quickly traveled to Keidan to save the child. When I arrived, I was informed that the police chief had moved to Germany. Some years later I was informed that Brochala had been removed from Christian hands by her aunt who lived in Vilna.

Upon my return from Keidan, a Christian woman approached me. In a pious tone she told me the dark secret of a house in which she knew a Jewish child was being kept. If I were to pay her so-and-so many American dollars, she would give me the details. Since I had no American dollars, I tried in every way I could to obtain the information by other means. Ultimately, I discovered in which Christian home the child was and, with G-d's help, she was taken to Israel.

I soon became aware of another Jewish child named Yehuda Eidelman. When I approached his Christian "mother," the boy, upon seeing me, began to wail that he wanted to "go home to the Jews." His crying brought a stream of tears to my eyes—they gushed uncontrollably as if from some limitless well.

When his real mother had given him over to the Christian woman, she had given him a note that read, "My child! I am leaving you forever. You are a Jew and remain a Jew. Better to die as a Jew than to live as a non-Jew!"

The situation was very delicate. Both the child and his adoptive "mother" had to be handled with tact. Every day the woman came to the community and asked for something for the child. We did our best to provide for him. Eventually, thanks to the self-sacrifice of the boy's aunt in the United States, Rebetzin Soloveitchik of Spring Valley, New York, the boy was transferred to her custody.

Rebetzin Shulman, before she set out from Kovno for Poland, told me that the priest who lived in Italias Street in Kovno would tell me where to find two Jewish girls, her niece Adina, the daughter of Rav Isaac Sher's son Yosef, and Shulamis Friedman, daughter of Rav Malkiel Friedman.

I went to the priest's house several times and did not find him in. When we finally met, he kept putting me off with excuses. Finally, I angrily demanded that he tell me where the children were. He replied that in two weeks they would be brought to Kovno. Two weeks passed, then a third, and the children were not brought. I ran over to his house again and raised a fuss. He ran out of the room and left me sitting there. I waited several hours until he returned and gave me the address of an orphanage run by nuns several miles outside Kretinga; where he said the children were.

I sent Bas-sheva Berkman, who worked for the community, and Rashl Deutsch to get the children. With G-d's help the girls arrived and were provided for. They had forgotten how to speak Yiddish and had to relearn their language. They were later transported to Rebetzin Shulman in Bnei Brak, Israel.

◆ ◆ ◆ ◆

Even the horrors of ghetto life had not deterred people from marrying and bringing new beings into their miserable world. And even in the ghetto, most baby boys had been circumcised. Some, however, because of difficulty in finding a *mohel*, were not. Then there were parents who calculated that if they left their sons uncircumcised it would be easier to put them in the care of Christian women.

Our community decided to circumcise the boys we had in our orphanage; however, there was not one *mohel* in Jewish Kovno in 1944. We were informed that in the town of Stoipitz near Vilna there was a *mohel* named Rav Noach Bokow. We brought him to Kovno and he brought 15 boys into the covenant of our Father Abraham.

Thus did we deal with and resolve issue after issue. After each new solution, a new communal problem would arise as we slowly rebuilt the Jewish community from the ashes. Seeking and implementing solutions did wonders for Kovno, and in particular for those who participated in the *mitzvos*.

Working to resolve the issues kept us too busy to mope about the tragic consequences of the Holocaust. Every solution we implemented gave us extraordinary satisfaction, a sort of compensation for some of the horrors we had suffered.

We regularly summed up everything we had accomplished: We had buried the Jewish dead, we had saved children from gentile homes, we had circumcised 15 boys. These and similar achievements gave our lives meaning and purpose. Our achievements freed us from the sense of inferiority we had developed. We began to plan a new achievement—the construction of a *mikveh*. During the Holocaust, the *mikvos* had been destroyed. Our new community decided to build a *mikveh* in the Choir-synagogue building on Azeskenia Street.

We threw ourselves into this holy work wholeheartedly. As the Talmud teaches, "One who comes to cleanse is aided from Above." Within a few weeks the *mikveh* was operative.

Immediately afterwards we began to think about matzos for Pesach—the holiday that commemorates that fact "that in every generation they rise up against us to annihilate us!"

Baking the matzos that year was more difficult for us than setting up the *mikveh* had been. The problems were two: we had no equipment with which to bake, nor did we have any money with which to buy flour. Flour was available only on the black market, which the Soviets called the "open bazaar."

This led to a further question: Who could provide *maos chitim?* There was no one among us who could contribute to such a fund, because we were all paupers.

We discovered broken parts of matzoh machines in two former matzoh bakeries. From these parts we pieced together a functioning matzoh machine. After a four-year interval, a matzoh bakery was reestablished in Zilber's cellar on Birshtan Street. Two weeks before Pesach we baked matzos with the very last *groschen* (Lithuanian coin) that the Jews of Kovno possessed. We also provided for the totally impoverished and for the children in our orphanage, and still had some matzoh left for the wounded Soviet soldiers who lay in the hospital.

In a spacious building on Mairana Street we organized a *seder* for those who lived alone. The purpose of these public *sedorim* was twofold—first, to give them a more festive character; and second, to provide for those whose entire families had perished. The *sedorim* were celebrated very festively. Jewish soldiers and officers of the Red Army joined us at each. They cried and sang along with us. I sensed that many of them were in effect "children who were raised in captivity among non-Jews."

On 9 Cheshvan 1945 we freely and undisturbedly bewailed our great losses. We observed the collective *yahrtzeit* (anniversary of a date of death) of our murdered brothers and sisters, of our nearest and dearest. Kovno's Jews came to Hoizman's kloiz to bewail their horrifying losses. Jewish soldiers and officers of the Red Army crowded in as well. The entire congregation, all of us orphans, together recited *kaddish*, a prayer of praise to G-d, one variant of which is recited in memory of the dead.

As the rabbi, I addressed the audience and offered words of consolation. Professor Rebelsky and others spoke. The Moscow cantor Misha Alexandrovitch recited the memorial prayer.

Children who survived the war hidden with Gentile families.

· 39 ·

RAV YITZCHOK ELCHONON SPECTOR

S tanding at the awesome mass Holocaust grave of Lithuanian Jewry, and reciting *kaddish* for the centuries-old Jewish communities martyred by Hitler, I recalled the rosiest period of Jewish life in Lithuania, the time of the great teacher of Jewry, Rav Yitzchok Elchonon Spector.

I shall try to draw a miniature portrait of this great and brilliant personality. I am incapable of providing a full, multidimensional picture, a complete evaluation, of this man who occupies one of the loftiest and most revered positions in the history of Lithuanian, Russian, and world Jewry—a unique giant in the annals of Jewish history. My source for much of the information below is the biography written by his personal secretary, Rav Yaakov Lipschutz.

Rav Yitzchok Elchonon grew renowned throughout the world as a genius in codifying Jewish law when he published his collection of responses, *Beir Yitzchok*. Major experts in halachah throughout the world followed his opinions. For example, during the famine year of 1869 he allowed the use of beans and peas on Passover. In 1875 he forbade the use of *esrogim* from Corfu in Greece, because the merchants were charging exorbitant prices that were beyond the means of the Jewish people.

In one of his most famous legal rulings, he found a way to allow Jews in the Holy Land to plow and plant during the *shemitah* year of 1889, although it is normally forbidden to work the land during a *shemitah* year.

When faced with the problem of an *agunah*—a woman who cannot remarry unless she provides evidence of her husband's death—Rav

Yitzchok Elchonon would immerse himself totally in the problem to seek a way to relieve the woman from her excruciating and often complex situation.

Rabbi Yitzchok Elchonon did not merely issue halachic rulings for the Jewish people; he personally involved himself in every individual's difficult situation. Wealthy gentiles also appeared before him for adjudication of their disputes.

He was not restricted to rabbinical, scholarly, and halachic problems. He was also an activist concerned with Jewish issues the world over. In 1870, during the Franco-Prussian War, he provided aid for the Jews of Strasbourg. In 1872, he arranged

Rav Yitzchok Elchonon Spector,
Kovno's rabbi, 1862-1896.

for the Alliance Israelite Universelle of France to provide assistance to Persian Jewry. Kovno suffered a major fire in 1881, and Rabbi Yitzchok Elchonon traveled to St. Petersburg to raise money for the victims and help rebuild Jewish Kovno.

In 1884, when Tsar Alexander III appointed a committee to "solve the Jewish problem," chaired by Baron Pahlen, Rav Yitzchok Elchonon was informed that the baron had once expressed his opinion that the Talmud was a demoralizing work. Rav Yitzchok Elchonon immediately turned to the esteemed Rabbi Samson Raphael Hirsch in Frankfurt-am-Main, and asked him to prepare an essay in German about the importance and the greatness of the Talmud. Rabbi Hirsch very soon published a short work entitled, "Regarding the Attitude of the Talmud to Judaism and to the Social Standing of Its Adherents." The work was sent to Baron Pahlen and, as was later learned, impressed him favorably.

When protest grew against Jewish *shechitah* (ritual slaughter) in Russia, Rav Yitzchok Elchonon pressured Dr. J. A. Dembo of the Alexander Hospital in St. Petersburg to write a book about the importance of *shechitah*. Dr. Dembo was able to demonstrate that the meat of animals that were stunned with a hammer before butchering—the "humane" method the Soviets were promoting—spoiled more rapidly than meat from animals killed by *shechitah*.

Rav Yitzchok Elchonon established a kosher kitchen for the many Jewish soldiers who were quartered in Kovno. The idea spread, and kosher kitchens were opened throughout Lithuania wherever Jewish soldiers were quartered.

Rav Yitzchok Elchonon frequently traveled to St. Petersburg where he participated in meetings to counteract decrees against the Jews and to cancel expulsions from the Pale of Settlement. Together with his brilliant son, Rav Tzvi Hirsh (Rabinovitch), he organized protest meetings in England and all over the world, where the pogroms and other anti-Semitic acts of the Russian government were publicly decried. Ultimately the czar accepted the resignation of the Jew-hating cabinet minister Ignatiev and replaced him with the novelist Leo Tolstoy.

In 1877, Rav Yitzchok Elchonon, together with Rav Yisroel Salanter, founded the Kovno *kollel* to strengthen Torah-study. Many of the ensuing generation's Torah leaders spent formative years in the Kovno *kollel*.

Rav Yitzchok Elchonon was loved and respected by ordinary people as well as by the great. When he lay ill, the street outside his house was covered with

Rav Tzvi Hirsh Rabinovitch, son and successor of Rav Yitzchok Elchonon; Kovno's rabbi, 1896-1910.

straw so that passing carts should not disturb the rabbi's rest. I remember Ora the Slobodka coachman telling me, "I merited longevity because Rav Yitzchok Elchonon rode in my cab and blessed me."

On 21 Adar 1896, the righteous genius passed away in Kovno at the age of 79. The funeral procession was extraordinarily large. Rabbis and communal activists from all over Lithuania came to Kovno. All of Kovno Jewry and that of its suburbs, young and old, escorted the sage to his eternal rest. Eulogies were held in almost all of Kovno's synagogues and houses of study, and in communities all over the world.

Throughout the decades after his death, his tomb was always piled high with written requests from people seeking his intercession on High for all kinds of difficulties.

In 1944, after my liberation I visited Rav Yitzchok Elchonon's grave. The tomb had been vandalized. The roof was broken and the grave had sustained damage. I had it repaired.

Let me mention the genius, Rav Tzvi Hirsh, Rav Yitzchok Elchonon's son and successor as rabbi of Kovno. He was a major Torah sage and an excellent speaker. He also helped his father greatly in his communal efforts.

· 40 ·

REMEMBER WHAT AMALEK DID TO YOU!

"Remember what Amalek did to you...never forget" (Deuteronomy 25:17,19). It is human nature to forget even the evil that one swore with seven oaths to remember. Because of this the Torah specifically commanded us not to forget it.

Remember what the German nation did to your brothers and sisters, to your old and and to your infirm, to your little children.

In Deuteronomy we find the description of what the Amalekite nation did to the Israelites on their way out of Egypt. Instead of making a frontal attack—the Amalekites attacked the Israelite camp in the rear where the weakest and most defenseless walked—women with children and the elderly. Because of this merciless behavior, the Torah commanded that every Amalekite should be killed in retaliation and also: "Write this as a memorial." Write in a scroll, in a book, what Amalek did to you. Because in book form it is more likely to be remembered.

It is natural to want to forget great evil. It is assumed that forgetting will make life easier and sweeter. In the instance of what the Nazis did to the Jews this would be an error which I'd like to prevent.

Remembering applies not only to what Amalek-Nazis did to six million Jews. It applies as well to what Amalek-Nazis want to do to the survivors, the Jews who remained alive. His fury has not yet abated. He is still not sated with the blood of two million children. That innocent blood is not enough for him.

Jews usually forgive their enemies. They do not desire or yearn for revenge. But in the case of Hitler the matter is entirely different. You may not forgive the Amalek-Nazi. As long as you live you must remember what he did to you. Do not be impressed by his civilized appearance or by his finely polished words.

Remember and do not forget!

Do not forget the outstretched hands of the children begging to save their lives. Do not forget the fathers and mothers, brothers and sisters.

Remember too our heroes and martyrs; remember their martyrdom!

Remember everything that your fellow-Jews wrote in their blood and suffering for posterity!

Do not forget what the Hitler-nation did to us!

We must keep these commandments forever.

"You will utterly eradicate the mention of Amalek." Sometimes after eradication there still remains a mark, a trace to remind you of what used to be there before. Concerning Amalek, however, G-d commanded that even the marks and the traces are to be eradicated.

Behind the barbed-wire fences of ghettos, Jews wrote in their diaries, "We will surely not survive. But those who are alive in the free world, and the few who may survive the ghettos, let them remember and declare throughout the world 'Remember what Amalek-Nazi did to millions of our people!'"

Let us also recall the martyrs, the sacred souls, the sacrifices, who died with courage and trust in G-d's will.

◆ ◆ ◆

In keeping with the Torah directive, "Remember what Amalek did to you!" I have written this book. Let our children and grandchildren be able to read and inform future generations what the modern Amalekites—the Germans—did to their forefathers and mothers.

Akmian•Alite•Aniksht•Birzh•Butrimants

Dorbian•Dvinsk•Ezherene•Gorzhd•

Kalvaria•Kamei•Keidan•Kelm•

◆ PART TWO ◆

Kretinga•Kupishok•Maliat•Mariampol•Mazheik

THE ANNIHILATION OF

Meretsh•Neishtot-Shaki•Plungyan•

LITHUANIAN JEWRY

Ponevezh•Possval•Radvilishok•Rakishok•Rasseyn•

The Cities and Towns

Riteve•Salant•Serey•Shadove•Shavl•Shirvint•

of Jewish Lithuania

Shkud•Shkudvil•Shvexna•Tavrig•Telz•Utyan•

Vekshne•Vilkomir•Vilkovishk•Vizhun•Vorne•

Yanishok•Yanova•Yurborg•Zhager

PREFACE

In writing these chapters about the towns and personalities whose lives and whose martyrdom earned them a place of honor in Jewish history, I have come to realize that many of these great people had already attained a place along the eastern wall of Lithuanian Jewish life during their lifetimes. Their martyrdom—the *kiddush HaShem* of their horrifying deaths at the hands of the Germans—elevates them to the highest rank of Jewry's noblest martyrs.

I cannot mention them all. I merely name the major Lithuanian rabbis, the true giants of Jewry, who were martyred. I shall present the facts straightforwardly, as I have entered them in my diary.

In each case the Yiddish name of the town is given, followed by the Lithuanian and Russian names. A variety of sources were relied on for population statistics including *Lita*, Culture Society of Lithuanian Jews New York, 1951; *Yahadut Lita*, Mosad Harav Kook, Jerusalem, 1959; *Yidishe Shtet un Shtetlech, etc.*, Berel Kahan, New York, 1991; *The Encyclopedia Judaica*, Keter Publishing House,1972, Jerusalem; *Lithuanian Jewish Communities*, Garland Publishing, Inc., New York, 1991; *Encyclopedia of the Holocaust*, Macmillan Publishing Co., 1990, New York.

AKMIAN

LITHUANIAN NAME: Akmene
LOCATION: In northwest Lithuania, a few miles northeast of Telz.
JEWISH POPULATION IN 1939: 100 Jewish families
JEWISH HISTORY: The Jewish settlement in Akmian dates back to 1839.
ECONOMY: Most of Akmian's Jews were shopkeepers, craftspeople, and farmers.
SPIRITUAL LEADERS: Akmian's rabbis included Rav Yitzchok Vunder, Rav Aharon E. Kahana, and the martyred Rav Nochum M. Verbovsky.
1939-45: Among the pitiful remnants of Lithuanian Jewry the story of "The Three Rabbis" is tragically well-known. These three rabbis, together at the head of their three communities, were able to write a noble page in the history of Jewish martyrdom. The story of their *kiddush HaShem* (martyrdom) needs to be told and retold.

The threefold cord—the holy trio of rabbis of whom I speak—were Rav Kalman Maggid, the rabbi of Vekshne; Rav Yosef Tzvi Mamiyaffe, rabbi of Mazheik; and Rav Nochum M. Verbovsky, rabbi of Akmian.

On or about the 25th of July 1941, the Germans ordered the Jews out of the neighboring towns of Akmian, Mazheik, and Vekshne. The Germans took them to Tirkshli, a small town near Mazheik, from where they were led into the nearby forest. The men, women, and children were separated. The communal leaders, the intelligentsia, and the rabbis were herded into a separate group.

The three rabbis, sensing that they were being ordered to their deaths, each donned his *tallis* (prayer shawl) and *tefillin* (phylacteries).

The eyewitnesses of that procession related how imposingly Rav Kalman Maggid, the old, gray rabbi of Vekshne, addressed the crowd. He told the Jews not to be sad, not to despair. "It is forbidden to show the Germans any sign of sadness. We must sanctify G-d. That is the loftiest, the holiest goal of a Jew. We must die as Jews, as holy people, as the members of G-d's people."

The rifles and the machine guns waited as the rabbi cried out, *"Shema Yisroel, Adonoy Elohenu!"* ("Hear, O Israel, the Lord is our G-d.")

The entire crowd responded, *"Adonoy Echad!"*

The guns spit forth their bullets and the souls of those holy Jews departed their bodies.

ALITE

LITHUANIAN NAME: Alytus RUSSIAN NAME: Olita

LOCATION: Alite, in southern Lithuania, was really two cities—the Polish Alite and the Russian Alite—separated by the Niemen River. Polish Alite belonged to the Suvalk governmental district, and Russian Alite belonged to the Vilna district. When Lithuania became independent, Polish Alite became a district capital since its population was greater and because it was more culturally advanced than its Russian sister city, which remained a small town. Alite, about 35 miles southeast of Kovno, was linked to Kovno by rail and bus lines. An asphalt highway connected these two cities, and buses left from one to the other every two hours.

Alite's main street.

JEWISH POPULATION IN 1939: 7,000

ECONOMY: Alite was surrounded by a large pine forest, and the city looked like a spa. It was considered strategically important, and fortifications were built in the forest. Barracks were built in both Alites to house the soldiers who manned the forts. Because so many soldiers were quartered in Alite, the city was economically secure. Jews drew much of their existence from supplying provisions for the army; others were shopkeepers, craftspeople, leather tanners, sawmill operators or lumber dealers.

INSTITUTIONS: Each Alite had its own Jewish communal structure, its own houses of study and worship, its own rabbis, and its own institutions. Alite was renowned for its nearly 400-year-old Jewish cemetery. Alite's institutions included an elementary school, a middle school, a library, a credit union, and Yosef Marshak's bank. These were in addition to the traditional *chadorim* (religious schools for young children) and the adult education religious seminars in the synagogues.

SPIRITUAL LEADERS: The roster of Alite's prominent rabbis includes Rav Zev Volf ben Moshe Yehoshua, Rav Chayim Nosson ben Moshe Levin, Rav Chayim Tzvi Broida (the father-in-law of Rav Zelig Reuven Bengis), Rav Yoel Zelig Zalkind, Rav Moshe Yaakov Rosenberg, Rav Yitzchok Noach Levinbrook (1890) and his son Rav Reuven (1909), Rav Eliyahu D.N. Kolodetsky, Rav Aharon Milevsky (later in Montevideo), the martyred Rav Betzalel Levin (in Polish Alite), and the martyred Rav Yehuda Yablonsky (in Russian Alite).

Polish Alite's leading citizens included Shmuel Potatovsky, the synagogue *gabbai*; Yaakov Yehuda Isrelsky; Yosef Marshak the bank owner; Chayim Kartzmar; and Kalmanovitch, the teacher. Russian Alite's leading citizens included Leiba Tkach, Reb Avrohom Chayim Kaplan, and Yitzchok Chazanovitch. Kaplan, who was respected by Jew and Christian alike, settled both Jewish and non-Jewish disputes, and all parties left his house satisfied with the services of "the compromise maker." He took no fee for this service.

The scholar Dr. Chayim Leib Peker, who survived the war and worked in the Weizman Institute in Rechovot, Israel, was originally from Alite. So too, was the famous New York communal activist, Shmuel Aharon Israel.

A *ger* (proselyte) named Kestig lived in Alite. A former officer in the German army, he had converted to Judaism during World War I. People recounted how observant he was, and that he frequently could be found in the Alite house of study.

1939-45: On the 22nd of June 1941, Alite was one of the first cities to be bombed by the Germans on account of its strategic location and fortifications. The Jews had no idea what was happening. They heard no news from abroad of impending war between Germany and Lithuania, because their short-wave radio receivers had been confiscated by the Russians.

The sudden bombardment upset everyone. No one knew what to do, for they had been unprepared for war. Higher Russian military officials, in the days before the war broke out, had been bringing their wives and children from deep in the interior of Russia to Lithuania in order to convince people that the reports about German forces building up at the Lithuanian border were merely British propaganda. The Russians were so effective in making people believe that the Germans could not invade that few Jews in the Lithuanian countryside were able to flee. From several dozen border cities there was not a single survivor.

The German bombardment damaged many houses, and the city

caught fire. Jews fled for nearby villages, but the roads were already dangerous for Jews. The Lithuanian fifth column was prepared to kill them on sight. The same was true in the villages—Jews could not remain there. And the Lithuanians were also shooting at the retreating Russian army. The confusion was very great: Where could one safely escape to? Before the Jews had decided that it was safest to flee deep into Russia, the Germans had beaten them to the punch. On Monday morning of June 23rd, Alite was in German hands. The city was in ruins from the German bombardment. The bridges had been destroyed. And it was difficult to communicate between Polish Alite and Russian Alite.

An entire mountain of trouble and anguish was suddenly dropped on the Jews. Old Dr. Abramovitch was arrested, as were Rav Levin and several citizens. The Jews were taken to work at cleaning up the city's rubble. Many of them were worked to exhaustion and then killed.

On the night of June 25th, several hundred Jews were rounded up and taken to work in Suvalk. They never returned. The murdering and robbing of Jews by Lithuanians increased to horrendous proportions. For a pair of boots, a Lithuanian would murder a Jew. Women were raped and thrown into the Niemen River.

Several hundred Jews were driven into a synagogue, and the synagogue was torched and the Jews burned alive.

This life did not last long. One night the Jewish houses were surrounded, and the men collected and led into the forest. They were held there for several days under the open sky without food, and then driven into pits they had been forced to dig themselves and killed. Several weeks later the women and the children were murdered the same way.

ANIKSHT

LITHUANIAN NAME: Anyksciai **RUSSIAN NAME:** Onikshty

LOCATION: Aniksht, in the Utyan district in eastern Lithuania, was one of the Lithuania's larger towns. The Shventa-Rika River flows through Aniksht on its way to the Niemen.

JEWISH POPULATION IN 1939: 400 families

JEWISH HISTORY: Jews settled in Aniksht in the 16th century.

ECONOMY: Aniksht was a manufacturing center for felt footwear for winter. Most of Aniksht's Jews owned or worked in the small factories that produced enough felt to supply all of Lithuania. Some of Aniksht's Jews also made a living poling rafts downriver.

INSTITUTIONS: Chassidim lived in town and had their own brick *kloiz* (small synagogue). In a town where all the houses were of wood, a brick synagogue was a novelty.

SPIRITUAL LEADERS: In 1704 the rabbi was Rav Gershon ben Abbele

Isserels. His successors include Rav Yekele ben Avrohom Emden and Rav Shlomo ben Yaakov Meir Schlossberg.

The town of Aniksht was renowned for its rabbis. These include Rav Moshe Yoel Guryon (1860), author of the halachic responsa *Roshei Besomim*; Rav Aharon Burstein (later rabbi of Tavrig); Rav Shmuel Avigdor Feivelson (later rabbi of Plungyan); Rav Eliyohu Ber Shor (who died in Israel in 1936); Rav Avrohom Mordechai Vessler (later rabbi of Plungyan, martyred in 1941 by the Germans); and the very last rabbi of Aniksht, Rav Kalonimos Kadishevitz, who was known as the Lottever Rav (Lotteva was a village near Aniksht) authored a work on the methods of thought common throughout the *gemora* (talmud) called *Toledos Yitzchok*. He was martyred by the Germans in 1943.

Rav Eliyohu Ber Shor of Aniksht.

Rav Kadishevitz's integrity and simplicity were astonishing. One Friday evening he was informed that the barber shop had not closed. He walked into the shop not long after candle lighting for Shabbos. The Jews who were sitting there dashed out, some of them in the middle of their haircuts, others in mid-shave. When someone asked him, "Rabbi, what are you doing here so late?" he replied, "I've come to wish the Jews a good Shabbos." That was his way of preventing Shabbos desecration in town. And it explains why he was so respected in Aniksht and in the rabbinical world.

As I have recorded, Aniksht was a felt-producing town. The owners of the factories mixed old fabric with wool to produce the felt footwear. Rav Kadishevitz informed the local Jews that they must not wear footwear that was not made from pure wool, because the fabric that came from old clothes might contain linen, and linen mixed with wool is forbidden to Jews to wear. He himself wore only clothing made of cotton (corduroy). He did not even wear leather boots since a boot's lining might contain wool mixed with linen. He would not even sit on an upholstered chair for fear that the fabric might contain the prohibited mixture.

Small wonder that Aniksht had very respectable citizens—men who were also philanthropists and scholars such as Yisroel Sheinzon (known locally as Yisroel Shimons), whose home was always open to the needy. Other notables were Mannes Gurevich, Yitzchok Charay, and Shimon Ratner.

Love for Torah abounded in Aniksht. Families took the best yeshiva students as sons-in-law. For example, the chief *shochet* (ritual slaughterer), Reb Chayim, took the *gaon* (genius) Rav Meir Eliyohu Veiner as a son-in-law; Rav Veiner served as rabbi of Vizhun and later of Yedvabna.

Aniksht families sent their sons to the yeshivos. Almost every yeshiva in Lithuania had students from Aniksht. When I studied in the Ponevezh Yeshiva, there were almost 20 boys from Aniksht there.

Before the end of the first world war, Aniksht had a Chassidic rabbi known as the Rav of Ushpal.

1939-45: The town continued normally until the Germans marched in on June 27, 1941. As soon as the Germans occupied the town, the Jews became the victims of torture and executions. These were directed, at

The Chevra Shas in Aniksht.

first, at Jewish refugees who had fled other cities and towns, such as Kovno, in an attempt to escape into Russia. Others came from towns that had been destroyed by the Germans. Many towns were cut off entirely; their townspeople had nowhere to flee.

Aniksht's refugee Jews were housed in the local houses of study and prayer. The Lithuanian fascists led the Germans directly there and pointed out "the Jews who are escaping to Russia." The synagogues were turned into slaughterhouses. Refugee Jews hiding elsewhere rushed out of town, but most were killed on the road.

When the Germans were done with the refugee Jews, they started in on the Aniksht Jews. They beat and raped women and imposed forced labor upon the men.

Not long after, on July 28, 1941, they assembled the Jews—men, women, and children, ill and well alike. The men were separated from the women and children, and tortured. They ordered the town rabbi to sing and dance for them, and then they tortured him. They led communal leaders to the Hasenberg, an area in Aniksht that had once housed the community's slaughterhouse. Along the same street that Jews used to lead their animals to the slaughter, now the rabbi and Yossel the *shochet* and Mannes Gurevitch and Yitzchok Charay and Shimon Ratner and the others were driven to their slaughter. Most were buried alive.

Several weeks later the women and children were also killed. Thus was an old Jewish community eradicated. The town itself went up in smoke.

BIRZH

LITHUANIAN NAME: Birzai RUSSIAN NAME: Birzhi

LOCATION: In northern Lithuania, north of Ponevezh, near the Latvian border. A district capital settled in 1415, Birzh was renowned for its 16th-century castle about which many legends abound, including that a treasure lies hidden in a cave below the castle that Napoleon once visited.

JEWISH POPULATION IN 1934: 3,000 (total population: 9,000)

JEWISH HISTORY: Jews first settled in Birzh in about the 16th century, when Prince Radziwill received the Jews in Birzh graciously. He helped them organize economically and protected them.

Karoim (Karaites) once lived in Birzh; they had their own cemetery and a synagogue. Two streets bore the name Karainsky. The Jews bought their synagogue from them when their population diminished.

ECONOMY: Jews in Birzh made their living from crafts and retail shops. The two large flour mills were owned by five Jewish partners. Jews used to come from the nearby towns of Possval, Pokroy, Linkova, Pumpian, Yanushkel, and Obalnik to buy packaged flour or to grind their own grain. Birzh also had a number of Jewish organ grinders who traveled around with their organs and such animals as squirrels, parrots, and hamsters, which performed clever feats such as drawing lottery cards.

INSTITUTIONS: Birzh had a Chassidic community with a *kloiz* of its own that followed the *Chabad* style of chassidism, which emphasizes intellectual and emotional facets in serving G-d. In addition to its *chadorim* and organized *shiurim* (Torah lessons), Birzh's Jewish institutions included Hebrew and Yiddish folk schools, an *OZA* (society for the protection of the health of Jews, a medical and child care organization) division, a Linas Hatzedek (guesthouse for wayfarers), a credit union, an old age home, a library, and other organizations.

Birzh also had a yeshiva for young boys. The deans were Rav Yehuda Leib Bernstein and Rav Binyomin Movsho. The students went on to the Slobodka Yeshiva and were some of its best students. Lithuania's well-known Oshry family was a Birzh family that produced rabbis and scholars. Birzh's scholars included Reb Nosson, the collector for the Slobodka Yeshiva (and the father-in-law of Rav Yehuda Leib Bernstein); Velvel Chenkin, Aharon Yuda Kramer, Eliyohu and Zundel Wien, Moshe Leib Chayat, Yitzchok Mindelevitch, Yitzchok Mass, Sholom Kripst, Leib Possvaletzky, and Mr. Chodosh.

SPIRITUAL LEADERS:
Birzh achieved great
renown because of its
rabbis. Among them
were Rav Tzvi Haleivi
Horvitz (who died in
1689); Rav Yechezkel
Katzenellenbogen, the
famed author of *Knesses
Yechezkel*, a book of rabbinic responsa, and in
1713 the rabbi of the
towns of Altona, Ham-

The big beis hamidrosh in Birzh.

burg, and Wansbeck; Rav Sholom Zak (who died in 1725); Rav Avrohom,
the brother of the Gaon of Vilna; Rav Shimon of Keidan (around 1820),
father-in-law of Rav Shmuel Salant, who himself was the son-in-law of
Rabbi Zundel of Salant—they moved together to Jerusalem in 1838; Rav
Azriel ben Gershon Ziv; Rav Yehuda Leib Levinson (around 1860) and his
son Rav Osher Nisson (author of a book of halachic insights, *Gan Na'ul*;
died in 1909); and Rav Pinchos HaKohen Lintop, who became rabbi for
the Chassidim in town in 1888.

Rav Osher Nisson's son, Menachem Nochum Nosson, was a brilliant
scholar known as the *iluy* (prodigy) of Birzh. One legend about him said
that he could tell at a glance how many bricks there were in a wall or how
many leaves there were on a tree. Rav Yisroel Lipkin of Salant (Reb
Yisroel Salanter) (1810-1883) once came to test the *iluy* and afterwards
commented, "His is one of the sharpest minds Jews have." Menachem
Nosson died at the age of 18. His original Torah insights were published
in his father's work *Gan Naul*, which includes his father's eulogy for the
prodigy.

Birzh's more recent rabbis included Rav Feivel Segal, a rabbinic judge;
Rav Eliyohu B. Shor, later rabbi in Aniksht; and Rav Binyomin Movsho,
later rabbi in Krekenova where he was killed by the Germans. The last
rabbi of the city was the martyred Rav Yehuda Leib Bernstein.

1939-45: When the Germans entered Birzh, the first victim was the
city's rabbi, Rav Yehuda Leib Bernstein. Lithuanian murderers called the
rabbi to the window of his house and declared, "Because you reported us
for once breaking the synagogue windows, and we were punished for
that, we've come to pay you back." And they shot him. As he collapsed,
he said to his wife, "You see? Because of a *mitzvah* I am privileged to be
buried among Jews." With difficulty and risk, the Jews buried him in the
Jewish cemetery.

The same bloody story ensued here as it had everywhere else. The men, women, and children were killed next to the castle. Bombardments reduced the city to rubble.

And so Birzh perished.

BUTRIMANTS

LITHUANIAN NAME: Butrimonicai RUSSIAN NAME: Butyrmantsy

LOCATION: In southern Lithuania, southeast of Kovno. Before World War I, Butrimants was in the Troki district; after Lithuanian independence, it became part of the Alite district. Not far from the town stood a tall hill where Napoleon had built a fort during his war with Russia. For a while Napolean actually lived there. People used to dig into the hill in quest of coins and other artifacts of that period.

JEWISH POPULATION IN 1939: about 200 families

JEWISH HISTORY: Butrimants was one of the older Jewish communities in Lithuania. The town's Jewishness and its poverty are encapsulated in an old Motka Chabad the Jester joke:

Motka tells a wealthy Vilna Jew, "If you want to live forever, move to Butrimants."

The rich man asked, "Why? Is the *Malach Hamovess* (Angel of Death) forbidden to enter that town?

Motka responded, "A tradition going back generations says that never since Creation has a rich Jew died in Butrimants."

ECONOMY: The Jews in town earned their living from commerce, from stores, as lumber dealers, as peddlers, and with crafts.

INSTITUTIONS: Besides its *chadorim* and *shiurim*, Butrimants had an elementary school, a credit union, a library, a Bikur Cholim (visit-the-sick) society, a hostel for visitors, and other religious and cultural organizations.

SPIRITUAL LEADERS: Among the town's rabbis were Rav Mordechai Lichtenstein, Rav Avrohom

Rav Avrohom Eliezerson,
rabbi of Butrimants.

Eliezerson, Rav Eliezer Strashun, Rav Yosef Yankelevitch, and the martyred Rav Avrohom Moshe Vitkin.

Many Jews in Butrimants were noteworthy scholars: Reb Gershon the cloth-merchant had *semichah* (rabbinic ordination) and sat all day and studied Torah while his wife ran the business. Reb Gershon was the unofficial rabbi of the New *kloiz*, and his opinion was well-respected by everyone in town.

Velvela Simcha was the Jewish landowner of a large estate. He always had an opinion and enjoyed offering it.

Then there were Simcha Pargament, the town elder, and Zisel the butcher, who was the *gabbai* of the Old Shul.

Remarkable was the modest, secret charity work of Feiga Glatkovitz. She collected money and food from the members of the community, which she distributed to the town's poor, particularly to families in distress and for underwriting *hachnosas kallah* (bridal charity).

1939-45: On June 22, 1941, the Russians were attacked by the Germans, and Butrimants soon fell into German hands. Robbery and murder of Jews ensued, on the part of both Lithuanians and Germans.

Young men and women were forced to work under horrifying conditions. Rav Vitkin's head was set on fire and, while it was afire, they made him run through the town. His Lithuanian "escort" kept shouting, "We're going to do this to all the rabbis!" Reb Gershon, too, was abused. Jews were beaten and shot while at work. But even that did not last long.

At the beginning of September 1941, a ghetto was established. The Jews of Butrimants and neighboring Stoklishka were driven into the synagogues and tortured. The Lithuanians dug pits a mile or so out of town and annihilated the Jews there.

The police chief took the town's doctor and his wife to a village where he locked them in a house. The doctor's wife went insane; the doctor managed to survive.

DORBIAN

LITHUANIAN NAME: Darbenai **RUSSIAN NAME:** Dorbyany

LOCATION: Dorbian, also known as Drobian, was in the Kretinga district in northwest Lithuania, six miles from the Latvian border and about 45 miles from Libau (Liepaja).

JEWISH POPULATION IN 1939: about 300 families

JEWISH HISTORY: The Jews began to settle in the town of Dorbian in the 19th century.

ECONOMY: The Jewish population made their living from commerce and from various crafts.

Dorbian's main street.

INSTITUTIONS: *Chadorim*, an elementary school, a Tiferes Bachurim, and other organizations.

SPIRITUAL LEADERS: Dorbian's early rabbis included: Rav Aryeh Leib Shalmon, Rav Eliyohu Margoliyos, the great scholar Rav Alexander and his son-in-law Rav Yisroel Isser Levin (who moved to America). Its last rabbi was the martyred Rav Isser Weisbord.

One of the town's outstanding Jews was Reb Shlomo Moshe Levy the *shochet*. He was a great scholar and an extraordinarily fine person.

1939-45: At the outset of the war Dorbian was occupied by the Germans. On June 29, 1941, the Germans shot all the Jewish men. The Germans locked up the women and children inside the synagogue. For

Dorbian's Chevra Shas.

more than two months they abused them.

At the beginning of September 1941, they began to take the women and children to the nearby forest and murder them. In November 1944 when the Russians liberated Dorbian their mass graves were opened, and alongside the remains the Russians found the iron rods and wooden clubs that had been used to kill them.

DVINSK

GERMAN NAME: (when under Prussian control): Denaburg **LATVIAN NAME:** Daugavpils **RUSSIAN NAME:** Dvinsk

LOCATION: East of the Lithuanian border, on the Dvina River, part of Latvia after World War I.

JEWISH POPULATION IN 1935: 11,106 (total population: 45,160)

JEWISH POPULATION IN 1946: 2,000

JEWISH HISTORY: Jews settled in Dvinsk at the beginning of the 19th century. Though Dvinsk became part of Latvia after World War I, it remained closely linked with Jewish Lithuania.

ECONOMY: Several thousand Jews were involved in the garment industry. Others were employed in construction and railroad workshops, and almost 5,000 Jews were artisans.

INSTITUTIONS: The city had a Chassidic community as well as a *misnagdic* (opponents of chassidism) one. Among Dvinsk's first Chassidic rabbis were Rav Aryeh Leib Hommler and Rav Yosef Levin.

Among Dvinsk's citizens was the philanthropist Shotza Hurvitz, who single-handedly supported a yeshiva known as Shotza Hurvitz's Yeshiva. Not to be outdone, a second wealthy man, Mr. Vittenberg, maintained a yeshiva at his expense which was called Vittenberg's Yeshiva. Together these yeshivos had hundreds of students from Dvinsk and from nearby towns and cities.

SPIRITUAL LEADERS: Dvinsk achieved world renown through its *gaonim*, Torah scholars who served as its rabbis. One of the best-known was Rav Reuven Halevi (who died in 1888), known as Rav Reuvela Denaburger. His successor, Rav Meir Simcha HaCohen, who served Dvinsk as rabbi for 38 years until his death in 1926, was the author of the widely studied *Meshech Chochma* on *chumash* (the Pentateuch) and *Or Someiach* on Maimonides' 12th-century seminal code of law and ethics, the *Mishneh Torah.* In *Meshech Chochma* (on *Parshas Bechukosy* [a portion in Leviticus]) he predicted the

Rav Meir Simcha HaCohen, rabbi of Dvinsk, 1888-1926.

rise of Nazism 15 years before Hitler came to power. Rav Cohen was admired not only for his scholarly genius, but also for his perceptiveness and cleverness.

Dvinsk's Jews related hundreds of pearls of Rav Cohen's wisdom. One story concerned Rav Cohen staying in the city during World War I while most of its citizenry had fled. They feared that the nearby fort would draw enemy bombs to the city. When some of the townspeople asked the rabbi why he hadn't fled, he replied, "Every bomb, every bullet, has its address. So there's nothing to worry about."

Dvinsk achieved further renown through Rav Yosef Rosen, known as the Rogatchover *Gaon* after the town of his birth, who served as rabbi of

Dvink's Chassidic community from 1889 until his death in 1936. He achieved a level of popularity beyond that of any rabbi of his time. His fame spread not only among Torah scholars, but into non-Orthodox circles.There was no corner of Torah knowledge that he was unaware of or did not command. Astronomy? He knew it from the Torah, Oral as well as Written. *Kabbalah*? He knew it. Anatomy, medicine, contemporary and ancient— he knew it all and knew it well. The Torah scholar, the halachist (one who studies Jewish law), and the scientist, too—as soon as they touched this genius's doorknob, they felt a wellspring of knowledge open before them.

Rav Yosef Rosen, the Rogatchover Gaon, rabbi of Dvinsk's chassidim, 1889-1936.

When I visited the Rogatchover Rav in 1935, I heard a well-known scientist, Dr. Scheffner, ask him about atoms. "There are two opinions about that in *Moreh Nevuchim* (Rambam's [Maimonides] philisophical *Guide to the Perplexed*); then there's an opinion of Tosofos (followers of Rashi, one of the most important commentators of the Torah) in tractate *Zevochim* and there's also a *gemora* in tractate *Horoyos*. The general problem is whether there exists any point that cannot be divided and subdivided ad infinitum."

One stood in wonder at the vastness of his knowledge, the clarity of his thinking, and the sharpness of his presentation. His mind was constantly reviewing the Talmud and the commentaries of many scholars. Rav Meir Simcha Cohen reportedly jested, "The Rogatchover has a good memory? Not at all. He never has to remember anything, because he's always just freshly learned it."

When I visited the Rogatchover Rav, he invited me to spend Shabbos as his guest. After Shabbos had ended and *havdolah* had been recited, Chatzkel the *shamosh* (caretaker of a synagogue) brought in the mail—22 letters and 10 postcards from all over the world containing questions on halachah (Jewish law). The Rogatchover opened each letter himself and commented on each one. Then he tucked some into his pocket and others into the drawer of his desk. He sat down immediately to write responses to the inquirers, every response from memory. He did not look at any of the letters or cards again, nor did he look into a single *sefer* (religious book). As he completed a reply, he addressed each one himself from memory, without looking at the original card or envelope, even though the addresses were in foreign languages, including a number from America. Reading, responding to, and addressing the letters took a total of two hours and 11 minutes!

Rav Meir Simcha Cohen was succeeded by Rav Elchonon Cohen, formerly rabbi of the town of Sumi in Russia. When he died in 1935, he was succeeded by his son Rav Binyomin Yehonoson Cohen, who was martyred in 1943.

1939-45: The destruction of Dvinsk was narrated in the *South African Jewish Zeitung* by a former citizen:

"On June 26, 1941, the Germans entered Dvinsk. On the 29th, the Jews, young and old, were ordered to gather at the city plaza, from which the men were driven to the prison yard. There they were compelled to participate in gymnastic exercises, such as jumping upon each other. Whoever did not perform "properly" was beaten brutally.

A group of 16- to 25-year-old girls was selected then. Their fate remained unknown. They were never again seen among the Jewish living.

Among the women who were arrested was Dr. Yakobson. The prison warden offered to free her, but she refused in order to share the fate of the her unfortunate brothers and sisters. She was shot that very night.

Since the prison was too small for so many Jews, many were locked into synagogues from which they were taken to be killed. All the gruesome, murderous acts were performed by the fascist Letts [Latvians]. The Germans did not participate actively.

By the 12th of July all the Jews in the prison had been shot except for the craftsmen. Among those killed were Rav Binyomin Y. Cohen; Rebbetzin Rosen, the Rogatchover's widow; Rav Alter Fuchs, the Rogatchover's disciple; Rav Sheftel Rosenholtz; Reb Lipa, a brother-in-law of Rav Cohen; the Rogatchover's daughter; Rav Yehuda L. Plachinsky, the rabbi of Pletzer, a suburb of Dvinsk, and his wife.

The teacher, Mrs. Kopengois-Neischloss, had been wounded by a bullet. Her fellow teachers carried her from the hospital to the prison and later to the annihilation area.

In the first round of murders almost all the teachers were killed: Kopilov, Plepka, Vishkin, Gallin, Tulbovitz, and others. Everyone was shot naked. Dina Pulkin, the military doctor's daughter, was shot by her father's best friend, a Lett. She begged him to allow her to be killed in her clothes, but he refused.

The students of the Novardok Yeshiva, which was headed by Rav Dovid Budnik, were also shot.

On the night of July 23rd, the Germans drove the male Jews into the ghetto, which they established in the ruins of barracks once used by artillerymen. The barracks were full of horse manure, but the Jews were so exhausted they lay down to sleep on it. Several days later the remaining Jews from the prison were brought into the ghetto.

The first *Akzion* (Nazi round-up) was directed at the old people. On the 12th of August 1941, the Jews who were not working were taken. Minna Aarons and her husband Damesek were shot along with their child. So was the Nitkin family of 34 Miasnitzka Street. The victims were dragged away violently. They were forced to dig their own graves, then shot behind the fortress.

In another *Akzion*, Jews were gathered from nearby towns and told they were going to be resettled in another ghetto. Every transport was accompanied by a Jewish doctor. One transport was accompanied by Dr. Gurevitz. As the transport traveled through the city, he was saved by a Christian friend. Here, too, all acts of horror were perpetrated by the Letts.

The leader of the annihilation was the mayor, Bluzman, whose brother was a baker.

Another *Akzion* took place on August 25, 1941. The following doctors were killed then: Dr. Bloch and his wife, Dr. Chatziantz, and Dr. Liebman. All were shot on the steel bridge near the fortress, and their bodies were thrown into the Dvina River.

Another time, the Germans put a grenade into a sick woman's bed, and the Jewish doctor, Dr. Donneman, was forced to write a report that the grenade was discovered in the bed although he had seen the Germans put it there.

On September 28, 1941, there was a fresh *Akzion*. The work battalions were discontinued, and the people who had been working till then were shot. Krill of the paper business was killed along with his entire family, as were Ida Silin, in the last month of her pregnancy, Manya Shapir, and others.

That same month there were more *Akzionen*, and by the end of the month, most of Dvinsk's Jews had been killed. They were buried in the Griva. On November 4th, 1941, the Letts began to sort out those who were not working. At that point the Germans involved themselves directly. Between November 6 and 8, the Jews who were not working were transported in trucks to Pahulianka.

It was common for the Letts to hang up Jewish children and use them for target practice. On the 9th, they took away the families of the people who were working. There were no more children left after that. Only the sick people in the hospital remained alive after that *Akzion*.

As of May 1942, there were only some 450 Jews left. On that day they went off to work as usual. When they returned, they found no one left in the ghetto. Everyone had been murdered by the Latvian killers. Everything the Jews possessed had been stolen. The surviving men were forced to bury the dead in a single grave. Some of the Jews died where they were, because they did not want to go to the execution area. Only a few women managed to hide and survive. That was the end of the Dvinsk ghetto."

EZHERENE

LITHUANIAN NAME: Zarasai **RUSSIAN NAME:** Novo Aleksandrovsk
LOCATION: On the northeastern Lithuanian border, slightly southwest of Dvinsk.
JEWISH POPULATION IN 1939: 2,000
HISTORY: When Lithuania was a Russian province, Ezherene was

View of Ezherene.

known as Novo-Aleksandrovsk. When Lithuania became independent, the Lithuanian name for the town was Zarasai, and it became a district capital. Nevertheless, it retained the name Ezherene because of the many nearby lakes (*ozhera*) where people came to skate in the winter. Because of its harsh winter climate, the area was known as the Lithuanian Siberia.

JEWISH HISTORY: Jews began to settle in Ezherene at the end of the 18th century.

ECONOMY: Jews made their living from the fish in the lakes and as shopkeepers and craftsmen. Before World War I the Ezherene district included many farms. After the war most of the farmland came under Polish rule; Ezherene lost its agricultural base and its economy suffered.

INSTITUTIONS: Jewish communal institutions included *chadorim*, adult education, an elementary school, a library, a credit union, a Bikur Cholim society, and a free guest house.

SPIRITUAL LEADERS: The town's rabbis included Rav Yosef Ashkenazi, a disciple of Rav Chayim of Volozhin; Rav Yoel Katzenellenbogen; Rav Levi Shapiro; Rav Refoel Shapiro, later rabbi and rosh yeshiva (dean of a rabbinic academy) in Volozhin; Rav Mordechai Feinstein; and the martyred Rav Eliyohu Resnik.

1939-45: Ezherene was one of the last towns in Lithuania to be occupied by the Germans. Jews from nearby villages were rounded up along with Ezherene's Jews and locked into the main synagogue from which they were taken out into the nearby forest and butchered.

After liberation in 1945, a monument was set up to commemorate 8,000 martyred Jews.

The mass grave of 8,000 Jews from the Ezherene region.

GORZHD

LITHUANIAN NAME: Gargzdai RUSSIAN NAME: Gorzhdy

LOCATION: Gorzhd, in the Kretinga district in northwest Lithuania, lay near the Prussian border. From the town one could see the tollhouse that marked the border with Germany, nine miles from Memel (Klaipeda).

JEWISH POPULATION IN 1939: 450 families

JEWISH HISTORY: The Jewish community in Gorzhd dates back to the massacres of 1648, when Reb Bendet Potkova found a haven there from Chmielnicki's pogroms. Moshe Markovitz, in his work profiling great Jewish leaders, *Shem Hagedolim Hashelishi*, related much about Reb Bendet. Reb Bendet was the father of Rav Shmuel Hechosid who lived in the town of Rasseyn where he studied with the *gaon* and *tzaddik* (righteous man) Rav Moshe, who later would become rabbi of Telz. He also studied with the *gaon* and *tzaddik* Rav Mordechai, later rabbi in Pokroy. Rav Shmuel Hechosid was greatly revered by the *Gaon* of Vilna who called him *"Der Zamuter Chosid."*

View of Gorzhd.

ECONOMY: Most Jews were merchants in trade with Prussia and later with Germany. Gorzhd was one of Lithuania's wealthier communities.

SPIRITUAL LEADERS: Gorzhd's rabbis included Rav Moshe Yoffe; Rav Yitzchok Y. Rabinovitz, later of Ponevezh; Rav Aharon Valkin, later of Pinsk; Rav Yitzchok I. Friedman; Rav Shabsy Shapiro; and the martyred Rav Meir Levin.

1939-45: During the night of June 22, 1941, the Germans entered Gorzhd and set the town afire. The entire citizenry was driven out into the marketplace. That morning the Lithuanians were separated, and the Jews—men and women, young and old—were surrounded by soldiers with machine guns. A motorcyclist drove up suddenly from Dovlin with orders to postpone the mass execution. The Jews were penned into a garden where they were held for three bitter days without food and water.

On Tuesday, June 24th, the men were led away to Lavgallen. There they were taken in groups of

The aron kodesh in Gorzhd.

25 and forced to undress before being shot to death. As they were being driven into the death pits, Rav Levin called out, "Fellow Jews! We are going to sanctify G-d; we are being killed because we are Jews!"

The women and children were taken to Analishka where they were enslaved in a labor camp under horrifying conditions. The children used to pull up grass to eat.

The women could not bring themselves to believe that their men had been butchered, even though the distance between the two locations was only half a mile. The German soldiers took the women over to Lavgallen and forced them to dance on the common grave of their husbands, brothers, and sons. This was typical of the degradation of the Jews practiced by the Germans.

On September 14th, the women and children were driven into the forest near Analishka. The Germans separated the children from the women, and shot the children. On the 16th of September they murdered the women. The mass grave of the women and the children is in the woods alongside the road that leads from Gorzhd to Kool.

These details were supplied by Mrs. Yami of Visatz, who escaped from the women's camp.

KALVARIA

Lithuanian name: Kalvarija **Russian name:** Kalvariya

Location: Kalvaria, not far from the Sesupa River, was in the Mariampol district in southwest Lithuania, a few miles southwest of Mariampol. Before World War I it had been in the Suvalk district.

Jewish population in 1939: 1,000

History: Kalvaria was known for its penal and mental institutions, to which people were sent from all over Lithuania.

Jewish history: Kalvaria's Jewish community dates back to the early 18th century.

Those of Kalvaria's Jews who emigrated to the U.S. maintained a closeness with one another as evidenced by their establishment of the Kalvarier Shul on Pike Street in New York City and of the Bnei Yaakov Shul in Chicago.

Economy: Around Kalvaria were large tobacco plantations, some of them owned by Jewish families—Kranz, Solomon, and others. The Kreingut family owned a bee farm and a factory where they produced artistic wax products. Kalvaria's Jews also made a living from pig-bristle products and other crafts, and retail trading. The town regularly quartered soldiers, and many Jews made a living from provisioning them.

Institutions: Among Kalvaria's Jewish institutions, besides the *chadorim* and the daily *shiurim*, were a credit union, a Linas Hatzedek, an elementary school and a secondary school, and a number of other cultural organizations. Kalvaria's main synagogue was decorated with artwork by Yaakov ben Shlomo, one of the town's leaders.

Spiritual Leaders: Kalvaria was known in Jewish circles for its respectful treatment of its rabbis, which is why many of its rabbis were among the greatest of their generation. In the days of the *Gaon* of Vilna,

Kalvaria's rabbi was Rav Shlomo, a member of the *Gaon's* inner circle of disciples and the teacher of Rav Abale of Possval, who became rabbi in Vilna. Rav Shlomo was not required to deal with questions of Jewish law or with *din*-Torah (litigation); these were the province of the town's *dayan* (judge). Nor did Rav Shlomo teach Talmud to the members of the *Chevra Shas* (Talmud study group). He taught and studied with the students in his yeshiva. The community supported him and his yeshiva respectfully.

Among its distinguished rabbis were Rav Aharon Broida and his son Rav Aryeh Leib (Reb Leibela), who built a *kloiz* of his own on his property. Reb Leibela also disbursed charity secretly through one of the town's wealthy men. After Rab Leibela died it became known that the rich man had been disbursing Reb Leibela's money.

Other well-known Kalvaria rabbis were Rav Shlomo Landa; Rav Yisroel Katzenellenbogen; Rav Leibela Shapiro, later rabbi in Kovno; Rav Yehoshua Eizik Shapiro, renowned as Rav *Eizil Charif* (sharp mind), who later became rabbi in Slonim; Rav Mordechai Meltzer; Rav Mordechai Hoffman; Rav Dovid S. Margoliyos; Rav Moshe G. Braver; Rav Ben-Tziyon Sternfeld; Rav Eliezer Simcha Rabinovich, previously rabbi in Lomza; Rav Zelig Reuven Bengis, who became rabbi of the Eida Hachareidis in Jerusalem; and the martyred Rav Moshe Mezigal. At one time the parents of the famous rabbi and scholar, the Chofetz Chayim, lived in Kalvaria and made their living from brushmaking.

Rav Ben-Tziyon Sternfeld, rabbi of Kalvaria.

How did the well known rabbi of the big city of Lomza, Rav Eliezer Simcha Rabinovich, come to accept the rabbinate of much smaller Kalvaria? Rav Rabinovich, who spoke perfect Russian, undertook a mission to the mayor of Lomza, and the mayor refused to grant the rabbi's request. Rav Rabinovich, a man of strong character, sharply rebuked the mayor, warning him that he would take up the matter with higher authorities in St. Petersburg, the capital. One word led to another, until the rabbi was compelled to leave Lomza. The government-appointed mayor was also transferred elsewhere. And this was how Rav Rabinovich ended up rabbi of Kalvaria.

Rav Eliezer Simcha Rabinovich, rabbi of Lomza and later of Kalvaria.

Kalvaria had a great many scholarly businessmen like Reb Elya Vistenetsky, who taught *gemora* daily.

1939-45: On June 22, 1941, the destruction of Kalvaria by the Germans began. As soon as nearby Suvalk was captured and occupied by the Germans, Kalvaria fell as well. Jews immediately began to flee to Kovno and Vilna.

Guided by their Lithuanian assistants, the Germans took hostage some of the Jewish community's most important people, including the town doctor. Upon their release, the hostages were nearly unrecognizable, they had been so beaten up. A few days later, they were again rounded up and taken away, and this time they never returned.

Men were rounded up for labor and sent to a place near Neishtot-Shaki. Many of them did not survive the labor. Those who remained in town were subjected to harrassment and torture, and were stripped of their possessions.

The men were led outside the town, where they were ordered to dig their own graves and to undress. Then they were killed. Afterwards the Germans also murdered the women and the children.

After liberation, in 1945, I visited Kalvaria and found on one of the ruined walls of the town synagogue the barely visible inscription, JEWS TAKE REVENGE!

KAMEI

LITHUANIAN NAME: Kamajai

LOCATION: In the Rokishok district in northwest Lithuania, a few miles west of Dvinsk.

JEWISH POPULATION IN 1939: 150 families

JEWISH HISTORY: The Jewish community dates back to the 18th century. The townspeople were divided into Chassidim and *misnagdim* (opponents of chassidism), which effectively meant that there were two communities, each with its own rabbi and *shochet* and synagogue. There was one yeshiva in town and its dean was the rabbi of the *misnagdim*, Rav Eliezer Luft.

ECONOMY: The Jews of Kamei occupied themselves with business, handicrafts, and fishing. Some Jews leased the fishing rights to the lakes around Kamei. Other Jews were peddlers, and there were also some flax dealers who exported flax to Latvia.

SPIRITUAL LEADERS: Among Kamei's rabbis were Rav Avrohom Hirshovitz; Rav Bunim Tzemach Silver, father of America's Rabbi Eliezer Silver; Rav Eliyohu Gordon; Rav Eliezer Zev Luft; Rav Yisroel Zissel Dvoretz; Rav Meir Fein; Rav Betzalel Cohen; and the martyred Rav Leib Sigar.

1939-45: On Thursday, June 26, 1941, the Germans entered Kamei and with the assistance of their Lithuanian allies they began their brutal extermination process. The Jews were rounded up and driven into the large synagogue, where they were held prisoner for two weeks without any systematic provision of food. After two weeks of starvation they were taken to Rakishok, where they were held under even more intolerable conditions.

On August 10th, 1941, the men were told that they were being taken to work along the highway to Smolensk. Instead they were taken to a spot outside of Boyar and shot to death. The women and children were taken out and killed 10 days later, on August 20th. Some 5,000 Jews from Kamei as well as a number of nearby towns—Rakishok, Abel, Fonadel, Sevenishok, and Dohuta—were butchered there. All that remains now of the Jewish community are seven mass graves.

KEIDAN

LITHUANIAN NAME: Kedainiai RUSSIAN NAME: Keidany

LOCATION: A district capital near Lithuania's center, a few miles north of Kovno.

JEWISH POPULATION IN 1939: 3,000

JEWISH HISTORY: The Jewish community in Keidan dates back to at least the 15th century. In 1495 the Jews were expelled. They were allowed to return in 1503, at which time many Jews settled there. Christopher Radziwill granted the Jews full rights in 1560 and they participated in communal life.

ECONOMY: Keidan's Jews were mainly vegetable farmers, and their cucumbers were renowned beyond the borders of Lithuania. The partners Movshovitz and Cohen owned a printing press—one of the few presses in Lithuania—where they primarily printed rabbinical works.

INSTITUTIONS: The communal institutions included the synagogue and several *batei midrosh* (houses of learning), a yeshiva, an elementary school, a high school, a credit union, and other cultural organizations.

The old *beis hamidrosh* was one of the most beautiful in Lithuania. The

Keidan's communal minutes and record book.

art work inside it was extraordinary. The walls were highly ornamented, and its *aron kodesh* was a masterpiece. The ceiling, too was covered with paintings, one of which depicted the Jewish exiles along the Babylonian riverbanks. Beginning in the 18th century, Keidan maintained a yeshiva that was under the aegis of the town rabbi. Its last rosh yeshiva was the martyred Rav Shimon Dubiansky,

The synagogue in Keidan.

*The sundial at the entrance
to the Keidan synagogue.*

*Keidan's aron kodesh—one of
Lithuanian Jewry's great treasures.*

The Keidan synagogue yard.

*The masterfully
designed omud.*

who was killed in Dachau.

SPIRITUAL LEADERS: Among Keidan's great rabbis and scholars was Rav Moshe Margoliyos, author of *Penei Moshe*, an 18th-century commentary on Talmud Yerushalmi that opened that Talmud to popular study. Rav Margoliyos sought out rare manuscripts and even studied botany in order to clarify abstruse passages. The *Gaon* of Vilna studied under him in Keidan at the age of eight, when Rav Dovid Katzenellenbogen—son of Rav Yechezkel Katzenellenbogen, 18th-century author of the responsa *Kenesses Yechezkel*—brought young Eliyohu there and arranged his marriage with the daughter of a local Jew. My grandmother Necha Margoliyos was Rav Moshe's fifth-generation descendant. Keidan's other famous rabbis include Rav Avrohom Shimon Traub, Rav Avrohom T. Kamei, and the martyred Rav Shlomo Feinzilber.

Rav Avrohom Shimon Traub of Keidan.

Rav Shlomo Feinzilber, Keidan's last rabbi, was born in 1871 in Bialovka. He served as rabbi of Parazava, Vekshne, and Keidan. His published works of Talmudic exegesis include *Nishmas Chayim*, a halachic perspective of the *bris milah* (circumcision) of a child; *Hashlomas HaMidos*, on the commandments that deal with human nature and emotion; and *Yerios Shelomo*, elucidations on the Temple services and sacrifices. He was chairman of the Union of Lithuanian Rabbis and one of Jewry's prominent personalities. His beautiful, patriarchal appearance with his long white beard emphasized his handsome, clever face.

Among Keidan's Jews were some very interesting people. For example, if you stepped into the pharmacy you found yourself *reddin lernin* (Yiddish for "talking learning," i.e., discussing Talmud) while the pharmacist prepared your medicine. When the pharmacist demonstrated his virtuosity in Talmud and Jewish law, people wondered, "What is such a great *gaon* doing in a pharmacy?" The townspeople soon enough made this pharmacist, Rav Avrohom Tzvi Kamei, their rabbi. He went on to succeed his father, Rav Eliyohu Boruch Kamei, as Rav and rosh yeshiva of Mir, and was martyred by the Germans.

1939-45: In 1940, Keidan's Jewish community warmly received the Mirrer Yeshiva's students when they fled Poland. From Vilna the students also moved to Keidan, where they stayed until they could move on. They eventually arrived in Shanghai where they survived the war.

On June 25, 1941 the Germans occupied Keidan. A ghetto was soon established into which the Jews of the nearby towns of Shatt and Yasven were shoehorned. The elderly Rav Feinzilber was the victim of much harassment.

I shall here relate briefly what happened to Keidan, as recounted by Chayim Rander in a letter to his sister:

"I am the only surviving witness of how they shot our babies, our aged, and our women; how they cut them in pieces, how they buried them half alive.

On August 15th, the Jews were driven out of the town and locked into a granary on a farm. They tormented us for three whole days. Old Rav Feinzilber was there as were 19 yeshiva students. They were students of the Mirrer Yeshiva, who had not been able to obtain Russian visas and were therefore unable to leave with the rest of the yeshiva. The *dayan* of Keidan, Rav Aharon Gallin, the Rav's son-in-law, was also there.

There were women and children and old people, weak and sick people. My ears still hear the groans of the shoemaker, Yossel Volpert, who was lying on the bare ground, ill and weak. I cannot forget the screaming and roaring of Sholom Chayat, who was carted in, ill, on a garbage handtruck, and dumped on the ground. Before my eyes still stands Hirshel Lubiatkin, who in his anguish, hanged himself. And still more and more tragedies passed before my eyes.

I saw how they shot Zalman Frank because he was too old. Reb Zalman Frank was a great scholar and the son of the rabbi of Nimenayetz. Malkala and Mottela they shot because they were too young; Gessa Rabinovitch's daughter because she was too beautiful; Benny Rander, Moshe Zalmanovitch, Feivel Friedland, and others because they "declared war" against the Hitler-cadre!

A hero's death was that of Tzodok Shliapobersky. He dragged the German commandant with him into the grave and slit the throat of a Lithuanian murderer, a policeman.

I returned to Keidan, weapon in hand, and stood at the mass graves—90 yards long, three yards wide, and three yards deep, on the Datnev Road, planted in oats. And I heard the voices of my old mother and my acquaintances calling to me, 'Chayim, Chayim, take revenge!' I swore on the spot, at their grave, that I will take revenge!"

KELM

LITHUANIAN NAME: Kelme RUSSIAN NAME: Kelmy

LOCATION: In the Rasseyn district in Lithuania, a few miles north of Rasseyn.

JEWISH POPULATION IN 1939: about 2,000

JEWISH HISTORY: The community was founded in the 17th century. Kelm was renowned throughout Lithuania and beyond as a *mussar* (the study of rebuke to improve one's character) town, because of its Talmud Torah—a yeshiva founded by a native of Kelm, the *gaon* and *tzaddik* Rav Simcha Zissel Ziv (Siev) (known as the *Saba MiKelm* [grandfather from Kelm]), who was born in Kelm in 1829 and died there in 1898. One of Rav Yisroel Salanter's foremost disciples, Rav Simcha Zissel taught the *mussar* concepts of his master to generations of students.

The classic *mussar* teachers systematically studied the complexities of the human mind and soul, their strengths and weaknesses. In their endeavor to achieve personal perfection, they demonstrated as well as taught the system developed by their teachers. This was done without recourse to modern psychology, even though some of the concepts seem to overlap.

The study of *mussar* in the Kelm Talmud Torah was in addition to and underlay the study of Talmud and codes that were the standard program of every yeshiva. Only students deemed capable of meeting the Talmud Torah's exacting standards were admitted. Their power of concentration in learning was developed as was their character.

Life in Kelm revolved very much around the Talmud Torah. Every year during the month of Elul and the Ten Days of Awe, rabbis and scholars from all over Lithuania, alumni of the Talmud Torah and others, converged on Kelm to make their personal soul-reckonings and to bask in the atmosphere of Kelm's *mussar*.

In its final years, the Talmud Torah was headed by the martyred Rav Doniyel Movshovitz. Besides his genius in Torah scholarship, he had a deep love for every Jew. He treated everyone with great respect and spoke to each as if to a brother. The *menahel* (principal) was the martyred Rav Gershon Miednik.

ECONOMY: Most Jews in Kelm were small shopkeepers or artisans and several were merchants and factory-owners.

INSTITUTIONS: Kelm had a yeshiva *ketanah*, a preparatory yeshiva, with some 150 pupils. It was founded by Rav Eliyohu Lopian—who eventually settled in Israel where he died in 1970—and the martyred Rav Eliyohu Kremerman, later rabbi in Kroz. In 1941 it was headed by the martyred Rav Shlomo Pianko and its *mashgiach* (dean and spiritual mentor) was Rav Sadovsky.

The main synagogue in Kelm had a clock, made by Kelm's rabbi, Rav Chatzkel, that was a masterpiece. Besides the hour and the minute, it displayed the day of the week, the date, the month, the year, and the *ma'amodos* (daily biblical and Talmudic passages) for that day. In the old, wood-

Kelm's big beis hamidrosh.

A synagogue in Kelm.

Yavneh School staff and students, 1925.

*The aron kodesh in
Kelm's Cold Synagogue.*

*Rav Nachum Zev Ziv,
son of the Saba MiKelm.*

*Rabbi Doniyel
Movshovitz.*

*Rav Tzvi Yaakov
Oppenheim.*

en synagogue there stood an extraordinarily beautiful *aron kodesh* (holy ark), carved from wood by the artist Yaakov ben Shlomo of Kalvaria.

SPIRITUAL LEADERS: Kelm's better-known rabbis were Rav Eliezer Gutman; Rav Yechezkel, who was called Reb Chatzkel by the townspeople; Rav Elyokim Getzel Horvitz and his son-in-law Rav Yitzchok Horvitz; Rav Eliezer Gordon, later rabbi and founding rosh yeshiva in Telz; Rav Tzvi Yaakov Oppenhiem; and Kelm's last rabbi, the martyred Rav Kalman Beinishevitz.

Another of Kelm's well known personalities was the famous *maggid* (preacher) of Kelm, Rav Moshe Yitzchok Darshon, who was known for his fiery sermons and his vivid portrayals of *Gan Eden* (the Garden of Eden) and of *Gehinnom* (Hell).

Then there was Rav Leib Ziegler, known as Reb Leib *Chosid* because of his extraordinary piety and humility. Reb Leib was considered a Lithuanian Rebbi—a *Rebbi* without a court, without a *tish* (table around which a *Rebbi's* followers gather on Shabbos and holidays to hear his sermons on the Torah). Reb Leib possessed a great mind and an extremely warm heart. There was always a smile on his luminous face and his eyes gazed lovingly at everyone. He spent day and night immersed in Torah study, always occupied with serving G-d. He was unusually humble—if someone called him "*Rebbi*," he would protest. Throughout Lithuania, Latvia, and White Russia, he was recognized as a *tzaddik*. He would retreat into isolation for long periods of time, often in the woods outside of town.

One day, preoccupied with his thoughts, he wandered into a field owned by a Christian. The man came riding along on his horse and, imagining that Reb Leib was trampling his plants, began to beat him. Reb Leib interrupted him, "Why are you wasting time with this? Better race home quickly to save your family. They are in great danger." The farmer panicked and raced home to find his house on fire. He barely managed to save his wife and children. Afterwards, the farmer sought out Reb Leib, begged his forgiveness, and presented him with gifts.

Reb Leib was once traveling and spent the night at an inn, where he simply put his pack under his head and went to sleep in the main room. During the night, some merchants came into the inn, saw him sleeping there, and began to poke fun at him. One lit a match and singed Reb Leib's beard. By the light of the match, a more sober merchant recognized Reb Leib, trembled visibly, and jumped up. Reb Leib turned to the decent fellow, "Leave him alone. He's enjoying it." Reb Leib died in 1894 at the age of 70.

In Kelm you could see a Jew walking through the streets wearing his *tallis* and his *tefillin*. Everyone in Kelm knew Reb Zeligel Tarshish. On the town's market day, Thursday, when the gentiles saw Reb Zeligel coming down the street in his *tallis* and *tefillin*, they would clear a path for him.

Non-Jews rejoiced when Reb Zeligel walked onto their fields. They said that his visit would bring them a successful year.

Kelm was rich in many types of Jews. Who didn't know Menda the Peiah? A simple man —tall and lean, with long, bushy *peios* (sidelocks)—Menda would walk from town to town inspecting *mezuzzos* (small parchment with biblical passages affixed to doorposts of Jewish homes). When he encountered a defective one, he would replace it free of charge.

Rav Zeligel Tarshish, known as the "Kelmer Kaddosh," davening in the forest.

Then there was Reuven the porter who, like so many others of Kelm's ordinary Jews, could be found every day studying Rabbi Avrohom Danzig's definitive halachic work, *Chayey Odom; Ein Yaakov,* a well-known 16th-century collection of *aggadic* (homiletical) material from the Talmud; the famous *mussar* work *Menoras HaMaor*; *Mishnayos* (tractates of the Mishnah), and Talmud. Another gentleman, known as "Reuven the bather" had mastered the entire Talmud.

1939-45: Kelm was unique and original in life. And it was unique and original in death.

In the second half of August 1941, the Jews of Kelm were herded into stables on three different estates. Men were herded into a large stable on Zundel Luntz's farm, women were herded onto Moshe Gelman's farm, and a third group was collected on the Kushelevsky farm. They were all shot to death. Kelm's Christians had much to relate about the courageous and proud march when the Jews were led to be butchered. Thoroughly inspired by a spirit of sanctifying G-d, the Jews of Kelm marched with their rabbi and the yeshiva students of the Talmud Torah at their head, and sang Psalms and *Adon Olom* (a medieval hymn, "Eternal Lord"). The hooligans were disappointed at not having the opportunity to enjoy Jewish fright and terror. The pious Christians went to their church and recited the Latin verses of the same Psalms; and the priest sprinkled them with holy water and "cleansed" them of their sins.

But bloodstains are not so easily washed away. The punishing Hand will fulfill His pledge: "Vengence will He return to His enemies" (Deuteronomy 32:43).

KRETINGA

LITHUANIAN NAME: Kretinga RUSSIAN NAME: Kretinga

LOCATION: Kretinga was a Lithuanian district capital near the German border in northwest Lithuania, the last stop on the railroad. From Kretinga buses ran to the nearby Palanga spa, six miles away on the Baltic Sea. Palanga, with its beautiful pine forest along the seashore, attracted tens of thousands of visitors during the summer months.

JEWISH POPULATION IN 1939: 800

ECONOMY: Many people stopped in Kretinga on their way to and from the spa, and the local Jews made a living from supplying them with necessities for their vacations and with gift items such as amber souvenir jewelry and cigar-holders. These items were also exported to Germany.

View of Kretinga.

INSTITUTIONS: Kretinga's secular Jewish institutions included an elementary school, a credit union, a Bikur Cholim society, a library, and a number of other cultural organizations. Its religious institutions also included Pirchei Shoshanim and Tiferes Bachurim groups.

SPIRITUAL LEADERS: Most of Kretinga's residents were also Torah scholars. The Haskalah movement[1] gained easy entry to Kretinga because of its proximity to Germany.

Kretinga became renowned in the Jewish world through its best-known native son, the *gaon* and *tzaddik* Rav Eliyohu Levinson. Born in Kretinga in 1821, Reb Elinka, as he was called, was the pride of

[1]The Enlightenment movement of the 18th century, which attempted to move Judaism away from traditional Talmudic observance and towards a more secular, emancipated way of life.

Lithuanian Jewry for two generations. A major Torah scholar, he refused to accept a rabbinical position, but made his living as a bookkeeper in a private bank. He went on to become an independent businessman and grew wealthy. Throughout his life he supported his former mentor, Rav Yisroel Lipkin of Salant (Salanter), enabling the latter to pursue his various endeavors on behalf of Jewry.

Kretinga's best-known rabbis were Rav Aryeh Leib, a grandfather of Reb Elinka; Rav Aryeh Leib Lipkin, a nephew of Rav Yisroel Salanter; Rav Shlomo Zak; Rav Tzvi Zev Shor; and the martyred Rav Chayim Binyomin Persky.

1939-45: The Jews of Kretinga lived peacefully until Sunday, June 22, 1941. At 4 a.m. German troops dragged many of the Jews out of their beds and began their standard series of cruelties. The town's rabbi, Rav Persky, was their first victim. They tied him to a horse hitched to a cart, and proceeded to drive the horse as quickly as possible through a swamp. The rabbi could not keep up with the horse. Whenever he stopped, the murderers whipped him onward. When he finally made it across the swamp in great anguish, they beat him again for having taken so long.

A few days later, the murderers made a great fire in town into which they threw the rabbi together with the rest of Kretinga's Jews.

KUPISHOK

LITHUANIAN NAME: Kupiskis **RUSSIAN NAME:** Kupishki
LOCATION: In the Ponevezh district in northeast Lithuania, a few miles northeast of Ponevezh.
JEWISH POPULATION IN 1939: 400 families
JEWISH HISTORY: Kupishok was settled by Jews in the 17th century. On the way into Kupishok was the new Jewish cemetery and, near the town, was the old cemetery, where the names on the graves were no longer recognizable. Only a few old worn out tombstones told of a 300-year-old past. Kupishok was one of Lithuania's oldest Jewish settlements, and it is where I grew up.

Kupishok reveled in Jewish living, Jewish tradition, and Jewish knowledge. I will tell you what *erev* Shabbos—Friday—looked like. Early Friday morning the village peddlers would return from their rounds, *daven* (pray) with an early *minyan* (quorum), and rush off to the market to buy fish at Yudel the Fishman's before he ran out. Housewives were at home baking *challah* (braided loaves of bread). The scent of delicious Shabbos dishes wafted out into the streets. Soon you could see Jews rushing to the communal bathhouse to clean up for Shabbos. Immediately after noon, Rav Sender Falk was at his seat in the *beis hamidrosh* reciting *Shir HaShirim* (Song of Songs) with a beautiful tune. When I was a child in Kupishok, I would hide with other children in the women's section and listen to Rav Falk's sweet *nigun* (melody). An hour before candle-lighting a loud horn was blown at Chona the Miller's mill to announce that the Shabbos Queen's arrival was imminent, and it was time to close the shops. A second blast on the horn announced candle-lighting time. Menda the *shamosh* would stand in the market, announcing, "To synagogue!" Every window glowed with Shabbos illumination as the men and the boys streamed into houses of prayer.

On Shabbos, every *beis hamidrosh* was filled with men and boys studying Torah. Daily Talmud lessons were given by the town's rabbi who was succeeded by the martyred Reb Moshe Zundel Leizerovitz. At the Chassidic *kloiz*, the *gemora shiur* was given by Reb Getzel Hoffman, who was succeeded by the Chassidic Rav. A scholarly Gemora *blatt* taught by Reb Zalman Pertzovsky was instituted at the Tiferes Bachurim.

Every year on the holiday Simchas Torah, the town's Jews rejoiced with the Torah and danced in the streets. Can I forget how Yisroel Moisheles used to don his coat inside out and dance in the street with us children around him? He would hand us pieces of kugel and honeycake he had collected from the nearby homes.

The rabbi was led to synagogue under a canopy, accompanied by a singing and dancing crowd. The custom was to go to the synagogue called the Cold *Shul*, where we *davened* in the summer, and say a *brocha* (blessing) there, after which the crowd proceeded to the *beis hamidrosh*. All the boys returned to Kupishok from their yeshivos all over Lithuania to join their families and their community and share in the celebrations of Yom Tov (holiday).

Menda (Birger) the *shamosh* of the *beis hamidrosh* was a short, bent Jew who carried his hundred years with equanimity. He *davened* without eyeglasses, and still possessed a full set of teeth. When he'd tell a story about life in town, and I'd ask him, "Reb Menda, when did that take place?" he'd reply, "Recently."

"And when was recently?"

"Around 85 to 90 years ago."

He knew everyone in town and remembered their fathers, grandfathers, and great-grandfathers. He displayed his virtuosity when calling men up for *aliyos* (the honor of reciting the blessing over a portion of the Torah) and when making *Kel Moley Rachamim*s (prayer for peace). When I asked him, "How does a 100-year-old feel?" he answered, "Like yesterday." He died a year before World War II began.

The town mailman was a *chosid* named Nochum Leib. His father had been a chassidic *moreh horoah* (rabbinic scholar of Jewish legal issues) who died young. In order to help the family earn a living, a number of community members signed a power-of-attorney authorizing Nochum Leib to pick up their mail for them from the post office. The people would give him a small sum of money when he brought them their mail. After World War I, Nochum Leib became the official letter carrier for the whole town, Jews and non-Jews alike. The Jews continued the habit of tipping him for delivering their mail, particularly when registered letters from husbands and sons in the U.S. and South Africa began to arrive. Nochum Leib, too, died before World War II.

Another interesting character was Heshel the tailor, who was called Heshel the *Bulbala* (Belorussian for the potato). He was an itinerant tailor who spent all week making the rounds of the nearby villages and farms. Because he ate no food in the Christian homes where he worked, he would cook a sackful of potatoes before leaving home, and eat them cold all week long. He was too poor to afford bread. Heshel was a short man with a very calm disposition.

When I knew Heshel, he was already the teacher of the daily *Mishnayos* class that took place between *Mincha* and *Maariv* (daily afternoon and evening prayers). Everyone enjoyed his class greatly, yet the man was not as knowledgeable in Talmud as in *Mishnayos*. When I once asked him about that, he told me, "As a child, I did not have the oportunity to learn Torah because my parents were extremely poor and I was left an orphan. I was apprenticed to a tailor when I was still a child. When I married, I used to travel around the villages sewing coats for the Christians, and therefore my only opportunities to sit at the table in the *beis hamidrosh* came on Shabbos and Sunday. Whatever I learned from Reb Nechemya Steinberg those two days I would review the rest of the week while working. By the time I had been doing this for thirty years, I knew all of *Mishnayos* by heart. After the [first world] war, when my *Rebbi*, Reb Nechemya, died, I became the *Rebbi* of the *Chevra Mishnayos* (Mishnah study group)." Heshel was tragically butchered when he was 80 years old.

Then there was Blind Zalman, blind in one eye and illiterate, with a unique memory for birthdates—including the hour—and *yahrtzeits* (anniversaries of deaths). Despite his disability and his illiteracy, Zalman worked for the credit union delivering letters and notices, and never mis-delivered a letter.

Love for Torah was visible at all times in Kupishok. How fortunate and proud was a mother whose son went away to learn in a yeshiva, and how much sacrifice that entailed! Can I forget the sacrifices my dear, martyred mother made so that my Torah study could be more comfortable? In order for me to receive a parcel of her freshly-baked goods for Shabbos, my mother would—after a wearying business day at the market on

Thursday—get up in middle of the night to do her baking. Then she would walk two miles to the train early in the morning—rain or shine, frost or heat—and beg passengers to take the parcel with them and deliver it to me at the yeshiva in Ponevezh that same day! Her joy was to get a report that I was a *masmid* (student devoted to Talmudic study) at the yeshiva, and that the yeshiva deans were satisfied with me.

The same was true for the other mothers in town. No wonder that Ponevezh Yeshiva—which was a preparatory yeshiva—normally had 30 to 40 Kupishok boys studying there every semester. We were the largest group of students from any one city or town. Older boys studied at the advanced yeshivos in the towns of Slobodka, Telz, Radun, and Mir.

And not only were our mothers proud of us. When we came home for holidays, the men of the town would greet us as if we were adults and look on us with respect. All the more so when I grew older and delivered my first sermon in the *beis hamidrosh* on the first day of Pesach, and the Jews in town expressed their pride in me: "You see, we've produced our own Rav." "The Rav is a native Kupishoker."

This warmth and concern for Torah extended to the kind treatment of *meshulochim*, the itinerant collectors who traveled from town to town to raise money for specific yeshivos. The townspeople were pleased and honored to share their paltry funds with these collectors. As Malkala from down the hill once said to me: "What I use to buy myself food is only temporary, but what I give for Torah is my eternal portion." How often did my mother give away her last coins to a *meshuloch*, because she feared she might not have done enough for Torah! When a *meshuloch* with whom I was well acquainted told her, "You don't have to give, you have your own *talmid chochom* (Torah scholar)," my mother retorted, "And making a *talmid chochom* out of someone else's child is not a *mitzvah*?"

You could almost literally weigh the fear of G-d, the genuine Yiddishkeit, in Kupishok. And today there is no place to set up a tombstone to commemorate our dearly beloved ones. Once there was a town named Kupishok; today it's no longer there. Uprooted were its holy souls…What we possessed and what we have lost!

ECONOMY: The Jews made their living as small traders, as flax-workers, and in crafts.

After 1925, many young people could not find employment in or around Kupishok. Most of those who emigrated settled in South Africa. Thus, several hundred families in Johannesburg and Capetown hail from Kupishok. Emigration saved their lives physically, and the contemporary *teshuvah* (repentance) movement is bringing their grandchildren back to *Yiddishkeit* (traditional Judaism).

INSTITUTIONS: Kupishok had many *chadorim* for the education of its children. It also had two elementary schools—including a Yavneh (religious) school; a preparatory yeshiva, a Talmud Torah; and the usual social and cultural organizations. Kupishok's Tiferes Bachurim was the place where the young married men came to study Torah in a *minyan* of their own after work.

Kupishok had an old, large synagogue, built of unfinished stone. Its *aron kodesh* was a masterpiece with eye-catching carvings. During the first fire in Kupishok, that irreplaceable ark was destroyed. Near the synagogue were a *beis hamidrosh* and a Chassidic *kloiz*. Down the hill there was another *beis hamidrosh*.

The old Kupishok synagogue in 1991.

Before World War I, Kupishok hosted many *perushim*, married men who left home with their wives' permission to study full-time for several months to a year. Many of them became famous rabbis.

When Rav Abba Yaakov Boruchov opened his yeshiva in 1886, the *mashgiach* was Rav Chayim Halpern. His base of support were former Kupishokers who had emigrated to America. One of the best known students of Kupishok's yeshiva was Rav Yisroel Abba Citron who married the daughter of the Rogatchover Gaon, Rav Yosef Rosen. In Kupishok he was known as the *iluy* of Utyan, his native town. He became rabbi of a suburb of Dvinsk, and later rabbi in Moscow, where he died.

The primary *gemora* teacher was Reb Moshe Mordechai, who taught two levels of boys. In the town's *beis hamidrosh* there were always men studying Torah, people like my grandfather Reb Moshe, who spent the last 20 years of his life in retirement studying day and night. No one arrived earlier than he did, and no one left later. He was a man of extraordinarily fine character; if anyone embarrassed him, he did not react, but immediately forgave him. He was particularly careful not to speak *loshon hora* (gossip and slander); he was a very silent man. He died on 28 Tamuz 1928.

Reb Zala Menda Alufovitz, another relative of mine, learned through the entire Talmud every year, making a *siyum* (celebration marking the completion of a scholarly work) on Simchas Torah.

Kupishok had a Chassidic community, mostly Chabadniks, who had their own synagogue, their own *shochet*, and their own rabbi—called *moreh horoah* so as not to diminish the stature of the town rabbi—the last of whom was the martyred Rav Yisroel Noach Chatzkevitch. Before World War I, the Chassidim had their own bathhouse and *mikveh* (ritual bath) near the river. They never had their own cemetery.

SPIRITUAL LEADERS: Among Kupishok's most famous rabbis were Rav Alexander Sender Kaplan, author of *Shalmey Nedorim* (1881), debates on the Talmudic tractate Nedorim which discusses vows; Rav Yitzchok Trivis; Rav Meir Segal Epstein, known as Rav Meir Shnipishoker, *moreh horoah* in Vilna; Rav Abba Yaakov Boruchov, author of the halachic responsa *Chevel Yaakov* (1881) and founder, in 1886, of Kupishok's yeshiva; Rav Leib Fein, later rabbi in Slonim, where he was martyred by the Germans; Rav Eliyohu Meir Feivelson, author of the halachic discussions *Pikuach Nefesh* and *Netzach Yisroel*, who was a founder of

Rav Abba Yaakov Boruchov, rabbi and rosh yeshiva in Kupishok.

Agudas Yisroel and a prolific polemicist; and Kupishok's last rabbi, the martyred Rav Zalman Pertzovsky.

Rav Eliyohu Meir Feivelson, rabbi of Kupishok, 1907-1928.

Kupishok's native sons became renowned scholars and rabbis. One of these was my uncle, Rav Nochum Gershon Oshry, who served Kupishok as a *dayan*. Another was Rav Elchonon Cohen who became rabbi of Dvinsk; during his student years at the Volozhin Yeshiva he was called the "*Iluy* of Kupishok." He married the daughter of the *gaon* Rav Mordechai Eliasberg, rabbi of Boisk. Others include Rav Moshe Etter, rabbi in Harrisburg, Pennsylvania; Rav Eliyohu Lutzki, rabbi of Zidik; the martyred Rav Lipa Zilber; and Rav Yonah Cohen of New York.

1939-45: In June, 1940, when the Russian government took over Lithuania and introduced its Soviet regime, the yeshivos came under immediate attack. The Baranovitch Yeshiva, headed by the martyred Rav Elchonon Wasserman, having escaped Soviet oppression by fleeing Poland, was compelled to disband. Its students formed small units, each of which moved into a different town in Lithuania in order to keep out of the Soviet regime's eyes. One group settled in Kupishok, and the story that follows was told to me by Rav Nosson Kotlowitz, who was a member of that group.

As the Germans approached, the Baranovitch yeshiva students did not know whether to stay or to flee. Rav Kotlowitz asked the local Catholic priest for advice. The priest told them that they should not leave, that he had enough food for them to last two years, and a cellar in which he could hide them. Rav Kotlowitz did not take the priest's advice and left town on one of the last coaches out. The rest of the Baranovitch students shared the fate of Kupishok's Jews.

On Wednesday, June 26, 1941, some 40 families managed to escape into Russia. Others fled into nearby villages to hide with Christians there until the bombardment would end, as they had done during World War I. Tragically, that is not how it worked out. As soon as the Germans occupied the town, the Jews began to suffer at the hands of their Lithuanian neighbors with whom they had once lived peacefully. One of the worst was Pezes, the secretary of the town council. All the Jews who had fled to the villages were stripped of their possessions and forced back into town barefoot and almost naked. A temporary ghetto was fenced in with barbed wire around the synagogue yard, and that is where the Lithuanians abused the women and the children, among them my dear mother and my beloved sisters, my precious little nieces and their parents, and the other friends and neighbors of my family.

They set upon the two rabbis, Rav Zalman Pertzovsky and Rav Yisroel Noach Chatzkevitz, chased them into the Chassidic *kloiz*, and put them through Job's tortures. Then they set a fire around them to burn their bodies, and then gruesomely led them out behind Kalman Levin's house, where the gentiles had a cemetery for atheists. The murderers insisted that the Jewish martyrs would have to be buried there. They also killed some of the most important members of the community, including Reb Moshe Zundel Leizerovitz the *melamed* (teacher); Avrohom Klip the *shochet*; Rav Meir Shteinbach, the son-in-law of the Chassidic rabbi; Isser Mechel, my brother-in-law; Yitzchok Mara; Hillel Zilber; Yitzchok Ezrach; Yisroel Gapanovitz; Gershon and Naftoli Meyrovitz. Two weeks later they killed the women and the children.

Rebetzin Chaya Leia Pertzovsky and her children, and Mrs. Bassa Meyrovitz and her children managed to hide in the home of Dr. Franzkevitch. But they were discovered and murdered six weeks later.

After my liberation, when I visited my hometown, the Christian woman Tonkicha, who had been my grandfather's neighbor, handed me a coat that she said had belonged to little Eliyohu Meir, Rav Pertzovsky's oldest child. Searching through the coat, I found a note that read, "They're taking us to be killed. Take revenge."

Nachum Shmid, the richest man in town and one of the most generous when it came to helping a fellow Jew, hid for three months in Shmilag, a village near Kupishok. After the Lithuanians stole his money, they reported him to the Germans. He was shot to death on the bank of the Kupa River.

Kupishok Jews were also murdered in the town of Rakishok, on their escape route to Russia. The pits in Rakishok are on the count's estate. Kupishok Jews were also murdered in the towns of Ponevezh and Payost.

Many of those who escaped to Russia and survived, returned to Lithuania and settled in Vilna, Kovno, and Ponevezh.

There used to be a town named Kupishok.

MALIAT

LITHUANIAN NAME: Maletai RUSSIAN NAME: Maljaty
LOCATION: In the Vilkomir district in eastern Lithuania, about 42 miles north of Vilna. The entire town was built along a single, long street.
JEWISH POPULATION IN 1939: 500 families
ECONOMY: The town's Jews drew their income from various retail shops, crafts, and trade.

The synagogue in Maliat.

INSTITUTIONS: It contained the institutions of an old-time Jewish settlement with its traditional lifestyle. Its inhabitants were Torah scholars and G-d-fearing people. There was a large Talmud Torah for elementary education, and then many Maliat families sent their sons to yeshivos out of town. The best-known *melamdim* in the Talmud Torah were Reb Yaakov Shachar and Reb Leib Ilofsky.

The modern era brought a number of modern institutions into the town. By 1940 Maliat had an elementary school, a credit union, and some other groups.

SPIRITUAL LEADERS: The town's rabbis over the decades included Rav Meir S. Guryon, Rav Eliezer Altzgut, Rav Nechemya Maliatsky, Rav Yisroel Heilperin, Rav Avrohom D. Reines, Rav Yitzchok A. Belitsky and his son, the martyred Rav Nota C. Belitsky.

1939-45: When the Germans occupied the town, the men were marched off to the town of Utyan

Rav Yitzchok Aryeh Belitsky.

Survivors at the mass grave in Maliat.

where they were murdered along with Utyan's men. Maliat's women and children were shot to death on the first day of *Selichos* (penitential prayers recited on the days preceding Rosh Hashanah), September 14, 1941, in the yard behind the mill where their mass grave is to be found. Individuals who managed to hide were reported by the Lithuanian farmers and killed after horrifying torture.

MARIAMPOL

LITHUANIAN NAME: Marijampole RUSSIAN NAME: Mariampol

LOCATION: Mariampol was a district capital in southwest Lithuania, about 30 miles southwest of Kovno. Before World War I it was part of the Suvalk district.

JEWISH POPULATION IN 1939: 35,000

ECONOMY: The economic life of Mariampol's Jews revolved around trade, retail shops, and handcrafts. The economic policies of the independent Lithuanian government often made business difficult for the Jews of Mariampol and similar towns and cities. But it did not lead to anti-Semitism on the part of the Lithuanian farmers. However when the Germans occupied Lithuania, the Lithuanians were ready and willing to participate in the process of annihilating the Jews.

INSTITUTIONS: Jewish community life in Mariampol was well organized. The community council directed religious and social life in town.

Besides the standard religious and cultural organizations and institutions, Mariampol also had the secular and non-religious institutions typical of most of Lithuania after World War I: there was a Hebrew-language high school, a credit union, a library, and local chapters of almost all the other parties.

SPIRITUAL LEADERS: Mariampol's residents included Torah scholars and men of secular knowledge such as Yitzchok Rosenthal, Eliyohu Eisikovitz, Peretz Bloch, Friedberg, and Meir London. The driving force in the community was the martyred Reb Chayim Velvel Kovisher, who was known in town as Chayim Velvel the *shochet*. A man of fine character, he possessed native intelligence and leadership ability. His good heart, loving smile, and respect for every person—manifestations of his love for every Jew—earned him a sterling reputation. The martyred Reb Yankel was the *shochet* and he used to assist Reb Chayim Velvel in many of his activities.

Mariampol's rabbis were world famous. Its first rabbi was Rav Chayim Shershover, who served the community for nearly 40 years. He was succeeded by his son-in-law, Rav Yehuda Leib Charlop. Later rabbis included Rav Yehonoson Eliasberg, son of Rav Mordechai Eliasberg, the rabbi of Boisk; Rav Yaakov Meir Gold; Rav Eliyohu Klatzkin; and Rav Avrohom D. Poppel, who was the first rabbi to serve as a deputy in the independent Lithuanian parliament. Mariampol's last rabbi, the martyred Rav Avrohom Z. Heller, was a *gaon* in Torah knowledge and an extraordinary speaker.

Rav Eliyohu Klatzkin.

Rav Shlomo Botnitsky was a *dayan* in Mariampol; his righteousness and good deeds are worthy of a whole chapter to themselves.

1939-45: Life in Mariampol went on normally until June 22, 1941, when the war broke out and the Mariampol-Kovno highway became impassable for Jews. Any Jew caught on that road was beaten and robbed. On June 23rd, Mariampol was occupied by the Germans. The Jews were abused, robbed, and murdered. Men were force-marched to labor, and their families were driven from their homes and forced into houses on Frenner Street.

The intelligentsia, the important citizens, and the rabbi of Mariampol—Rav Avrohom Z. Heller—were forced into the *beis hamidrosh* where they were placed under heavy Lithuanian guard. The courtyard around the *beis hamidrosh* was fenced in with barbed wire, and the stronger men were brought there. Then began some of the most horrifying "experiments" on the bodies of the men.

The famous Lithuanian journalist Antonas Ventzlova described the annihilation of Mariampol's Jews in the Soviet-Lithuanian newspaper, *Taribo Lietuava*, published in Kovno in October 1944:

"Along the bank of the Sheshupa River there are eight long pits, three meters wide and 70 meters long... The pits were dug by Jews forced by Lithuanian policemen acting under German orders... The extermination was very gruesome. The victims were forced to lie naked in rows in the pits, then they were shot to death with automatic weapons, and were covered with a thin layer of earth. First the men were murdered, then the women, the children, and the sick... The children's heads were bashed in with spades and rubber truncheons. There is no way to imagine the horrifying suffering of the victims.

Since during the extermination days the murderers were very drunk, more than a third of their victims lay in the pits wounded or even unharmed. The murderers would stomp with their boots on their living victims and cover them with earth to bury them alive... The racket of the machine-guns, the screams of the wounded and the dying, and the wild barbarity of the German [and Lithuanian] murderers, were enough to drive insane the forced laborers who were compelled to deal with the victims....

The laborer Maximov related, 'A Jewish man named Subotsky, lying with a chest wound under a thin layer of soil, pushed himself up on his hands and begged to be finished off, not to be buried alive.'"

According to information provided by a Christian, Rav Heller donned *tefillin* that he found in the *beis hamidrosh* and preached a fiery final sermon to his townspeople on the subject of how to die—not to become despondent and to sanctify *HaShem* joyously. The rabbi marched proudly at the head of the first group of Jews to their martyrdom. In all, 8,000 Jews were annihilated in Mariampol.

MAZHEIK

LITHUANIAN NAME: Mazeikiai **RUSSIAN NAME:** Mazheiki

LOCATION: A district capital in northwest Lithuania, Mazheik lies near the Latvian border and was the site of a railroad junction where trains arrived from a number of cities. It is a few miles north of Telz.

JEWISH POPULATION IN 1939: 300 families.

JEWISH HISTORY: Mazheik was one of Lithuania's newer Jewish communities.

ECONOMY: One of Mazheik's major manufacturing plants was a shovel factory which exported its shovels to other countries. Many of the town's Jewish families made their living from this factory. There were also a number of smaller factories which produced matches and other products for the region and for export.

SPIRITUAL LEADERS: Mazheik's first rabbi was Rav Zev Avrech, author of the responsa *Revid Hazohov*. Its other rabbis included Rav Moshe Zaks, dean of the local yeshiva; Rav Shmuel Moshe Rubinstein, author of *Toras Hakabbalah*, observations on the development of the Oral Law and its foundations in the written Torah; and the martyred Rav Yosef Mamiyaffe and his son-in-law, the martyred Rav Chayim Volk.

View of Mazheik.

1939-45: On July 24, 1941, the Germans entered Mazheik. But as in many other Lithuanian towns, the first to murder the Jews were the Lithuanians: they grabbed Jews from their homes and off the streets, beat them, abused them, and shot them. On July 14th, the Lithuanians went from house to house to round up the men. They took them to the synagogue, where they beat and tortured them. When they were finished, the Jews were led away, never to return. The next day they rounded up the women and the children, and took them to the town of Tirkshli, where the Jews of three towns—Akmian, Mazheik, and Vekshne—had been brought to be killed.

I have told the heroic tale of the *kiddush HaShem* of the rabbis of the three towns in the section on Akmian.

MERETSH

LITHUANIAN NAME: Merkine **RUSSIAN NAME:** Meretsch
LOCATION: Before World War I, Meretsh was in the Troki district; after Lithuanian independence it became part of the Alite district. Meretsh lies on the Niemen River in southern Lithuania, some 25 miles northeast Druzgenik, the Lithuanian spa famed for its mineral baths and mud baths. People suffering from arthritis, lumbago, sciatica, rheumatic diseases, and heart conditions used to travel there for the baths.
JEWISH POPULATION IN 1939: 300 families

JEWISH HISTORY: An older Jewish settlement.

ECONOMY: Many local Jews made their living from the river, shipping lumber on rafts to Germany. Others were grain dealers, shopkeepers, and craftspeople. The flour mill and sawmill were owned by Jewish merchants, the Alkenitzkys.

INSTITUTIONS: Meretsh had its own communal institutions: an elementary school, a credit union, a library, and a number of other organizations. Meretsh's primary residents, scholars and communal activists included Binyomin Alkenitzky, Reb Zalman the painter, and Reb Yudel Rochman. Mr. Hurvitz, also a scholar, utilized his friendship with the Alite district chief of police and other Christian officials to prevent trouble for the local Jews. Mr. Radovsky was the esteemed town elder. The town's younger activists included Eishishka, the leader of the Poaley Tziyon (a socialist movement) party, and Eliyohu Kadansky, an activist for the local elementary school.

SPIRITUAL LEADERS: Meretsh's rabbis included Rav Dovid Volpa, Rav Ben-Tziyon Sternfeld, Rav Yehuda Lipschitz, and the martyred Rav Michel Shtoppel, author of *Beir Mayim Chayim*, original explanations on the Talmud, and at age 84, one of Lithuania's oldest rabbis. I personally observed an episode that involved Rav Shtoppel at a meeting of the Union of Lithuanian Rabbis. The chairman proposed that the members rise to honor the memories of departed rabbis. Rav Shtoppel protested that doing so was forbidden as it is a gentile practice, not a Jewish one, and he brought halachic proofs of his position. The matter was removed from the agenda.

Rav Yehuda Lipschitz.

Mindel, a woman who lived on Vilna Street, personified *matan beseiser* (Hebrew for "secret giving to the needy"). She humbly made the rounds of the town to collect money and food which she judiciously distributed every Friday to the town's needy. One of Meretsh's native sons who achieved success in America was Eliyohu Dovid Stone—Chona the *Melamed*'s son—who later became attorney general of the state of Massachusetts.

1939-45: On June 23rd, 1941, Meretsh was occupied by the Germans. A few dozen families managed to flee and hide in the nearby villages during the initial bombardment. But they were compelled to return to town immediately after the Germans entered and robbed them of everything they had.

Young men and women were taken off to labor. There were reports from time to time about men being beaten or girls being raped, but otherwise matters were relatively calm—the calm before a storm. Two weeks passed, and suddenly the German commandant issued an order that Rav Shtoppel, who had fled town and hadn't returned, was to be brought to him. Fifty important citizens of the town were taken hostage to insure the rabbi's return.

The willingness of the hostages to let the Germans do whatever they wanted with them so long as the rabbi would go unharmed, frustrated and infuriated the murderers. So the order was issued to bring the rabbi to the commandant within 12 hours; if not, all the Jews in town—men, women, and children—would be dumped into the Niemen River.

Not one of the Jews in town was willing to go to the rabbi's hiding-place and bring him into town. As the story was told to me by a Christian from Meretsh, the Christian in whose home the rabbi was staying heard about the decree and told the rabbi what was going on. The rabbi immediately donned his good Shabbos clothes, his *kittel* (long, white robe), his white Yom Kippur *yarmulka* (skullcap), and his *tallis*. He bade his family farewell and told them not to cry for him since he was going in his 84th year to fulfill the greatest *mitzvah*—*kiddush HaShem*, to sanctify G-d with his life.

When the murderers saw the rabbi, they ordered him to sing and to dance. The old and gray rabbi danced with a Torah scroll, screaming at the top of his lungs, *"Ato hor'eiso loda'as"* ("In order to know G-d, He has shown us Himself through miracles," Deuteronomy 4:35) with the special tune reserved for Simchas Torah. The murderers went berserk and butchered him brutally. Only some of his limbs and organs were given proper burial, at great risk to those who managed to bring what was left of the rabbi to the Jewish cemetery.

The murder of the town's Jews had begun. Several hundred Jews were immediately forced into the synagogue where they were tortured. Others were cast into the Niemen River, where they drowned. A few weeks later the men were led out of the town and murdered. They were followed in short order by the women and children.

NEISHTOT-SHAKI

LITHUANIAN NAME: Naumiestis-Sakiai

LOCATION: Neishtot, in the Shaki district in southwest Lithuania, was also known as Neishtot-Kudirka. It lies right on the German border, southwest of Kovno; because of its proximity to the Shirvinta River, it was also known as Neishtot-Shirvint.

JEWISH POPULATION IN 1939: 200 families

JEWISH HISTORY: Jews settled in Neishtot in the early 19th century. The closeness to Germany influenced Neishtot strongly and kept it worldly.

The German influence is apparent in Neishtot's appearance.

Nevertheless, the old style of Jewish life was maintained there due to the large number of scholars and *bnei*-Torah (Torah scholars). A tombstone in the Jewish cemetery dated 1816 marked the final resting place of Rav Yehuda Leib, son of the Vilna *Gaon*. Enroute to Königsberg in Prussia for medical help, he passed away in Neishtot and was buried there.

ECONOMY: The Jews drew their income from trading with Germany. Some owned linen factories, while others were farmers and craftspeople.

INSTITUTIONS: Neishtot's institutions, besides its traditional religious ones such as *chadorim* and *shiurim*, included an elementary school, a library, a credit union, and other cultural organizations.

SPIRITUAL LEADERS: Neishtot's rabbis included Rav Abba Dayan; Rav Menachem Chorif; Rav Abba Abelson; Rav

A women stands next to the Neishtot synagogue.

Nachum Stern; Rav Aryeh L. Broida; Rav Yechezkel Volpert; Rav Shmuel Gochberg; Rav Eliezer Ragin, author of *Yalkut Eliezer*, sermons for special occasions, and *Siach Yitzchok*; Rav Sender Vilensky; and the martyred Rav Nechemya Fortman, author of *Divrey Chayim*.

1939-45: Within a couple of hours of the German occupation on June 22, 1941, five Jews had been murdered. On July 1st, the male Jews ages 14

and up were herded into the Jewish cemetery and murdered. The women and children were penned into a ghetto that included the synagogue and Bathhouse Street. Three months later, in September of 1941, most of the remaining women and children were marched out into the Parashnova Forest and murdered.

PLUNGYAN

LITHUANIAN NAME: Plunge RUSSIAN NAME: Plungyany
LOCATION: In the Telz district in northwest Lithuania, a few miles southwest of Telz.
JEWISH POPULATION IN 1939: 1,700 (total population: 5,000)
JEWISH HISTORY: Plungyan was one of Lithuania's oldest Jewish settlements. Its Jewish cemetery had tombstones dating back nearly 400 years, when the victims of the Chmielnicki pogroms fled to Lithuania.
ECONOMY: The Jews in Plungyan were occupied primarily in commerce as well as in crafts and agriculture.
INSTITUTIONS: Plungyan's yeshiva was founded by Rav Yechiel Heller, who built a building especially for the yeshiva. Its enrollment grew to 100 students, including local boys and boys from nearby towns such as Riteve, Kool, and others. Among its later roshei yeshiva were Rav Shlomo Itzel, Rav Zelik, Rav Ben-Tziyon Feldman (known as Rav Bentzil Vilner), and Rav Chayim Yitzchok Bloch, who later became rabbi in Jersey City, New Jersey.

Plungyan also had many secular institutions, including a Hebrew high school, an elementary school, and a branch of OZA. I particularly recall the children of the Pirchei Shoshanim, a youth organization for children aged five through *bar mitzvah* collecting money in

The big synagogue in Plungyan.

order to buy *seforim* for the local houses of study. And they achieved their goal. Throughout the Zamut region, *batei midrosh* contained bookcases full of sacred works that had been donated by the Pirchei Shoshanim. The donation of the *seforim* took place at a joyous ceremony every fall, immediately after Simchas Torah. Fathers would carry their children on their shoulders while the youngsters hugged the *seforim*, and mothers walked with pride at having such wonderful children. The Pirchei Shoshanim children became the builders of Jewish spirituality.

SPIRITUAL LEADERS: Plungyan was a humble town whose community members were not particularly well off, nor could they boast about their successful native sons. But the town did have some fine men to be proud of: Yisroel Itzes; Yaakov Dovid Zaks; Reb Yossel the *shochet;* Elya the pharmacist; Yeka and Leiba Metz; Reb Nachum Lurya; Avrohom Levovitz, the manager of the credit union; and others.

Rav Shmuel Avigdor Feivelson, rabbi of Plungyan.

The scholarly men in town took *talmidei chochomim* for sons-in-law. Reb Yisroel Elya Israelovitz's son-in-law was Rav Efrayim Epstein later an important Chicago rabbi. Reb Zundel was the *shochet* and he was very meticulous in his *mitzvah* observance, and a genuine G-d-fearing man. His son was the previously mentioned Rav Chayim Yitzchok Bloch.

Plungyan's rabbis included Rav Dov Ber Lipkin; Rav Yehuda Leib Ziv; Rav Moshe Zeitlin; Rav Yechiel Heller; Rav Moshe Yitzchok Segal; Rav Hillel Lifshitz; Rav Zevulun Barit; Rav Shmuel Avigdor Feivelson; Rav Shmuel M. Katz; the martyred Rav Levi Shpitz and the martyred Rav Avrohom M. Vessler.

Rav Levi Shpitz, rabbi of Plungyan, Vorne, and later Tavrig, where he was killed by the Germans.

1939-45: On June 25, 1941, the Germans occupied Plungyan. Before the Russian army retreated from Plungyan they had organized and armed a group of young leftist Jews to provide a kind of rear guard to help the Russians. When the Germans entered the town, the Lithuanians informed on those Jews. About 40 young Jews were quickly arrested, and the Germans proceeded to "experiment" on them in a manner I cannot put on paper. After my liberation, I was told the story by a Christian named Adamovicius, who considered himself a Communist. He showed me a knucklebone he had saved from one of these young martyrs. Their common grave is alongside the Riteve Road.

With the German occupation came random murders and robberies of Jews. Men above the age of 16 were separated from the women and the children and locked into barracks, from where they were herded off to labor every day. Abuse and beatings were part of the daily work routine. Some of the women were also taken to work. On July 5th, 1941, a German selected 30 of the prettiest women to "work" and they never returned.

When the day of their murder arrived, the men were ordered to dig pits; they were told that these were trenches to protect them from the Russians. Once the pits were ready, the men were taken out of the barracks and butchered.

After killing the men, the Germans set up a ghetto for the women and the children, assuring them that they could continue to live as long as they worked. Not so—they were butchered six weeks later. Thus were all the Jews of Plugyan killed.

PONEVEZH

LITHUANIAN NAME: Panevezys **RUSSIAN NAME:** Ponevezh

LOCATION: A district capital in central Lithuania comprising two parts, Old Ponevezh or Ferma, and New Ponevezh, north of Keiden. The two sections were connected by a bridge across the Neviazha River.

JEWISH POPULATION IN 1939: Over 10,000 (total population: 15,000)

Halkomir Street in Ponevezh.

JEWISH HISTORY: Jews first settled in Ponevezh in the 14th century.

ECONOMY: The Jews in Ponevezh occupied themselves primarily with retail merchandising, crafts, and exporting grain and flax. Two Jewish men named Rubinstein and Lev operated two large flour mills, and N. Feigenson ran a print shop.

*The big synagogue in Ponevezh with a sundial on its facade
for those who prayed vosikin (at sunrise).*

Ponevezh Yeshiva staff and students.

*Rav Yitzchok Yaakov
Rabinovitch, known as R.
Itzela Ponevezher.*

*Rav Eliyohu Dovid
Teomim-Rabinovitch.*

Rav Yeruchom Levovitz.

*Rav Yosef
Shlomo Kahaneman.*

INSTITUTIONS: On Remigala Street there was a colony of Karaites with two synagogues—an old one and a newly built one. Whenever they needed a *shochet* they used Reb Shimon Goldstein, who lived near them. And whenever they needed a *mohel*, they would also call on one of ours.

The Karaite synagogue.

Ponevezh achieved renown with its yeshiva and its founder, Rav Yitzchok Yaakov Rabinovitch, better known as Rav Itzela Ponevezher. Appointed rosh yeshiva in Slobodka-Kovno in 1889, he earned a reputation for his methods of Talmud study, which attracted many students. When he became rabbi of Ponevezh in 1898, he opened a *kollel*, a gathering of scholars, selected from the cream of the Lithuanian yeshivos, which met in Glickela's *kloiz* and was supported by Mrs. Miriam Gavronsky, daughter of the millionaire philanthropist Vissotsky of St. Petersburg. Two of Rav Itzela's most outstanding students were Rav Boruch Hurvitz, who became a rosh yeshiva in Slobodka, and Rav Naftoli Trop, who became the rosh yeshiva in Radun. Rav Itzel was succeeded in 1919 by the last rabbi of Ponevezh, Rav Yosef Shlomo Kahaneman.

SPIRITUAL LEADERS: In the roster of Ponevezh's earlier rabbis appear the names of Rav Avrohom Abbala Yoffeh; Rav Hillel Millikovsky (Salanter); Rav Shmuel Shapiro; Rav Moshe Yitzchok (Moshe Itzel) Segal; Rav Eliyohu D. Rabinovitch-Teomim (Aderes); Rav Moshe M. S. Shapiro and Rav Shaul Shapiro. Rav Shaul Shapiro never played favorites when it came to telling the truth; he was greatly concerned that he might behave inappropriately and that no one would reprove him out of misplaced respect, so he designated two prominent local residents to make him aware of his trespasses.

Ponevezh produced a number of extraordinary personalities deserving of mention. One was Reb Hertzel, whose book *Noam Hamitzvos* discussed the 613 *mitzvos*. He founded a preparatory yeshiva for young teenagers for whom he provided both spiritual and material sustenance. His goodness and scrupulousness were immeasurable. The story of the well he drilled in the yard of the synagogue illustrates both these traits. Reb Hertzel's well was drilled very deeply and people were able to pump up excellent water, which they used primarily for brewing tea.

Why did Reb Hertzel spend so much money to have a well drilled? He feared that he might inadvertently take public property or something belonging to another person without knowing from whom he took it. In either case, he could not fulfill the *mitzvah* to return what he had "stolen." So he had the well drilled deep enough to pump up the very best water in order that everyone should want to enjoy it. In that way he was able to "repay" any and all the people he might somehow have "robbed." On his tombstone was etched a well.

Another unusual person was my great-grandfather, Reb Efrayim Cohen, known in Ponevezh as Reb Efrayim the hay dealer. He used to walk around carrying two large baskets in which he collected food for the kosher kitchen that served Czar Nikolai's Jewish soldiers quartered in Ponevezh, boys who came from all over Russia. In old age, when he no longer had the strength to carry the two massive baskets on his shoulders, he struggled on to make sure the soldiers had kosher food. Before he died, he requested that the two baskets be buried with him.

Also in Ponevezh lived the physician Dr. Shachna Mehr, the brother of the *gaon* Rav Shlomo Ezra Mehr. Dr. Mehr was the medical director of the Ponevezh's Jewish Hospital and his reputation as a physician spread throughout Lithuania. He was born in the nearby town of Possval and he was gracious, friendly, and concerned for the health of all the poor he treated. In Ponevezh he was also active in communal matters.

Rav Shlomo Ezra, another Ponevezh resident, was a brilliant Torah scholar, an expert in Talmud and in codes. He had served in the town of Riteve as a *dayan* before becoming rosh yeshiva of Ponevezh's preparatory yeshiva. His pedagogical approach and his clarity of presentation made him one of the most gifted roshei yeshiva. He studied day and night in Glickela's *kloiz* and conversed very little, even with his brother.

Ponevezh's last rabbi, Rav Yosef Shlomo Kahaneman, was a leader of the Lithuanian *Agudas Yisroel* and a deputy in the Lithuanian parliament. Those duties did not keep this energetic man from developing the Ponevezh community to heights it had never before attained. He founded a yeshiva *gedolah*, developed the preparatory yeshiva, opened the Rav's *cheder*, and founded a Bais Yaakov school for girls. All of the city's institutions—the hospital, the old age home, the orphanage—expanded. The city itself blossomed economically as well as spiritually. The first *mashgiach* in the yeshiva was Rav Yeruchom Levovitz, later *mashgiach* in the Mirrer Yeshiva. He was succeeded by the martyred Rav Moshe Dov Tzfasman. The martyred Rav Osher Kalman Baron was the rosh yeshiva. Rav Kahaneman, who was a wonderful speaker, traveled to South Africa and to the United States to raise the money the communal institutions required.

After losing his community and his family in the Holocaust, the Ponevezher Rav, as he became known to tens of thousands of Jews the world over, built in Bnei Brak, Israel, the world's largest major yeshiva— the Ponevezh Yeshiva—and with it a complex of educational institutions that have generated the resurgence of Torah Jewry in Israel.

1939-45: On June 26, 1941, the Germans occupied Ponevezh, and their Lithuanian neighbors began to abuse and rob the Jews. A temporary ghetto was set up for the Jews beyond Shmilka Street, in the new Jewish neighborhood that the Christians called Palestinka. Enclosed with barbed wire, the area had all the trappings of a ghetto—yellow patches and beatings—but it did not last long.

From their Lithuanian informants the Germans learned which Jews to arrest, and the city jail soon overflowed with people. Every day Jews were led away from the jail, but no one knew where they had been taken. P. Yanusheitis, writing in the Lithuanian Communist journal *Tieso*, published in Vilna, February 1945, relates the following:

"One September morning in 1941, several dozen Jews were brought to the Ponevezh railroad station. In pairs, the Jews were forced to carry 200-kilogram barrels of gasoline. Those who were too weak to do this and collapsed while trying, were viciously murdered. Many of them were crushed to death when the murderers rolled those heavy barrels over their collapsed bodies.

When the last barrel had been loaded, the Lithuanian supervisor, Anjoulis, lined up the half-dead survivors and told them, 'For your good work, we will provide you a hot bath, and then you'll be able to rest in a cool spot.' They then drove the poor Jews to the municipal cement factories, where there were large pits which contained active lime. The murderers ordered them to fill the pits with water which the lime soon caused to bubble with hot, white puffs of whistling steam. The Jews were ordered to leap into the pits. Those who didn't were pushed in. The unfortunate victims were forbidden to stay in one place, but were forced to 'swim.' When they attempted to elude the acidic limewater that was consuming their skin and flesh by climbing out, the monsters forced them back in at bayonet point.

A thin little old man who could barely manage to keep his head above the billowing limewater was perceived by the murderers as seeking to protect his grey beard from being eaten away by the acid. One of them hit the poor man over the head until he sank under the water. By the time his fellow victims picked his head up out of the water, both his eyes had been eaten away by the lime. When the victims were allowed to climb out of the pits, the weakest ones were sent off to Payost to be executed, while the rest were returned to the jail to await the next sadistic orgy."

Later that September the murder of over 500 of Ponevezh's Jews took place in Payost, a village about three miles outside the city. The Jews were force-marched there in columns of 200, forced to their knees at the edges of the freshly dug pits that were to be their graves, and machine-gunned to death. The above article also cites the testimony of a neighboring villager, Narbutis Adomas, who described some of the horrors of the extermination from the viewpoint of a Lithuanian Christian: "We saw from afar how the pits were dug, but we did not believe that such gruesome butchery would take place. Yet we saw and lived through shocking scenes when the executioners clubbed their victims as they dragged them to the pits. The murderers used to grab babies out of their wailing mothers' arms and, throwing them into the air above a pit, use them for target practice. Because the murderers were drunk, they often missed the babies, who then fell into the pit alive. Some of the murderers used to lift children by their hair and smash their skulls with revolver shots. Shocked by the gruesome murder scenes, we, the neighboring villagers, could not get back to ourselves for a long time."

Russian prisoners of war were brought in to cover the mass graves. In one pit they discovered a live boy and tried to hide him in the bushes. But their Lithuanian guards noticed this and beat them for it. The Lithuanian partisan Dambrauskas decided that it was "better to kill the boy. Otherwise the blood will avenge itself." So he put his revolver to the boy's brow and shot him dead. Part of Dambrauskas's words had already been fulfilled: Many participants in the butchery were executed by the Germans themselves so that there should be no living witnesses to their crimes.

The Jews of the nearby towns—Ramigola, Shadove, Rogeva, and others—were cynically tricked into riding to the Payost pits with their possessions. As they emerged from their cars and carts, they were robbed of their property and thrown into the open pits. Some of the Jews were butchered in the Yasnegurka Forest.

Thus was the beautiful Jewish life in Ponevezh—its inhabitants, its scholars, its activists, its rabbis, and its roshei yeshiva—brutally extinguished.

POSSVAL

LITHUANIAN NAME: Pasvalys **RUSSIAN NAME:** Posvol

LOCATION: In the Birzh district, in northern Lithuania, a few miles north of Ponevezh. Possval was named for the Possval River that flows nearby. It was known for its large markets and fairs which drew people from the nearby towns and villages.

JEWISH POPULATION IN 1939: 700

JEWISH HISTORY: The Jewish settlement, which began in the 18th century, was preceded by a Karaite settlement led by Shlomo ben Aharon. There were still some Karaite families left when the Germans came marching in, and they were deported.

ECONOMY: The Jews of Possval made their living primarily from retail shops.

INSTITUTIONS: Among the things that made Possval famous was its Martyr's Cemetery in which were buried Possval's martyrs as well as those of many of the surrounding towns of Yanishkel, Vashki, Linkeva, Pumpian, Salat, and Vabolnik.

SPIRITUAL LEADERS: Among the people who made Possval famous was the *gaon* Rav Abbala, a native Possvaler, who served his hometown as rabbi before moving on to become Vilna's rabbi. Among Possval's other rabbis were: Rav Zalman Zak; Rav Avrohom L. Mintz; Rav B. Binyomin Dimant; Rav Yaakov Kretchmer, author of *Toldos Yaakov*; Rav Mordechai Rabinovitch; his son and successor, Rav Moshe Rabinovitch; and Rav Moshe's son-in-law and successor, the martyred Rav Yitzchok Agulnik.

The martyred Rav Yitzchok Agulnik.

Lithuania was renowned for its *maggidim* (preachers), who traveled from town to town to utilize their Torah knowledge, their *mussar* inspiration, and their skill at vivid imagery—and, perhaps most significant, their wonderful tunes—to arouse and inspire their hardworking, worried, and Redemption-hungry brethren. Perhaps the sweetest of the *maggidim* was Rav Chayim Yaakov Bialostotsky, the *maggid* of Possval.

Possval was also well-known for its doctor, my relative, Dr. Shachna Mehr, whose home always seemed to be under siege by the local citizenry, gentiles as well as Jews. He later moved to Ponevezh where he became medical director of the Jewish Hospital and a well-known communal activist.

1939-45: On July 4, 1941, the murder of Possval Jewry began with Lithuanian and German officers demanding that Jewish girls be handed over to them. A huge bribe bought off that demand. A ghetto was set up around the 15th of July. During the ghetto's brief existence, food was provided by the city council to the newly created ghetto cooperative under the direction of the town rabbi, Rav Yitzchok Agulnik. Several weeks before their murder, Jews were brought into the ghetto from the nearby towns of Yanishkel, Pumpian, Vashki, Salat, and Vabolnik. The extraordinary and possibly sole instance among Lithuanian Jews of 40 Vabolnik Jews converting to Catholicism ended tragically. When brought to Possval they were kept apart from the rest of the Jews; but they were taken out to be killed together with their brethren.

On August 27th, the Jews were herded into the *beis hamidrosh* that stood outside the ghetto. The women and children were separated from the men and led away to the Lithuanian elementary school on Vilna Street. That very day the 1,649 martyrs—1,349 from Possval and 300 from the nearby towns—were taken out to the Zeidekan Forest, about two miles outside of Possval where they were butchered by Lithuanian partisans supervised by Germans. At the last moment, five women managed to escape and survive: Anna Maraz, Tzipa Davidovitch, Tana Balan, and two Todes sisters from the town Yanishkel.

The Lithuanian murderers whose names were recorded are Petras Bieluskas, Veitkus the shoemaker, Strazdas Yuozas the tailor, Metzkus, Ignatz Augentas, Godas Leonas, Antonas Birkauskas, Yanas Vilimas, and Visatzkis.

The only Lithuanian in that region known to have risked his life to save Jews was a man named Baniolis. He hid and fed three Jewish girls in a barn for three years.

RADVILISHOK

LITHUANIAN NAME: Radviliskis RUSSIAN NAME: Radzivilishki

LOCATION: In the Shavl district in northern Lithuania, with a train junction where trains connected to Tilsit, Berlin, Moscow, Kovno, and Dvinsk. Radvilishok is located a few miles west of Ponevezh.

JEWISH POPULATION IN 1939: 250 families

ECONOMY: Radvilishok had a large military garrison. The Jews made their living primarily from shops that served the local populace, the soldiers, and travelers who had to spend time in town between trains. As a whole, the Jews of Radvilishok maintained a higher standard of living and were more worldly than their brethren elsewhere in Lithuania. Nevertheless, many of the families were pious and scholarly, and sent their children to yeshivos.

INSTITUTIONS: Besides the daily and Shabbos *shiurim* and the local Tiferes Bachurim, the town had an elementary school, a credit union, and other religious and cultural organizations.

SPIRITUAL LEADERS: One of Radvilishok's early rabbis was Rav Reuven Yosef Gordon, known as Rav Yossel *der tzaddik*. Before becoming Radvilishok's rabbi, he had been rosh yeshiva in Shavl. When he died, the Jews of Radvilishok carried him on their shoulders the entire 12 and a half miles to Shavl for burial, because Radvilishok did not have its own Jewish cemetery.

Its roster of rabbis includes: Rav Yitzchok Hurvitz; Rav Yaakov Rabinovitz; Rav Meir Maltz; Rav Doniyel Zaks, author of the halachic *Chemdas Doniyel*, who later settled in Jerusalem; Rav Yochonon Zupovitz, who later settled in Tiberias; and the martyred Rav Yitzchok Begun, author of the halachic *Sedeh Yitzchok*.

1939-45: When the town was occupied by the Germans, the Lithuanians arrested the rabbi and other important community members. In jail they abused and killed them. The surviving Jews—men, women, and children—were taken to the Yanishok marketplace from where they were taken away to be murdered.

RAKISHOK

LITHUANIAN NAME: Rokiskis **RUSSIAN NAME:** Rakishki
LOCATION: A district capital about 13 miles from the Latvian border, a few miles southeast of Birzh.
JEWISH POPULATION IN 1939: 3,000

The central square in Rakishok.

JEWISH HISTORY: The famous Russian air hero, General Shmushkovitch, was a native Rakishoker, the son of Gershon Shmushkovitch. Just before the outbreak of the war with Germany, he moved his entire family from Rakishok to Moscow, including his brother Elozor, who was learning in the Slobodka Yeshiva.

ECONOMY: The Jews occupied themselves with retail shops, small trading, leather production, peddling in the surrounding villages, handicrafts, manufacturing, and exporting grain and flax.

INSTITUTIONS: Rakishok's uniqueness lay in its large Chassidic population. They were "heise" (fervent in Yiddish). Lubavitch Chassidim, with their own rabbi and *shochetim*. And this in a Lithuania whose cities and towns were decidedly not Chassidic. Rakishok arranged for the Lubavitcher *Rebbi* to visit Rakishok after he escaped from Russia and settled in Riga, Latvia's capital in 1915. Rakishok was proud that the *Rebbi* chose to stay there when he visited no other Lithuanian town or city, not even the large city of Kovno.

Rakishok's Jews were dedicated Torah Jews. Reb Bertchik Zalkind, a somewhat scholarly Jew, founded a yeshiva in Rakishok. Not only Rakishok boys studied there but also students from the nearby towns—Kamei, Fonedel, Abel, and Shvadost. The 60 students were taught by Rav Moshe Sidrer and the martyred Rav Mechel Veiner. Mr. Zalkind undertook to maintain the yeshiva students and the roshei yeshiva. Zalkind himself taught a daily *shiur* in the Mittelste Synagogue.

Many Rakishok boys studied in major yeshivos out of town, and some of them became renowned authorities. One of those was the martyred *gaon* Rav Zelik Ruch, who became rosh yeshiva in the Lomza Yeshiva.

SPIRITUAL LEADERS: Among the town's rabbis over the years were: Rav Eliyohu Margoliyos; Rav Isser Margoliyos; the martyred Rav Betzalel Katz, rabbi of the Chassidim for many years till the Holocaust; Rav Yitzchok Gorr, who settled in Hebron, Israel, and died there; Rav Shmuel Leviton, who settled in New York where he died in 1974 at the age of 91; the martyred Rav Avrohom Meirovitz; and the last

Rav Betzalel Katz and Lithuania's President Smetana at the dedication of the newly built Rakishok depot.

rabbi of the *misnagdim*, the martyred Rav Zelig Arlovitz, a native of Rakishok, who overcame the handicap of "I remember him as a boy" to become the town rabbi. Another native of Rakishok, Rav Shmuel Abba

Snieg, served as a chaplain in the Lithuanian army. He survived the war and became the rabbi of post-war Munich, Germany.

1939-45: During the early days of the war, Rakishok filled up with refugees from the surrounding towns—Skopishok, Kupishok, Kamei, Vishinta, Fonedel, and others—all seeking to cross the Latvian border into nearby Dvinsk and from there to cross the Russian border into Shebezh. But the Germans were faster than them and occupied Dvinsk, thus blocking that escape route. A few people managed to escape into Russia by train.

On June 25, 1941, the Germans occupied Rakishok. The day before, the Lithuanian fifth column began to beat and rob the Jews along the roads where they were desperately trying to escape by horse and wagon. Refugees whom the local Lithuanians pointed out to the Germans were warned to return home, but were murdered en route.

Baron Pzezdetsky's Palace—where the Jews of Rakishok and its region were incarcerated by the Germans before they were driven to their death-pits.

The local Jews were driven out of their homes and forced into the synagogues and houses of study. Several weeks later the men were separated from their wives and children, and marched out of town to dig their own graves before being murdered. A few weeks after that nearly all the women and children were killed. A few women somehow survived, among them Rochela Zhager and Mrs. Zokenstein.

RASSEYN

LITHUANIAN NAME: Raseiniai **RUSSIAN NAME:** Rossieny
LOCATION: A district capital in west central Lithuania, a few miles west of Keidan.
JEWISH POPULATION IN 1939: 2,000 (total population: 5,000)
JEWISH HISTORY: Rasseyn was one of Lithuania's oldest Jewish communities. A large number of its Jews arrived in the 17th century, although the Jewish community in Rasseyn dates back to the 14th century.
ECONOMY: Jews made their living exporting lumber and grain, farm-

ing, and from small businesses. When a railroad line was built outside Rasseyn, a new city, Shavl, developed nearby that soon outstripped Rasseyn.

Vilna Street in Rasseyn.

INSTITUTIONS: In 1863 a Talmud Torah was established and poor children were provided with shoes as well as an education. A trade school was also established to teach children locksmithing. In 1878 a Jewish hospital was built, followed in 1879 by the establishment of a Bikur Cholim society. The large free loan fund was established in 1880.

Rasseyn had its own yeshiva for boys from Rasseyn as well as for boys from nearby towns—Eiragala, Cheikishok, Betagala, Guirtegala, and others. The Rasseyn Yeshiva was headed by Rav Moshe Zaks, Rav Nisson Yablonsky, Rav Dovber Sheinfeld, Rav Chayim Zev Yoffe, and the martyred Rav Shlomo Z. Ossofsky. When the Kamenitz Yeshiva, Knessess Beis Yitzchok, escaped to Vilna in 1940, it was compelled to seek a home in a town outside Vilna. Rasseyn warmly received the yeshiva.

Rav Alexander Moshe Lapidos.

SPIRITUAL LEADERS: Rasseyn was renowned as a G-d-fearing and scholarly community. The roster of Rasseyn's rabbis includes: Rav Avrohom Lisker; Rav Nosson Nota Rabinovitz; Rav Mordechai Rabinovitz; Rav Moshe Zeitlin; Rav Avrohom S.

Rabinovitz; Rav Alexander Moshe Lapidos; Rav Moshe Soloveitchik; Rav Yehoshua Klatzkin; and the martyred Rav Aharon S. Katz. The town *maggid* was Rav Boruch Garfinkel.

One of Rasseyn's most interesting personalities was a shoemaker named

*Moshe Markovitz, the shoemaker who compiled
Shem Hagedolim Hashelishi.*

Moshe Markovitz. Although unable to write, he always carried a notebook with him, and whenever he garnered fresh information about any Lithuanian rabbi, past or present, or wanted his ideas written down, he would take his pencil from out of his boot and ask someone to write down the information. Ultimately in 1910 he compiled and published two volumes, *Shem Hagedolim Hashelishi*, a biographical encyclopedia about the rabbis of Lithuania. His son, Rav Tuvya Markovitz, was rabbi of Antaleft and was murdered in Kovno's Ninth Fort together with his son Rav Chayim Shimshon, author of *Divrei Chayim*, who was renowned for his phenomenal memory and encyclopedic knowledge.

Rasseyn was blessed with Jews whose level of piety was so high that they were widely called "*chosid*," even though they did not belong to any Chassidic group and were in fact *misnagdim*. Relatively recently there was Reb Osher the *Chosid*, and there used to be Reb Shmuel the *Chosid* and Reb Mottela the *Chosid*.

Reb Osher was an extremely knowledgeable scholar who persevered at his Torah studies day and night. His wife ran a fabric store to support their family. Reb Osher had an extraordinary reputation in town: Do you need advice? See Reb Osher. Did some tragedy take place, G-d forbid? Is someone ill? See Reb Osher the *Chosid*. He could always be found in the *beis hamidrosh* studying Torah. And there were always guests around his table, especially on Shabbos. He and his wife were eager to offer both meals and lodging.

One Friday night, his wife heard their houseguest walking through the house and collecting the silver items. She woke her husband, "Osher! The guest has collected our silver and is about to leave. Do something!" Reb

Osher replied, "Don't be afraid. Whoever needs can take what he wants," and he did not get out of bed.

1939-45: On July 28, 1941, the Germans occupied Rasseyn. Even before their arrival, Lithuanians had begun robbing and murdering Jews. Kovno Jews fled into the country, and Jews from the country fled into Kovno. But to no avail—every city and town had a Lithuanian fifth column that assisted the Germans.

The men were sent to forced labor, and women were raped. Jews were driven out of their homes, which were quickly taken over by their neighbors. The old rabbi, Rav Katz; the primary citizens of the town; the teacher, Cohen; and the town doctor were brutally tortured to "reveal where the Communists are." When they returned home they were barely recognizable, so severely had they been disfigured. Within several weeks the entire intelligentsia of the town and its scholars, including the old rabbi, were taken out to the marketplace and forced to dig a pit, in which they were buried alive. After that the remaining men were separated from their wives and children, and then a few days later they were killed. The women and children were killed soon after.

There were some survivors: Yeshaya Krum and his family, the Ziv sisters, Cohen the miller, and others. Yeshaya Krum was caught, and in 1943 was brought to the Kovno Ghetto with his family. Later, during the liquidation of the Kovno Ghetto, he was again fortunate enough to save himself and his family, and they indeed survived the Holocaust to be among the few witnesses to testify what happened to the ancient Jewish community of Rasseyn. Not only are the Jews no longer in Rasseyn; the city itself was entirely destroyed.

RITEVE

LITHUANIAN NAME: Rietavas **RUSSIAN NAME:** Retovo

LOCATION: In the Telz district in western Lithuania, slightly south of Plungyan.

JEWISH POPULATION IN 1939: 200 families

JEWISH HISTORY: Riteve was settled by Jews as early as 1662. Most of the men were Torah scholars, and the *beis hamidrosh* was always full of them sitting and studying Torah. Their businesses, mostly retail and craft shops, were operated by their wives.

Among Riteve's important men was Moshe Itzkovitz, known in town as Moshe Yeshias. He was the richest man in town and the major activist. Whenever Baron Aginsky, the landholder who owned Riteve, made trouble for the Jews, Moshe Yeshias would visit him and resolve the matter—and take home with him the baron's contribution to the *Maos Chitim* fund. Mr. Itzkovitz's son-in-law was the town doctor, Doctor Linde.

Riteve's main street.

INSTITUTIONS: Riteve had a yeshiva of its own. Its roshei yeshiva included some of Riteve's most important community members—Rav Mordechai Yitzchok Segal (son-in-law of Dovid Uzhpaler) and Rav Nachshon Hendler (known in town as Nachshon Bere-Shmuels). Also renowned in town was Rav Boruch Kreines, a great *tzaddik* and a very humble man who was conversant in the Talmud. After World War I another yeshiva was founded and headed by Rav Moshe Shurin, son-in-law of Rav Moshe Aharon Davidovitz.

SPIRITUAL LEADERS: Riteve's rabbinic roster includes Rav Leibchik Chorif and his son-in-law, Rav Aharon Burstein, later rabbi in Tavrig and rosh yeshiva in Yeshivas Merkaz HaRav in Jerusalem; Rav Yitzchok Eliyohu Geffen; and the martyred Rav Shmuel Fondiler, one of the most famous *mussar* teachers of the era.

The martyred Rav Shmuel Fondiler, last rabbi of Riteve.

1939-45: On June 23, 1941, the Germans occupied Riteve. The first Jews they shot to death were the communal leader Bere Zaks and his wife. According to an eyewitness, Rav Fondiler was brought into the *beis hamidrosh* and ordered to shred a Torah scroll and other sacred works in front of the other Jews. The rabbi's heart gave out and he died on the spot. The Germans then set the *beis hamidrosh* on fire and incinerated those Jews who were inside.

Some of Riteve's Jews were taken away to Telz, northeast of Riteve. There the Lithuanians separated the men from the women and made an offer to spare anyone who would pay them 5,000 rubles. One of the

Riteve women announced, "Don't worry, Jews, I have enough money to redeem us all." The Lithuanians took her money and on the next day, the 20th of Tamuz, murdered them.

The Jews who had remained in Riteve hoped their lives had been spared. But a few days later, the men were separated from the women and children and were killed, followed soon after by the women and children.

Thus ended the history of the lovely, scholarly Jewish community of Riteve.

HaRav Zvi H. Shurin, a native of Riteve who currently lives in Jersey City, N.J., and is the rabbi of Congregation Sons of Israel there, provided the following information about the dramatic re-interment of Rav Shmuel Fondiler and Rav Abba Rabinowitz, the shochet of Riteve:

> "More than 53 years after the Rav of Riteve, Rav Shmuel Fondiler, one of the generation's Torah giants, was brutally murdered together with Rav Abba Rabinowitz, the shochet of Riteve, their remains were laid to rest in Israel on the 19th of Av, 5754 (July 27, 1994) on the Bais Almin of Har Hazaisim (Mount Olives) in Jerusalem.
>
> Thousands of people, among them *rabonim*, roshei yeshiva and *bnei* Torah from all walks of life, as well as many survivors from Lithuania who reside in Israel, came to pay their respects as the coffin containing the remains of both men passed the Yeshiva of Ponevezh in Bnei Brak where they were eulogized by the rosh yeshiva HaRav Avrohom Kahanaman and HaRav Aaron B. Shurin, professor at Yeshiva University in New York and a close personal friend of Rav Fondiler, and the Hebron Yeshiva in Geulah, Jerusalem, where they were eulogized by the rosh yeshiva HaRav Chaim Sarno. Many close friends of the Rav and shochet delivered emotional eulogies there as well, including HaRav Yisroel Shurin, Rav of Efrat, Israel; Mr. Nathan Katz; Honorable Dov Shilansky, deputy speaker of the Knesset and a native of Shavl; and myself.
>
> A Lithuanian schoolteacher by the name of Ruibys Jonas-Vaclovas led to the discovery of the burial place of the Rav and the shochet. He responded to an ad Mr. Lifschitz, the head of the Jewish Committee of Shavl, had placed in one of the Lithuanian newspapers inquiring about the burial place of the Rav of Riteve at the request of Mr. Nathan Katz, a Riteve native who survived the Holocaust. Before he died, Mr. Katz's father had asked his son to do all that he could to find his beloved Rav's grave and bring his remains to a proper burial

in Israel.

Mr. Jonas-Vaclovas disclosed in his letter the exact location of the Rav's grave and notified the searchers that the shochet was buried there as well. Through a fence he had seen the brutal murders take place in June 1941 near a monument in Auginsky's Park, the city park of Riteve, when he was 12 years old.

Once the burial place of these two great men was established with a notarized statement by the teacher, a ruling concerning their removal to Israel was given by HaRav Aaron Soloveichik, head rosh yeshiva of Brisk in Chicago, Ilinois, and of Yeshiva University; the Agudas Harabonim of the U.S.; the Vaad Harabonim of Greater New York; as well as by the elder *rabonim* of Jerusalem, HaRav Y.S. Elyashiv, HaRav Shlomo Zalman Auerbach, and the chief rabbi of Jerusalem, HaRav Yitzchok Kulitz.

After two years of strenuous work and with the help of Mr. Rafael Genis, a native of Riteve who currently lives in Telz, all necessary permits were obtained and digging in Riteve's park proceeded. Two Chevra Kadisha men were sent by Kehilas Yerushalayim of Har Hazaisim, with the help of HaRav Chaim Dvir of Jerusalem [son-in-law of Rav Z.H. Shurin], HaRav Kulitz, and myself, to supervise the removal of the remains. Mr. and Mrs. Nathan Katz, who had undertaken and financed the entire cost of this endeavor, as well as former natives of Riteve and friends of the Rav and shochet, among them HaRav Aaron B. Shurin from New York, HaRav Yisroel Shurin from Efrat, Israel, and myself, stood by during the entire period of the digging. After six hours of exhausting digging, the remains of the Rav and the shochet were found and carefully put into a single coffin for their final journey to a proper burial in Israel."

SALANT

LITHUANIAN NAME: Salantai RUSSIAN NAME: Salanty

LOCATION: In the Kretinga district in northeast Lithuania, a few miles west of Telz.

JEWISH POPULATION IN 1939: 500

JEWISH HISTORY: Salant already had 279 Jewish inhabitants in 1765. In 1831, during the Polish rebellion, the Salant philanthropist Eliyohu Gutkind saved 12 Jews from being hanged. He walked into the Salant church, which was packed with Catholics, and asked the priest to save

The synagogue in Salant. Inset: Its aron kodesh.

the Jews. The priest, at the head of a large procession of his congregants, walked to the gallows and prevented the hanging of the 12 Jews.

ECONOMY: The Jews of Salant earned their living as flax merchants, craftspeople, and shopkeepers.

INSTITUTIONS: Salant had a wonderful Tiferes Bachurim branch where young married men studied every evening after the day's work. The teachers at the Tiferes Bachurim were Reb Nosson Berkovitz and the Salant rabbi's son, Reb Mordechai Klaf.

The Tiferes Bachurim in Salant, 1930.

SPIRITUAL LEADERS: Salant's most famous rabbi was Rav Tzvi Hirsh Broida, renowned as Reb Hirsh *Tosofos* for his phenomenal knowledge. His best-known students were Rav Yisroel Lipkin (Salanter), Rav Shmuel Salant, and Rav Eliyohu Levinson (Reb Elinka Kretinger). Other

Rav Gavriel Feinberg.

Rav Mordechai Yitzchok Izaak Rabinovitz.

well-known Salant rabbis were: Rav Broida's son-in-law, Rav Shmuel Avigdor Tosefta, later rabbi in Karlin; Rav Yoel Yitzchok Katzenellenbogen; Rav Hillel Millikovsky (Salanter); Rav Gavriel Feinberg; Rav Yosef Yoffe; Rav Meir Atlas, later rabbi in Shavl—the son-in-law of Rav Eliezer Gordon of Telz, and the father-in-law of both Rav Chayim Ozer Grodzensky of Vilna and Rav Elchonon Wasserman of Baranovitch; Rav Mordechai Yitzchok Izaak Rabinovitz; and Rav Bera Hirsh Klaf, the last rabbi of Salant.

SEREY

LITHUANIAN NAME: Seirijai RUSSIAN NAME: Seree

LOCATION: In the Alite district in southern Lithuania, about 50 miles southwest of Vilna.

JEWISH POPULATION IN 1939: 800

ECONOMY: The Jews made their living primarily from the lakes around Serey. They raised and marketed fish to as far away as Kovno and even Germany. Other Jews were merchants, crafters, or farmers.

INSTITUTIONS: I must mention the secret charity work of Chiesa Prusak and Mrs. Henya Tzvilling. Each collected money and food, which they then distributed to the town indigent or to those temporarily in difficult straits. Other Serey institutions included a credit union, a Bikur Cholim society, a guest house, and a large library. Young people were active in a number of cultural and religious organizations.

SPIRITUAL LEADERS: Among Serey's rabbis were Rav Avrohom Broida, who was a colleague and a *mechuton* (in-law) of the *Gaon* of Vilna whose son was married to Rav Broida's daughter; Rav Chayim Vasserzug; Rav Gershon Ravinson; Rav Yechezkel Volpert; Rav Avrohom P. Eliasberg; Rav Yisroel Goldin; Rav Sholom Yitzchok Sczupak.

Among Serey's communal leaders were Levi Pinkovsky, Mordechai Bordovsky, and Chayim Menda Keily. Keily was a quiet, modest activist. Yossel Garbarsky, a powerful Jewish land-owner, was a *gabbai* in the town *beis hamidrosh*; a former student in Volozhin, he taught a daily *shiur* in town. Yehuda Leib Bielas-totsky was a modern Jew who opened a mod-

Serey's beis hamidrosh.

ern *cheder* in Serey. He had considered himself nonreligious for a while, then became pious and taught a Talmud *shiur* in the *kloiz*. For many years the *gabbai* of the *beis hamidrosh* was Bera Tzvilling. The younger activists were Meir Evakovsky, Yeruchom Garbarsky, and Shmuel Koleka.

After Rav Sczupak's death, Serey had difficulty choosing a new rabbi. The town's temporary rabbi was Rav Sczupak's brother-in-law, Rav Karna, the rabbi of Mushnik, who was known throughout Lithuania as a very wise man. He was also physically very strong, and when he greeted you it was sometimes a bit difficult to free your hand from his. And so Jewish life continued in Serey until June 23, 1941, when the Germans occupied the town.

1939-45: Prior to their occupation, the Germans bombarded Serey with incendiary bombs, which burned down half the town. When the Germans entered Serey, the Lithuanians informed them that a Jewish member of the Communist Youth Party had shot at the Germans and at them from Garbarsky's granary. The Germans pulled Yossel Garbarsky out of his house and shot him. When his son Yeruchom, the town doctor, ran out to save his father, he too was shot. That same day Eliyohu Aminodov, Kovalsky, and other young men were shot.

The town's Jews had nowhere to go. They were crowded together in the Christian art school like herring in a barrel. Whoever was young and strong was taken off to labor; many never returned. Young women were raped.

This all occurred in 1941 until two days before Rosh Hashanah, when the remaining Jews were ordered to strip naked. They were driven through the streets and forced through a gauntlet of their Lithuanian neighbors who were armed with clubs and boards. The Lithuanians beat the Jews, all the while spitting on them and insulting them. In Galunishok, near the river, the bleeding, wounded Jews were finally driven into pits and to their deaths.

SHADOVE

LITHUANIAN NAME: Seduva **RUSSIAN NAME:** Shadov

LOCATION: In the Ponevezh district in north central Lithuania, a few miles west of Ponevezh.

JEWISH POPULATION IN 1939: 800

JEWISH HISTORY: Shadove was one of the oldest Jewish settlements in Lithuania. There is evidence of Jews living there as early as the mid-fifteenth century. In recent pre-war years, people from Shadove in the United States and South Africa sent home money to support their families in Shadove. Baltimore still has a Shadove synagogue and New York a Shadove committee, vestiges of that period.

View of Shadove.

ECONOMY: Many of Shadove's Jews made their living from retail shops and crafts. Some were vegetable farmers. They rented land from the gentiles, and planted, harvested and marketed their own produce.

INSTITUTIONS: Shadove was proud of its old synagogue and beautiful *aron kodesh*. There was also a large brick *beis hamidrosh*, once the yeshiva founded by Rav Yosef Leib Bloch when he was rabbi of Shadove. After Rav Bloch moved to Telz, the yeshiva was led by the town's new rabbi, Rav Aharon Bakst, until World War I. The *gaon* and *tzaddik* Rav Moshe Kravitz, later rabbi in Fayura, founded a preparatory yeshiva in Shadove.

Rav Yosef Leib Bloch, rabbi of Shadove and later of Telz.

Shadove's institutions, besides its *chadorim*, yeshivos and daily *shiurim*, included a Tiferes Bachurim where the young men studied and prayed. There were also a Hebrew elementary school, a credit union, a library, and a variety of cultural groups.

SPIRITUAL LEADERS: The roster of Shadove's rabbis includes Rav Gershon Kremer; Rav Eliezer S. Rabinovitz; Rav Shaul Shapiro; Rav Simcha Horovitz; Rav Yehuda L. Riff; Rav Noach Rabinovitz; Rav Avrohom A. Burstein; Rav Dov Y. Kanovitz; Rav Aharon Bakst, later rabbi in Shavl; Rav Chayim B. Notelovitz; and the martyred Rav Mordechai D. Henkin.

Shadove's community members included many scholars and lovers of Torah. The town philanthropist was Bena Mehr, my uncle. He loved Torah and respected rabbis and their disciples. His son Avigdor, a major Torah scholar, married the daughter of Rav Malkiel Tzvi Tenenbaum, the rabbi of Lomza. Yisroel Elya Mirvis took the brilliant Rav Yaakov Meskin for a son-in-law. Rav Meskin emigrated to America and served as a rabbi in the Bronx, New York, where he died in 1956. Shlomo Yossa the shoemaker was up at 4 a.m. daily, the sound of his *Tehillim* resonating through the town.

1939-45: As soon as Shadove was occupied by the Germans on Thursday, June 26, 1941, the local Lithuanians went on a rampage, pillaging and murdering their Jewish neighbors. The rabbi and prominent men were abused and tortured. The men were taken out of the city and murdered. The women and the children were locked into the synagogue, abused, and then killed.

SHAVL

LITHUANIAN NAME: Siauliai RUSSIAN NAME: Shavli

LOCATION: The second largest city in Lithuania, and a district capital in northern Lithuania. Shavl is located slightly northeast of Kelm.

A Shavl street.

JEWISH POPULATION IN **1939:** 8,000 (total population: 32,000)

JEWISH POPULATION IN **1945:** 500

JEWISH HISTORY: The Jewish settlement in Shavl dates from the 17th century.

ECONOMY: Shavl's wealthiest Jews were involved in leather production. The Turok brothers owned one such factory. Another was owned by Chayim Frankel, whose factory became one of the largest leather factories in Russia. A generous man, Frankel helped establish the Talmud Torah in which 250 children studied. He also provided many of the children with food and clothing.

INSTITUTIONS: Shavl had a yeshiva, founded in 1909, that was supported by the Moscow philanthropist Refoel Shlomo Gotz. Another yeshiva was founded by Rav Levitan and headed by Rav Yehuda Shapiro, son-in-law of Rav Atlas, and by Rav Yehuda and Rav Yerachmiel Levitan. Shavl also had a *kollel*, in the Landkever *kloiz*. The *kollel*'s most renowned member was Rav Zelig Reuven Bengis, later Rav in Jerusalem.

SPIRITUAL LEADERS: Shavl's rabbis included some of Lithuania's greatest Torah scholars: Rav Yechezkel Luntz; Rav Yitzchok Isaac Rabinovitz, author of the responsa, *Ateres Yitzchok*; Rav Yosef Zecharya Stern, one of the greatest geniuses of his generation, whose brilliance

Rav Yosef Zecharya Stern.

Rav Aharon Bakst.

still surprises scholars who study his works; Rav Meir Atlas; Rav Osher Nisson Levitan; and the martyred Rav Aharon Bakst. Shavl also had some very famous *dayanim*. They include Rav Michoel Deitch, Rav Eliezer Luntz, Rav Seima Stern, and Rav Avrohom Nochumovsky.

Shavl was also the home of the famous Lithuanian kabbalist Rav Shlomo Elyashiv, author of the kabbalistic, *Leshem Shevo Ve'achloma*, who eventually settled in Jerusalem. His grandson is the renowned halachic authority, Rav Yosef Sholom Elyashiv.

Another citizen was Mottel the winemaker. A scholar and a *tzaddik*, his fine character led to the spinning of a web of legends of which he is the hero. His charity and his hospitality were renowned throughout Shavl and beyond.

1939-45: The Germans entered Shavl on Thursday, June 26th, 1941. As soon as the Russians fled Lithuania, many of the Jews' Lithuanian neighbors and friends turned against them and began to rob and murder many Jews. The Lithuanian fascists, who had been illegal under the Russian administration, served as a fifth column for the Germans. To the surprise of the Jews, the fascists had the support of the majority of the Lithuanian people.

Very few Lithuanian gentiles did not participate in this mass extermination of their Jewish neighbors, with whom they had lived in supposed friendship for hundreds of years. All the friendships of the past were forgotten. The Jewish share in the battle for Lithuanian independence after World War I, the aid Lithuania received from the United States thanks to Lithuanian Jews, the Jewish share in the renewal of the Lithuanian language and the development of Lithuanian culture—all were forgotten as soon as the Germans marched into the country.

A Jew who survived the Shavl ghetto told of the first pogrom days in Shavl immediately after the German occupation. "On the first day everything portable in Jewish homes was taken away," he reported. "That night the murdering began. Even that butchery was mild compared to the planned pogrom that began on the first of July. On Shabbos, June 28, 1941, at noon, Lithuanian partisans together with Gestapo soldiers surrounded the house of the city's rabbi, Rav Bakst. In the house they found the rabbi's son-in-law, Rav Isaac Rabinovitch; the *dayan*, Rav Avrohom Nochumovsky; and a number of residents of the city. All of them had been participating in a Torah discussion with the rabbi when the murderers entered the house and arrested them. A few days later, the SS murderer, Gottschalg, entered their prison cell. Noticing Mr. Todes, one of the prominent citizens, he scoffed, 'And what are you doing here, Herr Direktor?' Noticing the rabbi with his patriarchal visage and beard, he screamed, 'Who are you?'

"The rabbi replied simply, 'I am the rabbi.'

"The SS man became furious. '*Ja*, you are the *Rabbiner!*' And he laughed like a devil. '*Schweinhund*! You are one of the lazy ones, the lazy rabbis!' And he cackled like a maniac.

"Seeing *Dayan* Nochumovsky, another German shouted, 'You too? Are you also one of the rabbinical gang?' And they began to slap both him and the rabbi.

"Then they took them both out into the prison yard. They hitched the *dayan* to a wagon and beat him with a whip to make him pull the wagon faster. The abuse and torture of the rabbi, the *dayan*, and others went on for several days. Whenever they didn't move fast enough, the Germans and Lithuanians threw stones at them. On July 11th they were taken out into the prison yard and shot."

SHIRVINT

LITHUANIAN NAME: Sirvintos RUSSIAN NAME: Shervinty

LOCATION: In the Vilkomir district in eastern Lithuania, a few miles southeast of Vilkomir.

JEWISH POPULATION IN 1939: 700

JEWISH HISTORY: Shirvint was settled by Jews in the 18th century and achieved renown in Lithuanian through its *maggid*, Rav Dovid Kretinger. Shirvint had promi-

A peddler with his horse and wagon on a street in Shirvint.

nent community members who were scholars and Torah students. They would marry their daughters to yeshiva scholars and send them back to yeshiva to continue their learning.

ECONOMY: The Jews of Shirvint made their living from handcrafts, trading, and retail shops.

INSTITUTIONS: Besides its *chadorim* and guest house, Shirvint's institutions included an elementary school, a library, a credit union, and a number of other religious and cultural organizations.

The Shirvint Talmud Torah.

SPIRITUAL LEADERS: Shirvint's rabbis included Rav Mendela Shirvinter; Rav Yitzchok Grodzensky; Rav Yitzchok Eliezer Shereshevsky; Rav Yaakov Glazer; and the martyred Rav Aryeh Leib Grossbard and his son-in-law, Rav Zundel Krok.

1939-45: Berel Garber, who survived and was witness to the destruction of Shirvint, tells his story:

"The Germans, together with the Lithuanian police, entered the *beis hamidrosh* and ordered Mrs. Rishel Koniges and her son Yona, who lived in the building, not to leave. Then they set the building on fire and incinerated them. They dragged the

The Shirvint beis hamidrosh.

old rabbi, Rav Grossbard, and his son-in-law, the young rabbi, Rav Krok, over to the burning *beis hamid-rosh* and cast them both into the fire. The old rabbi managed to yell out the words "*Shema Yisroel*" before the flames consumed him.

On July 12th, the so-called Jewish Committee—which had been established by the Germans—received an order that the Jews must move into a single quarter of the city, leaving their possessions in their original dwellings. Three days later a new order was issued that the Jews must surrender their gold and silver as well as any papers of value. The order stated that if any documents or money were found during a search of the houses, 100 Jews would be killed. The town's 700 Jews, frightened to death, surrendered everything in order not to have on their consciences the murder of innocent Jews because of them.

One Friday night the Germans collected the town's important Jews and locked them into roofless barracks. A meticulous watch was placed around the barracks and no food was allowed in. The Germans demanded that these Jews "reveal their secrets." By the third day the men could no longer tolerate their suffering. They tore their shirts, made ropes of them and hanged themselves.

On August 10th, the Germans issued an order that Jews who owned horses and wagons should prepare themselves for a journey the next morning. The order was carried out precisely. The Germans caught Jews aged 14 through 30 and put them into the wagons. Many Jews resisted, among them my brother Hirsh Berel. The Germans poured gasoline over the rebellious Jews, then set them on fire and forced them to run. This was done in my mother's yard. The Germans forced her to watch as her flaming son ran. The next day they shot my mother to death.

The situation in town remained fairly static till September 18, 1941. Healthy men and occasionally women were taken to work every day in the Sesolker Yard, some six miles outside the town. They were forced to walk there and back. Every day fewer people returned from work because the Germans shot people for the most minor "infractions."

From the woods we would frequently hear wild, confused screams, "Jews, save me!" These usually came from young Jewish women whom the Germans were raping. The next morning there would be no trace of them. The well on the boundary between Yatzkovitch's estate and the priest's land was full of dead bodies, most of them Jewish women.

At 2 a.m. on September 18th, the Jewish quarter was surrounded by Lithuanian police, Gestapo officers, and *Wehrmacht* (German armed forces) soldiers. They beat the Jews brutally and forced them onto trucks: sick and old, little children and nursing babies, together with their mothers and what was left of their families. The trucks set off in the direction of Vilkomir. Two miles outside of Vilkomir is the Pivonia Spa Forest. That was where the Germans had chosen to dig a mass grave for the Jews of the Vilkomir district.

Truck after truck with its military escort arrived in the forest. The Jews were ordered to strip naked next to the long, deep pits. Group by group, they were forced into the pits. At the last moment Jews bade brother and sister farewell, hugged and kissed one another, cried and wailed. Any who resisted the orders were horribly tortured and buried alive. Those who refused to hand over their babies had them torn out of their hands. The babies were thrown up into the air and shot at.

By 10 a.m. on September 18th there was not a trace left of Shirvint Jewry. That same day the Germans hung a sign at the entrance to Shirvint: *Judenrein*.

G-d! Avenge their blood!"

SHKUD

Lithuanian name: Skuodas **Russian name:** Shkudy

Location: In the Kretinga district in northwest Lithuania, a few miles north of Salant.

Jewish population in 1939: 2,500 (total population: 5,000)

Jewish history: Shkud's Jewish settlement began as early as 1694. Shkud's two parts, Old Shkud and New Shkud, were connected by a bridge across a river. As the economic situation of New Shkud improved, there was an overflow of wealth into Old Shkud. This led to Shkud Jewry building itself a new brick synagogue. Increasing industrialization led to the unification of both Jewish communities into a single community.

Economy: Shkud was a busy town because of its closeness to Libau, a resort city in Latvia, and to Memel in Germany. Shkud's primary industries were a button factory and several shoe factories.

Institutions: In Shkud's Cold Synagogue there was a chandelier with room for 366 lights. Every Shabbos and Yom Tov 366 were kindled; 365 for the number of days in the year and one as a memorial light for the Jews who were martyred in the war between Russia and Germany.

Besides a Talmud Torah, *chadorim* and a Pirchei Shoshanim group, Shkud had a library, a credit union, and cultural organizations.

Rav Yechiel Michel Havsho.　*The martyred Rav Chayim Yaakov Teruskin.*

SPIRITUAL LEADERS: Shkud's rabbis included Rav Aharon Horovitz; Rav Tzvi Hirsh Zak; Rav Yisroel Zelig Teplitz; Rav Yechiel Michel Havsho; and the martyred Rav Chayim Yaakov Teruskin. Rav Yaakov Yoffe and Rav Ben-Tziyon Aryeh were renowned as *dayanim* in Shkud.

1939-45: The Germans entered Shkud on the night of July 22, 1941. Lithuanian partisans caught the rabbi and the chief citizens and locked them into the synagogue where they harassed and abused them. The Jewish men were rounded up and taken off to work from which they never returned. The women and children were rounded up and taken out to the river, where they were kept out in the open for more than a week. After that, they were shot to death next to their open graves.

SHKUDVIL

LITHUANIAN NAME: Skaudvile RUSSIAN NAME: Skadvile

LOCATION: In the Tavrig district near the German border in western Lithuania. Shkudvil is slightly northeast of Tavrig.

JEWISH POPULATION IN 1939: 1,017 (total population: 2,000)

JEWISH HISTORY: Shkudvil was unique in that the whole town studied Torah; it was one big yeshiva. When you walked into a shop you could engage the shopkeeper—whether Leibchik the watchmaker, or Moshe Rivkin, or Lifshitz—in a Torah discussion and be amazed by his scholarship, particularly his understanding of the Talmud. Three Talmud *shiurim* were given daily for the public. The town rabbi taught one *shiur* for the older men. Binyomin Stein and Leibchik the watchmaker taught the younger men. And another Talmud *shiur* was taught by the town's scholars in rotation.

INSTITUTIONS: Shkudvil's Tiferes Bachurim was an extraordinary chapter of that organization. Their *rebbi* was Reb Moshe Rivkin, who had a great influence on his students. There was also a Chevra Kinyan Torah, where every day they studied *Mishnayos* and *Chayey Odom*.

SPIRITUAL LEADERS: When I visited Shkudvil in 1939, I found almost every Jew of the town in the synagogue Friday night studying Torah. It is therefore no wonder that Shkudvil's rabbis were major Torah scholars. Their roster includes the *gaon* and *tzaddik* Rav Eliyohu Yissochor Yoffe and his son-in-law, Rav Avrohom Y. Perlman.

1939-45: On June 22, 1941, the Germans entered Shkudvil. Almost no one managed to escape. The details were provided me by Rav Chayim Stein, rosh yeshiva of Telz Yeshiva in Wickliffe, Ohio.

On July 16, 1941, an announcement was made that all the town's citizens, Jews as well as Lithuanians, should gather at the marketplace. The Jews, however, were immediately encircled by Lithuanian partisans who chased the women away, and herded all the men they could catch into a building a mile away from town. On July 18th, they were murdered by SS men.

Three days later, on 26 Tamuz, the Lithuanians began to search for the men who had evaded the first *Akzion*. Some of the older men caught then were Moshe Boruch Broida, Binyomin Stein, Shmuel Eliyohu Bret, and Yaakov Dorfman. They were taken to the Jewish cemetery in Ufina where they were murdered together with the rabbi of Ufina, Rav Yitzchok Yoffe.

That same day the Lithuanians, with the approval of the German commandant, issued an order that all women and children must leave their homes. Some 800 women and children from Shkudvil were taken to Bloika, a village not far from the town of Botoka, and locked into a roofless barracks. They were kept there, under horrifying conditions of hunger and filth, for seven weeks. A number of children were born without any medical assistance. On the night of September 15th, the surviving women and children were killed by the Lithuanians and buried in a mass grave.

SHVEXNA

LITHUANIAN NAME: Sveksna **RUSSIAN NAME:** Shvekshni
LOCATION: In the Tavrig district in western Lithuania, east of Kelm.
JEWISH POPULATION IN 1939: 500
JEWISH HISTORY: Shvexna's Jewish community dates back to the 17th century.
ECONOMY: The Jews made their living as merchants, shopkeepers, and craftsmen.
SPIRITUAL LEADERS: An old-time Zamut town, Shvexna's inhabitants were scholars and upright people. Yosef Ber Shtutzin and Yaakov Shenkers were examples of this. This is why their rabbis had to be men of high caliber. On the other hand, because it was a small town with limited means, its rabbis usually moved on to larger towns or to cities. The roster of Shvexna's rabbis includes Rav Menachem Mendel Hurvitz; Rav

Yosef Yoffe; Rav Yissochor Ber Gavransky; Rav Moshe Yitzchok Segal; Rav Eliyohu Hacohen; Rav Chayim Tzvi Broida; Rav Shmuel A. Feivelson; Rav Ben-Tziyon Velvel Krenitz; Rav Yisroel Tanchum Fortman; and the martyred Rav Sholom Yitzchok Levitan.

Rav Ben-Tziyon Velvel Krenitz was a great Torah scholar and a *tzaddik*. During his tenure as Shvexna's rabbi, he maintained a yeshiva in town for about 35 students, some of whom came from nearby towns and villages. Rav Ben-Tziyon Velvel treated every *bachur* like his own son. If a boy needed money, he would say to him, "Go to the box on my bureau and take as much as you need." His son-in-law, the martyred Rav Yisroel Tanchum Fortman, succeeded him as Shvexna's rabbi, and then moved on to become Zhezhmir's rabbi. The last rabbi of Shvexna was Rav Sholom Yitzchok Levitan, author of the homiletical works *Yalkut HaDerush* and *Divrey Sholom*. Rav Levitan had previously served as rabbi in Oslo, Norway.

Rav Yosef Yozel Hurvitz, the founder of the Novardok (Novogrudek) yeshiva network and its system of *mussar*, lived in Shvexna for many years, and had been one of its prominent merchants. An encounter with Rav Yisroel Lipkin (Salanter) led him to rethink the purpose of his life and define new goals.

1939-45: The Germans occupied Shvexna on June 23, 1941. Robbery, rape, and murder followed immediately. The able-bodied people, including the rabbi, were taken away to Heidekrug on the border between Lithuania and Germany, where the Germans had set up a labor camp. Jews were brought to that camp from the towns of Varzhan, Neishtot-Tavrig, and Loikeva. There were very few survivors of that camp. The Jews who remained in Shvexna were annihilated.

TAVRIG

LITHUANIAN NAME: Taurage **RUSSIAN NAME:** Taurogen
LOCATION: A district capital in western Lithuania, about 17 miles from Brickenkop near Tilsit, Germany. Tavrig is slightly southwest of Shkudvil.
JEWISH POPULATION IN 1939: 3,000 (total population: 18,000)
JEWISH HISTORY: As the nearest city to the border coming from either Tilsit or Memel, Tavrig had the aura of a German city. Therefore its residents were both Torah scholars and secular scholars like Hirsh Motta Berman, who died in Siberia, where the Russians had exiled him.

Tavrig was a very charitable city. When I visited at the end of 1939 to appeal for help for Polish Jews who were suffering under the Germans, the response was extremely generous. Later help was sent to the ghetto of Lublin as well. I recall walking with Rav Levi Shpitz after my appeal, when a woman stopped us to request that we should make sure to collect her contribution as well. This is how she put it, "*Rebbi*, I have five pillows and I want to contribute three of them for suffering Jews." Rav Shpitz replied calmingly, "We will come to you as well."

"No, no!" the woman replied. "*Rebbi*, I want to come to your house to deliver the pillows." When the woman had walked away, Rav Shpitz said to me, "Do you know who this woman is? She collects for herself from house to house."

In Baltimore, Maryland, Mr. Shmuel Ladan, Secretary of the Litvisha Farband and a native of Tavrig, directed the sending of packages to concentration camp survivors and new arrivals in Israel. He and his wife turned their home into a shipping bureau where all tasks were performed by the Ladans with the assistance of Mrs. Ethel Sokolsky. Baltimore also has a Tavrig synagogue.

ECONOMY: Tavrig's Jews made a living by trading with Germany. The lumber factories were owned by Beikovitz, Gitkin, and Hirsh Cohen. Lithuania was rich in forests, and the wood was exported to Germany. Tavrig also had brick and other factories where Jews made a living.

INSTITUTIONS: Tavrig's Jewish institutions included a free loan fund, a guest house, a Talmud Torah, and a very fine chapter of Tiferes Bachurim where some 50 to 60 young men would come after work to study Torah. The Tiferes Bachurim *rebbi* was Rav Kopshtein. There were also a Jewish credit union and a Hebrew high school.

SPIRITUAL LEADERS: Tavrig was renowned for its world-class rabbis who included Rav Mendel Ziv; Rav Aharon Burstein, who later became rosh yeshiva in Yeshivas Merkaz HaRav in Jerusalem; Rav Yitzchok Isaac Friedman, later rabbi in Nachlas Yitzchok near Tel Aviv; and Tavrig's last rabbi, the martyred Rav Levi Shpitz.

Reb Shmuel Yaakov Mann was a paradigm of the Jewish nation—A Torah scholar, a man of fine character, he was always ready to help anyone. When he helped someone, you had to peer very closely to determine who was being helped and who was doing the helping, for he always made it seem as if the recipient were doing him a favor. By looking at Reb Shmuel Yaakov Mann, one had no way of knowing that he was a major activist, for he performed his activities in an absolutely unassuming manner. Nevertheless every community matter went through his hands. This humble man was murdered along with his brethren in Tavrig.

Aryeh Leib Beikovitz provided the money for the communal free loan fund. He also paid for publishing the volumes of Rav Yitzchok I. Friedman's book on commentaries of the Mishnah, *Hegyoney Yitzchok*. Wherever a large contribution was needed, Beikovitz was asked, and he granted it graciously and lovingly.

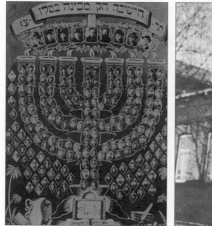

The preparatory yeshiva of Telz, 1937.

The Telz Yeshiva building.

Telz Yeshiva staff and students, 1932.

Students learning in the Telz Yeshiva.

Tzvi Hirsh Gitkin, one of Tavrig's foremost citizens and the scion of a great rabbinical family, loved Torah and Torah scholars, and demonstrated that love with much financial support. Other well-known activists were Shachna Mast, Alter Gudel, Zalman Passal, Hirshel Shlomov, and Zalman Dubchansky.

1939-45: At 4 a.m. on June 22, 1941, Tavrig's Jews jumped out of their beds in surprise when the Germans bombed the city as the Russians withdrew. Families and individuals fled with the Russian army or into nearby villages. Tavrig was immediately occupied, and the Jews came under the oppression of the Germans and the Lithuanians.

One of the Germans' first victims was the town rabbi, Rav Levi Shpitz. He was asked to inform on the Jewish Communists. When he told them that he didn't know any, they beat him so brutally that his face was completely destroyed. Then they ordered him to run—shooting him in the leg when he did. When he ran into a house and collapsed, the Germans set the house afire and cremated the rabbi.

The young people were immediately rounded up for labor, from which many never returned. A group of 300 young people was told that they were being taken for labor in Heidekrug, a city on the border between Lithuania and Germany. They selected a group of 60 young girls and led them away. Some of their mothers were shot on the spot when they refused to be separated from their children; they realized that they were being taken to brothels.

They herded the Jews into Chveidan Street, and separated the men from the women and children. They killed the men first. A few weeks later, the women and the children were killed.

TELZ

LITHUANIAN NAME: Telsiai **RUSSIAN NAME:** Telschi

LOCATION: A district capital in northwest Lithuania, a few miles northeast of Plungyan.

JEWISH POPULATION IN 1939: 2,800 (total population: 15,000)

JEWISH POPULATION IN 1945: 150

JEWISH HISTORY: Jews began to settle in Telz in the 17th century.

INSTITUTIONS: Telz's crown was its yeshiva, founded in 1875 by three rabbis—Rav Meir Atlas, later rabbi of Shavl; Rav Tzvi Yaakov Oppenheim, later rabbi of Kelm; and Rav Shlomo Z. Abel. The Telz Yeshiva distinguished itself by its method of study, by its division of students into grades by level, and by the individualized attention given each student.

Renowned throughout the Jewish world for its yeshiva, which drew students from everywhere, the city of Telz came to be considered a Torah

Rav Shimon Shkop.

Rav Chayim Rabinovitz.

Rav Avrohom Yitzchok Bloch.

Rav Zalman Bloch.

Rav Eliezer Gordon.

Rav Yosef Reizin.

citadel. The yeshiva's most famous teachers were Rav Meir Atlas, Rav Shimon Shkop, and Rav Chayim Rabinovitz. The heads of the yeshiva who were martyred by the Germans were Rav Avrohom Yitzchok Bloch, Rav Azriel Rabinovitz, Rav Zalman Bloch, and Rav Moshe Olshvang.

Telz had a *kollel* of major Torah scholars who continued their Torah studies after marriage. It also had a preparatory yeshiva that was attended by 150 young teenagers under the principalship of Rav Avner Oklansky and Rav Efrayim P. Helfant. It also had a Yavneh high school for girls, and a teachers seminary which produced excellent religious teachers. *Hane'emon,* an Orthodox Hebrew-language weekly, was published in Telz.

The town also had a hospital, a chapter of the OZA, a credit union, and a number of other cultural and religious groups.

View of Telz.

SPIRITUAL LEADERS: Telz's rabbis included Rav Yehuda Leib Ziv; Rav Moshe Telzer, a kabbalist who was renowned as one of the pious men of Zamut; Rav Avrohom Shapiro; Rav Avrohom Margoliyos; Rav Zev Volf, father of Rav Yisroel Salanter; Rav Yosef Reizin; Rav Yehoshua Heller.

Rav Eliezer Gordon in 1881 took responsibility for Telz's yeshiva and was tireless in developing it; Rav Yosef Leib Bloch, Rav Gordon's son-in-law, helped develop the yeshiva even further. The martyred Rav Avrohom Yitzchock Bloch, Rav Yosef Bloch's son, succeeded his father in 1929 and was Rosh Yeshiva of Telz and Rav until its destruction.

Telz was also home to such Torah scholars and men of importance as Reb Leib Gertzovitz, Reb Chayim Helfant, and Reb Avrohom Krenitz.

1939-45: The annihilation of Jewish Telz is one of the most gruesome chapters in Holocaust history. Because Telz was so important as a Torah center—a center for wisdom and perception, for knowledge and analysis—it was shamefully debased by the Germans. However great the *kedushah* (sanctity), so much greater must the *tumah* (defilement) be to overpower it.

At the beginning of 1940, the yeshiva was closed by the occupying Russians and its students were forced to disband. They regrouped in a number of nearby towns and continued their studies in secret. When German troops entered Telz anarchy broke out and Lithuanian fascists began robbing and murdering their Jewish neighbors.

Late one Friday afternoon, Lithuanians led by Gestapo officers drove the Jews out of their homes. The rabbi, the heads of the yeshiva, the old and the young, were herded down to the lake where they thought their end had come. The Germans did not make dying simple. The commandant informed the rabbi that the women and the little children could return home, and that the men would be taken to a labor camp. The families were separated with great cruelty, and the men were dragged off into the forest outside the city.

But before the miserable women and children could settle into their new situation, they were once more driven out of their homes into the forest, where they saw their men under a special guard. Their anguish grew greater yet as they helplessly watched their husbands, fathers, and sons being abused for the next eight days.

Many people died during those days; some were murdered. The survivors were released. On 19 Tamuz 5701, July 14, 1941, the Germans dragged out several hundred men, supposedly for labor, and killed every one.

The next day they collected several hundred more men—among them the rabbi, some of the roshei yeshiva, and yeshiva students—and took them to a place where graves had already been dug. The night before these Jews were exterminated, a vicious, sadistic and bloody orgy took place: Jews were forced to crawl on all fours and lick the ground; they were forced to dance for hours until many collapsed; children were forced to beat their parents, and adults were forced to beat each other until blood flowed. When they had been abused unto exhaustion, they were forced to undress and march into their graves.

In an impressive speech made by Yitzchok Bloch (not related to the Rav) to the Jewish victims of Telz before he was shot to death, he expressed the pathos and anguish of a people on the brink of annihilation, and demanded that it be justly avenged.

What took place at the mass annihilation is too gruesome to describe. The living and the half-alive were driven into their graves and forced to

LITHUANIAN TOWNS ◆ 261

bury one another alive. Witnesses testified that all the following night, they heard cries of *"Shema Yisroel!"* rising from the mass graves.

Dr. Mikulskas, the military doctor in Telz—who over the years had close contact with the Jewish community since he spoke Yiddish well, had friends who were Jews, and his beard even made him look like a Jew—this perfidious hooligan organized and carried out the annihilation of Telz Jewry.

In the winter of 1941, 500 Telz women cooped up in a camp attempted to escape. They were hunted down and shot to death. Mrs. Sarah Friedman, who survived and fled to the ghetto of Shavl and later to the Kovno ghetto, provided me with these facts.

The daughter of Rav Avrohom Yitzchok Bloch, Rebbitzin Chaya Ausband of Cleveland, Ohio, was just 17 years old when the Nazis entered Telz and shattered its Torah world. She recounted the events that violently disrupted her life:

"On Friday afternoon, June 27, 1941, the Germans commanded all the Jews of Telz to gather in the city marketplace. They pulled them out of their houses by force, threatening to shoot anyone who resisted. It was nearly impossible for the Jews to hide since their Lithuanian neighbors showed the Germans which homes they lived in. In the marketplace the Jews were ordered to line up in columns of six. All the while the Germans taunted them and ran after them with their guns aimed. Shamelessly, the Germans took pictures of their merciless actions.

Rav Avrohom Yitzchok Bloch didn't pay any attention to the rifles pointed directly at him despite the Germans' repeated orders that every Jew stand still and not make a sound. Instead he turned towards the crowd of Jews and spoke words of encouragement and strength. The crowd listened to every word the Rav was saying. When the Germans saw this, their attitude towards him changed. They didn't try to restrain the Rav, but allowed him to speak uninterruptedly. They even stopped taunting the Jews.

As it came close to sundown, with Shabbos approaching fast, the Germans took the Jews to the shore of the lake in Telz. They asked for a volunteer from the crowd to translate their commands from German to Yiddish for everyone else. The Rav immediately came forward and volunteered. The Germans spoke to the Jews, accusing them of siding with the Russians and giving them secret signals. The Rav denied these false accusations again and again. Then the Germans warned everyone that they would soon hear shooting, but they shouldn't worry about it—it was just an exercise.

Rav Avrohom Yitzchok called on his brother Rav Zalman and a prestigious young kollel man, known as the Tukemer *iluy* (the *iluy* from Tukem), to discuss what to do about the dangerous situation. After their short meeting, Rav Avrohom Yitzchok turned to the people and advised them that at such a dangerous time their only hope lay in doing *teshuvah*. He pleaded with everyone to take upon themselves three important *mitzvos*: *kashrus*, Shabbos, and *taharas hamishpochah* (basic marital laws). Every Jew agreed without a second's hesitation. This moment was like Kabolos HaTorah, when all Jews accepted the Torah and its laws in the Sinai Desert centuries before. At that instant all the Jews of Telz, though from different congregations and schools, were united.

The Germans watched as all the Jews *davened* the Shabbos prayers together. They didn't shoot or proceed with their exercise as planned. Instead they allowed the women to return to their homes. The Rav was allowed to return with his family, but he refused. He would not leave his congregation at such an uncertain time.

The women returned to their homes and found them completely ransacked. Everything had either been taken away by Lithuanian looters or destroyed beyond use. They crowded into the few homes still intact. The Rav's large home provided shelter for so many people that most had to sleep on the floor. Miriam Oklansky, the oldest person there and a relative of the Rav, urged everyone to make *kiddush* despite the oppressive gloom. It was, after all, Shabbos and there were *mitzvos* to do. The women made *kiddush* over *challah* since they had no usable wine.

The Rav's wife disguised herself as a peasant and removed the *sefer* Torah and some *seforim* from the synagogue. She put them together with her personal possessions and later brought them to the men.

Meanwhile the men were taken to the Rein farm, a large farm that belonged to a wealthy Lithuanian singer. There they were crowded into barracks-like barns and an unfinished, abandoned house. The next morning the women were taken to the Rein farm where they joined their husbands and sons. Many families were crowded together and each person had just enough room to lie down.

The Lithuanians were put in charge of the Jews on the farm. They forced them to clean the corpses of murdered Russian prisoners and prepare them for burial. These bodies were mutilated and decomposed beyond recognition since the Lithuanians had tortured them and then left them to rot. Every morning groups of men were called to this filthy, back-breaking labor and returned late at night, exhausted.

During this time, a young man named Yitzchok Bloch was part of an organized committee that mediated between the Jews and Lithuanians. The committee was able to secure some food for the Jews—every day they received only dry, hard bread and soup. *Seforim* and *siddurim* were also brought to the Jews through various middlemen.

One morning the Rav was called for labor. Yitzchok Bloch volunteered to go in his place. He didn't feel it befitted the Rav of Telz to be forced to do such work. When the Lithuanians saw this exchange, they took neither man.

For two weeks the Lithuanians continued to order the Jewish men to clean the Russian corpses. At one point they separated a large group of young men and women and brought them to a second farm, the Dusaic farm. There they forced them to make burning material for ovens out of squares of wet earth.

On July 14th a Lithuanian officer announced to everyone on the Rein farm that they had to relinquish all their gold and silver jewelry. Many Jews tried to defy the Lithuanians by breaking their gold watches into small pieces. They didn't want to just hand their valuables over to such an evil enemy. Those who refused or who tarried in giving up their jewelry were taken to a field in the center of the farm and were tortured. The Lithuanians forced them to jump, run, and dance like animals. Many fell as they became tired, but they were not allowed to stop or rest. Anyone who could not jump as fast or as high as the Lithuanians wanted was shot and killed. The father-in-law of Rav Meir Bloch, the Rav's younger brother, was too old to keep up with the officer's orders. Rav Avrohom Yitzchok and Rav Zalman Bloch carried him under his arms and jumped for him.

After they had enough of this brutal activity, the Lithuanians told the men to go inside and say goodbye to their wives and children because they were to be killed the next day. Several young men were ordered to stay awake and dig huge pits for their graves during the night.

The Rav returned to his family. He was too exhausted to learn Torah, so he called one of his daughters to read out loud from a *sefer* of *Rambam* about the *halachos* of *kiddush HaShem*. She read to him for an hour. Instead of bemoaning his fate, the Tukemer *iluy* raised his hands towards the sky and cried out to G-d, *"Du bizt gerecht, Riboinoi Shel Olam! Deine maasim zeinen gerecht!"* ("You are right, Master of the World! Your actions are right!") [At a time of terrible suffering, when it would be hard to understand G-d's judgment, the *iluy* didn't question His justice.]

The next morning, July 15th, a Lithuanian soldier called out, "Rabbis and half-rabbis, come out now!" The Rav's wife and daughters thought the men were merely being called to labor as usual and began preparing food for them. He told them that food was not needed right now, and instead asked for water to wash his hands. There is no way to know how many men kept from their families this terrible secret. Even at this critical moment, they tried to protect their loved ones....

After leading the men a few thousand feet to their freshly dug graves, the Lithuanians shot at them randomly. Suddenly it began to rain, forcing the soldiers to stop and run for shelter. The few Jews that were still alive were sent back to the barracks, where they described to the families of those who had been murdered the sad details of their loved ones' deaths. One of the Rav's students told the Bloch family that the Rav had been reciting Shema as he was shot. The same student told Rav Zalman's family that he had died with a peaceful smile on his face. People told this student to run away and save himself, but the student replied, "No! My father and my rebbe are already buried. I have no reason left to live."

The next day the women were taken to a nearby town called Geruliai. Among them were ten men who had saved themselves by masquerading as women. They were kept in barracks there with thousands of other Jews from the surrounding area until Shabbos, August 30th, when they were taken out and shot. Only 500 people survived from those barracks. They were returned to Telz where they were placed into a ghetto near the lake. Among these 500 Jews were the wife of Rav Avrohom Yitzchok, his two daughters, and a four year old son disguised as a girl. A total of 17 family members of the Rav returned to Telz.

The Rav's wife arranged for six young girls—two of her daughters, two nieces, and two other girls—to be smuggled into the Shavl ghetto in the wagon of a Lithuanian man. She sent two wagons, three girls on each, before she herself was caught and later killed by the Germans."

In this tragic manner did Jewish life in Telz come to its end.

The mass grave of Telz's Jews in the Girula Forest.

UTYAN

LITHUANIAN NAME: Utena **RUSSIAN NAME:** Utsjany

LOCATION: A provincial capital in eastern Lithuania, a few miles east of Aniksht.

JEWISH POPULATION IN 1939: about 5,000 (total population: 15,000)

JEWISH HISTORY: Utyan was one of Lithuania's first Jewish settlements. Its cemetery contained tombstones that date back to the 16th century.

ECONOMY: The Jews in Utyan traded flax, skins, and boar bristles.

INSTITUTIONS: Utyan had a number of Jewish institutions. Its communal affairs were run by an organization called Adas Yisroel. Among its institutions were an elementary school, a credit union, a Linas Hatzedek, and a Tiferes Bachurim.

SPIRITUAL LEADERS: Utyan's great and righteous sage, Rav Avrohom Tzvi Hirsh Eisenstadt (1813-1865), achieved renown in the world of Torah scholarship with his classic work *Pischei Teshuvah* on the *Shulchon Oruch* (the authoritative 16th century halachic encyclopedia). Hundreds of tales

A view of Utyan.

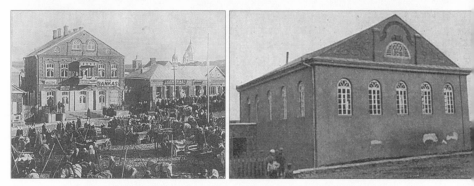

At the market in Utyan.

Utyan's old synagogue.

A kloiz in Utyan.

are told about his charity, piety and insights. One concerns a woman who entered the Cold Synagogue (that was the name by which the townspeople called the old synagogue) where he was in the habit of studying Torah until midday. She came in wailing, "*Rebbi*, tell me, where is my husband? He's already been gone over a year. I've searched everywhere for him and haven't found him!"

The rabbi replied, "I don't know." But the woman kept wailing and demanding that the rabbi tell her where to find her husband. The rabbi's statements that he did not know were to no avail; the woman would not leave. The rabbi's attendant's threats were also to no avail. The woman continued to disrupt the rabbi's studies. Finally, Rav Eisenstadt raised his bushy eyebrows and said to the woman, "Don't cry, Jewish lady. Travel to Kovno, and you'll find him there."

She traveled to Kovno and found her husband, and brought him back to town.

When the story spread everyone in Utyan grew excited—the rabbi had performed a miracle! That Shabbos morning, before the Torah reading, the rabbi went up onto the platform and asked for silence. Everyone in the synagogue was surprised, for the rabbi delivered only two sermons a year—on Shabbos HaGodol (the Shabbos before Pesach) and on Shabbos Shuva (the Shabbos before Yom Kippur). He said, "Do not be surprised to hear me speaking now. Since a rumor has spread through the town that I am a miracle worker, I wish to inform you that I am nothing of the kind. Since the woman kept on disturbing my studies, and I knew that in Kovno the Russian czar was having fortresses built around the city for which laborers are needed, I simply guessed that her husband had probably gone there."

Rav Eisenstadt's dedication to Torah study is clear from the following story: The Jews of Ponevezh asked him to be their rabbi and offered him a salary of 25 rubles a week. He turned down the offer and remained with Utyan's salary of three rubles per week because the big city's demands would deprive him of time for Torah study.

Utyan was privileged to have Rav Eisenstadt's son,

Rav Avrohom Tzvi Eisenstadt.

The grave of Rav Binyomin Eisenstadt, Utyan's rabbi from 1868 to 1920.

Rav Binyomin, succeed his father in 1868 and serve as rabbi until his death in 1920. Rav Binyomin was in turn succeeded by his son, Rav Avrohom Tzvi, who served until his death in 1938. The last rabbi of Utyan was Rav Nachman Hirshovitz. Some of Utyan's early rabbis were Rav Shmuel ben Chayim; Rav Dov Ber Yoffe, father of Rav Mordechai Gimpel Yoffe; and Rav Yaakov Matz.

1939-45: Tzodok Bleiman, who miraculously survived the Kovno Ghetto, had previously witnessed and survived the extermination of Utyan Jewry. He relates how the Jews of Utyan were killed. Among them were his father, Rav Tzvi Bleiman, the rabbi of Aran, who was visiting his daughter in Utyan, and Rav Nachman Hirshovitz, Utyan's rabbi. Tzodok Bleiman's report:

"When the war broke out on June 22, 1941, I was in Kovno. On June 23 I fled Kovno, which the Russians had left and where the Lithuanians had begun to act like owners. At 10 a.m. on June 26, I arrived outside Utyan, but could not enter the city because it was under bombardment from the Germans. After waiting several hours, I entered town. There were no Jewish losses then except for several damaged houses. At 2 p.m. the Germans entered. And from then on, Jewish troubles began. Immediately Jews were impressed into service, primarily to seek mines in houses forsaken by the Russians. A number of Jews were killed while doing this.

On the morning of the 27th, the Jews were driven out to work. The work was not necessarily labor; it was organized solely for abusing the Jews. Driving Jews to work was constant during the entire period, and was intensified as part of the annihilation process.

Every day was worse than the previous one. On every Jewish home the word "Jews" was painted. That opened the way for every Lithuanian and German hooligan to rob and murder us. Every German army unit, particularly the SS unit and SA unit, on its way to the battlefront, saw it as a "sacred" duty to "make a reckoning" with the Jews.

In a single tragic evening, Lithuanians and Germans destroyed every house of prayer and study, and tore and burned the Torah scrolls. Then they came to my father, led him to the synagogue, and ordered him to sing and dance and help shred the *sifrei* Torah. It goes without saying that he did not do so. They cut off his beard and tortured him, and then they shot him. We later found him in a river of blood, barely alive. Thanks to my brother-in-law, Dr. Ephraim Yudelovitz, the best doctor in the region, Father was operated on and would still be alive. But they executed him later along with everyone else. Who knows how they tortured him again before killing him?

In a situation fraught with murder, hunger, and fear, matters grew worse till the 14th of July, by which time the jailhouse was full of Jews. The ruins of the houses of study and prayer were turned into jails for Jews, Communists, and Russians, who were kept in filth and hunger, and tortured. At 6 a.m. on July 14, 1941, notices were pasted up that read:

'All Jews in Utyan must leave for the forest in the direction of Maliat, by 12:00. You may take along as many of your possessions as you wish, but you may not damage any property. Whoever is discovered in the city after 12:00, will be shot on the spot.'

(signed) *Dr. Stefanovitch*, Mayor of Utyan and
Commandant *Pulkinikas*.

I reread that notice several times. I found it incredible that they would drive us out so quickly. A few hours after the notices were posted, they were beating Jews and driving them from their homes. People ran as quickly as they could into the forest, not imagining that it was their last journey. Two thousand Jews left the city. The Lithuanian press immediately reported joyfully that Utyan was the first city to become *Judenrein*.

Before setting out for the forest, all Jews were searched and their gold, silver, money, and other valuables were taken away. Then they were allowed into the forest. We were guarded by Lithuanians to make sure we didn't escape. We were told that we would remain in the forest for three more days and afterwards be sent back into town where a ghetto would be established for us on Azira street.

For two whole weeks we lay under the open skies. It rained. It was also rather cold, and kept getting colder. Many people fell ill, but there were no doctors with us to treat them, because the Jewish doctors had been arrested several weeks after the Germans marched in and had then been shot.

For food they brought us only bread. We were completely cut off from the outside world. The guards treated us worse and worse, with increasing callousness. Daily, they drove people to labor, and at night they would shoot into the air, frightening everyone and not letting us sleep. Their intent was to weaken us physically and to demoralize us spiritually as quickly as possible.

It is noteworthy that the behavior of the Jews to one another was exemplary. They shared their morsels of bread. In one labor area, milk was given out to the laborers at the end of their day. None of them ever drank the milk himself. They brought it back and divided it among the children and the sick. There was no fighting or arguing among the Jews, nor any of the other negative developments that take place under abnormal circumstances.

That remained the situation until the first of August; we were still trying to sleep under the open skies. During the day, Lithuanian policemen came and took the names of the men and women aged 17 to 55. While that registration was taking place, I was led away with 10 other men into the city to work. We worked till night. During the evening we were led past a group of 500 Jews from the forest, among them the former Jewish vice-mayor of Utyan, Mr. Jiret, and his two sons; Rav Nachman Hirshovitz; the *shochet* Yudel Shafstein, and other distinguished citizens. After work we were taken back into the forest.

At 3 p.m. the next day, we Jews in the forest heard shooting. We fantasized that the Russians might be approaching, but none of us imagined that the Jews who had been led away yesterday were being shot today. Another week passed, and although we heard nothing from those Jews, we still assumed they were alive.

It rained very hard the night of August 6th. Besides, the guards kept firing shots all night in order to shatter our nerves. Early in the morning, the able-bodied men were chased off to work. Weary, wet, and lacking sleep, we went to work unaware that it was our last time. My mother handed me a coat and said, "Perhaps your group will be out long." I replied that I would surely be returning soon. My mother's heart had sensed that it was the last time; I never returned to the forest.

Instead of herding us off to work, we were led off to the Utyan jail, where they took our papers away as well as the belts from our trousers. We were left waiting in the jail yard. At two o'clock a Gestapo officer came and ordered us to stand in rows of four—100 rows of four. The warden of the jail, a Lithuanian, told us to remove our coats since we would be working.

We were then led out of the jail yard. We were lined up behind a group of Jewish women. We were heavily guarded by armed Lithuanians, among them high-school and university students. As we moved along, they beat us harshly in order to march us faster and faster. The women who could not keep the pace were shot on the spot. After having run several miles, the men were ordered to lie face down on the earth, and the women were ordered to go on ahead. We heard screams and the shooting of machine guns. About 15 minutes later, the men were ordered forward and I witnessed the following scene: Several pits had been dug. Next to one of the pits stood a German with a machine gun. Not far from the pit stood a Lithuanian with a mask over his face and a whip in his hand; he whipped every person who passed to drive him faster toward the pit. Then the German would do the "terminating."

At the side, standing by a light car, were the local Lithuanian leaders: the mayor, the doctor, the warden, and several Germans who had come to see the bloody spectacle.

I realized that within seconds I, too, might be in my death throes along with the other Jews. I immediately decided that if I was going to die, one of "them" would go with me.

My friend, Kalman Katz, who was standing next to me, also began to run toward the German. He was immediately shot and fell, screaming, "I'm dying!" I got a bullet in the leg and fainted from the pain, and rolled down into swampy ground. The pits had been dug on a hill above a swamp. I gained consciousness as I was rolling downhill. I crawled through the tall grass till I fell into a deep puddle surrounded by tall grass. I lay there, deathly afraid lest they find me and shoot again. It was a Divine miracle that they never noticed me. That night it poured. I crept out, wounded and chilled from the cold water, and began to wander through the darkness of the night.

On that day, August 7, 1941, most of the Jews were murdered. To judge by the shooting I heard while lying in my puddle, many groups of Jews were brought to the pits and shot. The rest of the women and the children were murdered two weeks later."

This is how Tzodok Bleiman described the extermination of Utyan's Jews. I present it without comment. What can anyone add to his words? May mentioning them be a blessing.

VEKSHNE

LITHUANIAN NAME: Vieksniai RUSSIAN NAME: Wekschni
LOCATION: In northeast Lithuania, between Mazheik and Akmian.
JEWISH POPULATION IN 1939: 500, making it one of Lithuania's smaller Jewish settlements.
JEWISH HISTORY: The Jewish cemetery has gravestones dating back 300 years.
ECONOMY: Many of Vekshne's men were Torah scholars who earned their living as shopkeepers, traders, lumber merchants, and craftsmen.
INSTITUTIONS: Vekshne's yeshiva was headed by Rav Yekusiel Zalman Levin, assisted by Rav Boruch Levinger and Rav Moshel Chorif. The town *maggid* was Rav Chayim Yosef Yoffe.
SPIRITUAL LEADERS: Vekshne's roster of rabbis includes Rav Avrohom Yoffe, Rav Moshe Shapiro, Rav Abba Yaakov Boruchov, Rav Yekusiel Z. Levin, and Rav Shlomo Feinzilber, later rabbi of Keidan where he was martyred in 1941. Its last rabbi was the martyred Rav Kalman Maggid. Born in 1872 in Vorne, he had previously served as rabbi of the Crimean town of Barmiansk, and then of Kroz. He was an active member of the Mizrachi movement in Lithuania.
1939-45: On July 23, 1941, the Germans occupied Vekshne. They ordered the Jews out of the three towns of Mazheik, Vekshne, and Akmian and to Tirkshli, a small town near Mazheik. From there they were led into the nearby forest, where they were separated into three groups: men, women, children, and the communal leaders, intelligentsia, and rabbis.

The three rabbis of the towns, sensing that they were being ordered off to their deaths, each donned his *tallis* and *tefillin*. Rav Kalman Maggid, the old rabbi of Vekshne, addressed the crowd, urging them not to be intimidated. He told them not to be sad, not to feel despondent. "It is forbidden to show the Germans the least sign of sadness. We must sanctify G-d. That is the loftiest and holiest goal of a Jew. We must die as Jews, as holy people, as the members of G-d's people."

The rabbi cried out, "*Shema Yisroel, Hashem Elokenu!*" and the entire crowd of Jews responded, "*Hashem Echod!*"

The guns spit forth their bullets and the souls of those holy Jews departed their bodies.

VILKOMIR

LITHUANIAN NAME: Ukmerge RUSSIAN NAME: Vilkomir
LOCATION: In east central Lithuania, a few miles east of Keidan.
JEWISH POPULATION IN 1939: 8,000 (total population: 15,000)

HISTORY: Vilkomir was a Lithuanian district capital on the Sventoli River dating back to the early Russian czars, serving many towns near and far. If someone needed a government office, to appear in court, or to obtain a passport, he had to travel to the district capital.

JEWISH HISTORY: Vilkomir's Jewish community was one of Lithuania's oldest, dating back to the late 16th century.

ECONOMY: Most of Vilkomir's Jews made a living from the town's many leather factories; Zelig Krok owned one of the largest of them. Chayim Frankel of Shavl, who owned the largest leather factory in Lithuania, was originally from Vilkomir.

INSTITUTIONS: Vilkomir maintained a yeshiva of about 200 young students from Vilkomir itself and from the surrounding district towns. Its roshei yeshiva, Vilkomir natives, were the martyred Rav Moshe Gratz, Rav Alter Broida, and Rav Gordon. The yeshiva's alumni included many rabbis and *shochetim*.

One section of Vilkomir lay across the river, and had its own rabbi and two *batei midrosh*. Its last rabbi was the martyred Rav Chayim Yaakov Resnik.

Vilkomir also maintained a hospital, and two high schools, besides the usual communal institutions.

SPIRITUAL LEADERS: Vilkomir's rabbinical roster includes some of Jewry's greatest Torah geniuses: Rav Refoel HaCohen, author of the halachic insights and responsa *Toras Yekusiel* and later rabbi of Hamburg; Rav Yehuda Leib Zalkind, a frequenter of the *Gaon* of Vilna; Rav Binyomin Rabinovitz, author of *Mishnas Rav,* answers to questions on the Mishnah; the *gaon* Rav Shoulka; Rav Aryeh Leib Rubin, who was known as Rav Leibela Vilkomirer; and the martyred Rav Yosef Zusmanovitz, Vilkomir's last rabbi and the author of *Chelko Shel Yosef* and other works.

Rav Aryeh Leib Rubin was a genius in both Torah scholarship and humility. He was at home with every type of Jew, especially with those who prayed next to the stove or behind the *bimah* (synagogue podium). When I sought him out to ordain me, I found him studying next to the synagogue stove.

An expert in the halachic codes, his opinion was consulted on every difficult question. In fact, Vilkomir itself had a reputation as a town that possessed a tradition of insightful decision-making in finding necessary halachic leniencies, as in the case where Rav Aryeh Leib Ginzberg, the author of the frequently quoted responsa *Shaagas Aryeh*, issued such a ruling during a visit to Vilkomir.

Rav Aryeh Leib Rubin was also a gifted speaker whose sermons inspired the people, whom he spoke to with the plainness of genuine humility. It wouldn't be unusual to find him in the street on his way home from synagogue, his *tallis* bag under his arm, advising a Jew to buy a wagonload of wood because the price is right or negotiating the price of a load of hay for his own animals. His sons-in-law were Rav Yosef Kahaneman, the rabbi of Ponevezh; the martyred Rav Osher K. Baron, rosh yeshiva in Ponevezh; and the martyred Rav Shraga F. Hurvitz, rosh yeshiva in Slobodka. Rav Aryeh Leib's wife was martyred in Ponevezh together with her daughters, Rebetzins Kahaneman and Baron, and her grandchildren.

Vilkomir's eminent residents included Reb Aharon Kaufman (Reb Ahrela Shloimas), a great Torah scholar who was the *de facto* leader of the Jewish community; Reb Boruch Nissons, one of the city's leading scholars; Reb Shlomo Kaufman, Reb Ahrela's son; and Reb Moshe Cohen, a Torah scholar who had studied in Volozhin. Even Vilkomir's secular scholars knew how to study Torah. These included Dr. Katzenellenbogen, the local physician, and Gerstein the pharmacist.

1939-45: On June 26, 1941, Vilkomir was occupied by the Germans. The Jews were immediately victimized and abused. Jewish refugees from other towns and cities who sought refuge in Vilkomir suffered most. Jews were taken to work, many of whom never returned. Young women were raped and murdered near the river.

The Jews lived in dread for two weeks. Then the Germans arrested Rav Zusmanovitz, Dr. Karlinsky, and the Jewish lawyers, high-school teachers, and prominent citizens. The Germans abused them in the most gruesome ways. For example, they would insert a rubber hose into a victim's mouth and fill the person with water until he burst. They then selected several hundred communal leaders including Rav Zusmanovitz, Dr. Karlinsky, Rabbis Gratz, A. Broida, Reznik, V. Broida, the *shochet* Reb Yaakov Zalman Gordon, and the other *shochetim*. They herded them into a barn in the Pivonya Forest, a spa two miles outside Vilkomir, and set it afire, incinerating everyone inside.

The city's Jews were forced to move into the section of the city that lay across the river, into which they were compressed like herring in a barrel. Rebetzin Leah Zusmanovitz recounted a dream in which her late, martyred husband appeared and instructed her that the Jews should make a Yom Kippur-like day on which they should fast and pray to G-d, and in that way they would be saved.

The Germans collected the Jews from the towns surrounding Vilkomir, tossed them into wagons and trucks, and drove them to the Pivonya forest. Vilkomir's Jews followed soon after, first the men, then the women and infants. They were buried half-alive. The Germans also uprooted tombstones in the Jewish cemetery and leveled the soil in which Vilkomir's dead rested.

VILKOVISHK

LITHUANIAN NAME: Vilkaviskis RUSSIAN NAME: Vilkovishki
LOCATION: A Lithuanian district capital in southwest Lithuania, near
Germany. It is a few miles northwest of Mariampol.
JEWISH POPULATION IN 1939: 3,609 (total population: 8,020)

View of Vilkovishk.

JEWISH HISTORY: Vilkovishk was one of the
country's oldest Jewish settlements, dating back to
the 16th century. Because of Vilkovishk's proximity to Germany its Jews were among Lithuania's
earliest secularists. That is why Vilkovishk's citizens were both Torah scholars and secular scholars: Moshela Haskel; Reb Yechezkel Yafu; Rav M.
Grodzensky; Avrohom Mokovsky; Reb Yaakov
Rosenholtz; Reb Shlomo Kaptzevsky; Mordechai
Garmaise; Avrohom Orenberg; Bendet Rabinovitz,
the vice-mayor; Yaakov Chmilevsky; Tzvi
Chmilevsky; and others.

*An ancient tombstone
in Vilkovishk.*

Vilkovishk had its unusual individuals—Yossel
Rabinovitz was always busy helping the poor, the
ill, and the suffering. Unmarried and with no other
obligations, he dedicated himself to helping unfortunate people. Even in
the Vilkovishk ghetto, he aided the elderly and ill as much as he could
until his last breath. Reb Yochonon the shoemaker, called by the Hebrew
for shoemaker, "*Hasandlor*," lectured, every day between *Mincha* and
Maariv, in Talmud for the members of the Chevra Shas. Shimon Dovid the
porter, a pauper, was well-known for never sitting down to his Shabbos

table without poor people as his guests.

ECONOMY: Vilkovishk's Jews made their living from a variety of occupations. Hundreds were employed in brushmaking, papermaking, the production of iron, and the processing of silk and tobacco. Binyomin Rottenberg owned a silk factory, and the major brush manufacturers were Abba Sobolevitz, Mr. Rosen, and Mr. Vindzberg. Much of Vilkovishk's production was exported to Germany. Vilkovishk's factory workers were organized in a trade union.

INSTITUTIONS: Vilkovishk had fine communal institutions, including an old age home, a Bikur Cholim society, a Maskil El Dol (providing for the poor) society, a Hebrew high school, a trade school, and a library. A monthly magazine edited by A. Filipovsky was published in Vilkovishk in 1939.

The Vilkovishk synagogue.　　　　*The Vilkovishk beis hamidrosh.*

SPIRITUAL LEADERS: Vilkovishk's rabbis included Rav Tzvi Hirsh Rapaport; Rav Yisroel Katzenellenbogen; Rav Boruch Mordechai Lipschutz; Rav Eliezer Landa; Rav Yaakov Dovid Vilavsky, renowned by his acronym, *Ridbaz,* and for his commentary on Talmud *Yerushalmi;* Rav Hirsh Mah-Yofis; and the martyred Rav Eliyohu Green, Vilkovishk's last rabbi.

Its *dayanim* included Rav Elchonon *der porush* (the explainer), a very righteous man and a great Torah scholar; Rav Berel Kamaika, whose son Leon edited *Der Togblat* in New York; and the martyred

Rav Yaakov Dovid Vilavsky, the Ridbaz.

Rav Avrohom Piltinov, formerly rabbi in Vistinetz, Vilkovishk's last *dayan.*

1939-45: On Sunday, the 22nd of June 1941, the Jews of Vilkovishk were awakened at five a.m. by artillery fire. The Germans were bombarding Vilkovishk from positions in the Prussian border towns of Stalupin and Gumbinnen. The Jews fled. Because the Russian resistance was desultory, the Germans took the city at eight o'clock that morning. As soon as the Germans entered Vilkovishk, they set fire to Jewish homes and synagogues, including the 400-year-old Old Synagogue. When the Jews returned to town the next day, all they found of their homes and houses of worship were ashes and smoke.

They squeezed into the few habitable houses, into Abba Sobolevitz's factory building, and into sheds. The Germans immediately forced the Jews to work. Returning from their forced labor at midnight that Monday, they were compelled to run a gauntlet of Lithuanians armed with clubs and rubber truncheons. Yossel Tzicher hit a Lithuanian who struck him, and was shot to death on the spot. By the time the Jews made it to their residences, after two consecutive days of uncertainty, terror and backbreaking labor, they were totally distraught and exhausted.

At that point they were ordered to give up their possessions: money, watches, knives, belts, suspenders. No objects could be retained. At 5 a.m. the Jews were lined up in rows of four. Certain that they were going to be marched to their execution, they were relieved when the German commandant instead ordered them marched off to labor.

The men were transferred to barracks where they were held for about two weeks. One Shabbos the men were ordered to dig pits near the barracks. The following Monday, 4 Av 5701, July 28, 1941, they took 111 men off to labor. Then 780 of the remaining men were led out to the pits and shot. Among those killed that day were the *dayan* Rav Avrohom Piltinov and the members of the *Judenrat* (a German-selected Jewish council): Chayim Hoffman, Yaakov Rosenholtz, Bendet Rabinovitz, and Mottel Zimansky.

Afterwards, the women and children were moved into the barracks, and the survivors were told that this would become a ghetto. Yisroel Zilber was designated the Jews' representative. On the second day of Rosh Hashanah, September 23, 1941, while the Jews were praying, German troops surrounded the barracks. The next day they butchered the women and children so savagely that the area was strewn with fingers, toes, and other broken and sliced limbs.

About 100 Vilkovishk Jews managed to escape. Among them was Eliezer Lapidos (who settled in Montreal, Canada), the eyewitness who provided the above details.

VIZHUN

LITHUANIAN NAME: Vyzunos
LOCATION: Vizhun is a picturesque town, nestled in a valley in the Utyan district in eastern Lithuania with hills circling the town. Right outside town was a forest with a round lake at its center. Vizhun is slightly

Kovno Street in Vilkomir.

Rav Refoel HaCohen.

Rav Shoulka.

The Vilkomir Yeshiva.

northwest of Utyan.

JEWISH POPULATION IN 1939: 367, making it one of Lithuania's smallest Jewish communities.

JEWISH HISTORY: Vizhun was one of Lithuania's oldest Jewish communities, and is mentioned in the minutes of the Vaad Lita (Jewish Council of Lithuania, organized to collect taxes and oversee Jewish affairs) of 1670. One of Vizhun's claims to fame was the great Rav Aryeh Leib Ginzberg, born there in 1695 and the author of *Shaagas Aryeh*, the classic responsa on diverse halachic issues, which is still frequently quoted.

ECONOMY: Vizhun had a large brandy distillery owned by three Jews—Palavin, Stern, and Leviad—which employed many of the town's Jews. In addition, some of its Jews were shopkeepers and craftspeople.

INSTITUTIONS: Vizhun's synagogue was several hundred years old, and famous for its beautiful *aron kodesh*. This synagogue also had a room that was called Eliyohu's Room, because that was where *brissim* were held. The synagogue's entrance hall displayed a chain that remained from the stocks that had existed when sinners were punished by the local rabbinic court.

Vizhun's Chassidim had their own synagogue which they called the Chassidic *Minyan*.

SPIRITUAL LEADERS: Vizhun's roster of rabbis includes Rav Osher Ginsburg; Rav Tzvi Hirsh Horvitz; Rav

The old synagogue in Vizhun, renowned for its beautiful aron hakodesh (inset).

Eliezer Ginsburg; Rav Eliezer Don-Yichiya, author of the halachic responsa *Even Shesiya*; his son, Rav Chayim; Rav Meir E. Veiner; and the martyred Rav Zalman Meltzer, the town's last rabbi. Rav Eliezer Don-Yichiya was renowned as Rav Leizer Lutzener, because his last rabbinic position was in Lutzen, Latvia. He was reputed to be physically very strong, and could break an old Russian five-kopek coin in half with two fingers.

Vizhun's Jews were Torah scholars and secular scholars: Bera Menda Shmid, the community leader and the town aristocrat; Rav Eliezer Zilber, the government-recognized rabbi; Reb Leibtzik Kretchmar; Reb Leibtzik Laies; Chona Yodeia; and Reb Eliyohu Finkelstein, a shoemaker by trade who dedicated himself to Torah study with great perseverance and earned ordination as a rabbi.

1939-45: On July 27, 1941, the Germans occupied Vizhun. The Lithuanians immediately painted the word *"Jude"* on every Jewish house as a service to the Germans. Abuse, torture, robbery, rape, and murder followed. A ghetto was established in Vizhun which was liquidated between Yom Kippur and Sukkos of 1941.

It is said that Vizhun's Jews were herded to a place five miles outside of Utyan, where they were butchered together with Jews from nearby towns. There were no survivors of this extermination. The only Vizhun Jews who survived the Holocaust were those who had fled to Russia at the outset of the war, or those who went through the concentration camps and managed to survive. The Germans watched as the Lithuanians killed the Jews. Then they burned the town and destroyed the Jewish cemetery.

VORNE

LITHUANIAN NAME: Varniai **RUSSIAN NAME:** Vorni
LOCATION: In the Telz district, a few miles south of Telz.

A view of Vizhun's marketplace.

JEWISH POPULATION IN 1939: 700

SPIRITUAL LEADERS: Vorne's rabbis included Rav Binyomin; Rav Yehoshua Heshel Melamed; Rav Yosef Bloch, later rabbi and rosh yeshiva in Telz; the martyred Rav Levi Shpitz, later rabbi in Tavrig; Rav Yaakov Rabinovitz and his son-in-law, the martyred Rav Abba Shor, Vorne's last rabbi.

Among Vorne's prominent men were Rav Nochum Lipa Chananya, a scholar, a *tzaddik*, and a man truly concerned with the study of Torah, so much so that he maintained his own yeshiva in Vorne. He taught the students himself, and arranged for them to eat at the homes of the townspeople. He also founded several societies, and got the community to accept pious practices. He lived a life of poverty, fasting Mondays, Thursdays, and during the Ten Days

The old synagogue in Vorne.

of Repentance. Others were Reb Artzik, Reb Moishel the Rav's, Yisroel Itzas (Golomba), and Yosha the shoemaker. Yosha was the *rebbi* of the Chevra Mishnayos. He taught in the synagogue every day between *Mincha* and *Maariv*.

1939-45: Vorne was occupied by the Germans on June 24, 1941. They abused the rabbi horribly, forcing him to sing and dance for them, before they executed him. The men of the town were killed almost immediately, followed by the women and children several weeks later.

YANISHOK

LITHUANIAN NAME: Joniskis **RUSSIAN NAME:** Yanishki

LOCATION: In the Shavl district in north central Lithuania, east of Akmian.

ECONOMY: Yanishok developed as an important city because of its proximity to the Latvian border. Jews were able to make a good living there by exporting to and importing from Latvia. A major business was the geese and eggs trade between Yanishok and Riga. Other Jewish occupations were retail shops and crafts.

INSTITUTIONS: Yanishok had a yeshiva headed by the brothers Rav Yaakov Leib and Rav Yehuda Matz.

Yanishok's communal institutions included a Tiferes Bachurim chapter, a Bikur Cholim society, an elementary school, a high school, a library, a credit union, and chapters of various other cultural and religious organizations.

SPIRITUAL LEADERS: Yanishok's rabbis were Rav Meshulom Z. Katzenellenbogen; Rav Sholom Rabinovitz; Rav Avrohom Heller; Rav Yechiel Mechel Wolfson, author of the halachic responsa *Sefas Hayam*, and his son-in-law, the martyred Rav N. Betzalel Dzimitrovsky, Yanishok's last rabbi.

Yanishok had many distinguished citizens who were also Torah scholars. Reb Avrohom Ziv, a scholar and a zealot, made extraordinary sacrifices so that his sons could study in yeshivos. He was exiled to Siberia in 1941. My friend, the martyred Rav Mordechai Yoffe, was a great scholar and a man of very fine character.

Not content to study Torah on their own, the Yanishokers sought first-rate scholars from the major yeshivos as sons-in-law. Rav Zingerevitz, for example, possessed both Torah and wealth. All his sons studied in yeshivos, and his sons-in-law were all great scholars. One was the martyred Rav Boruch Kaplan. Another was Rav Shnayer Dovid Volt who, together with his brothers-in-law, Rav Moshe and Reb Shlomo, miraculously survived the war and settled in Saõ Paulo, Brazil, where Rav Volt became the chief rabbi and the Zingerevitzes became communal activists.

1939-45: When Hitler's army attacked Lithuania on June 22, 1941, Yanishok was the city via which fortunate Jews were able to flee to Russia. But before Yanishok's own Jews realized what was happening, the Germans had occupied the city.

There was no organized robbery or mass murder in Yanishok during the first days of the occupation. The signal was given suddenly on the 16th of July, when the old, sick rabbi, Rav Dzimitrovsky, was arrested. In broad daylight the white-bearded rabbi was handed a broom and a dustpan, and forced to sweep the street. Other Jews were arrested and abused, and the first murders were soon reported. Several hundred younger men were herded off to a labor camp in the town of Zhager.

On the 23rd of July, the rabbi and a number of others were led outside the city and shot to death. The women and children of Radvilishok as well as all of Shavlan's Jews were brought to Yanishok. They were treated to a death-speech along with the rest of Yanishok's Jews, then taken outside the city and killed.

YANOVA

LITHUANIAN NAME: Jonava RUSSIAN NAME: Janovo
LOCATION: In the Kovno district in central Lithuania, a few miles northeast of Kovno.
JEWISH POPULATION IN 1939: 3,000 (total population: 5,000)
JEWISH HISTORY: Yanova's Jewish community was founded in 1775.

ECONOMY: Most of Yanova's Jews worked at producing the furniture for which Yanova was famous throughout Lithuania. Some Jews made their living steering rafts down the river to transport goods from Vilna to Kovno. Before buses, when horse-drawn carriages conveyed passengers from city to city, Yanova's Jewish drivers and their coaches were very popular. Jews also worked as traders and storekeepers.

Yanova's raft drivers.

The Jewish credit union was an important local institution that lent money at cheap rates. This allowed craftsmen and merchants some leeway until they could collect, and at the same time gave peddlers enough time to make their rounds of the villages.

INSTITUTIONS: Yanova had a yeshiva for its own young men and for boys from nearby towns. It was headed by the martyred Rav Mendel Teitz. When the Kletzk Yeshiva headed by Rav Aaron Kotler was forced to escape the Communist regime, Yanova welcomed it warmly. When the Russians occupied Lithuania in 1940, the Kletzk Yeshiva moved to Solok in the Ezhereni district. Some of the yeshiva's students were later exiled to Siberia by the Russians, but the majority of them, as well as the yeshiva's *mashgiach*, Rav Yosef Leib Nenedik, were killed by the Germans in Solok. Rav Aharon Kotler and his family, along with a group of his students, managed to escape to the United States via Japan.

SPIRITUAL LEADERS: Yanova's rabbis included Rav Avrohom Broida; Rav Yehoshua H. Eliashzon; Rav Alexander M. Lapidos; Rav Chayim Y. Blumental; Rav Yosef Z. Fried; Rav Yitzchok Lipkin, son of Rav Yisroel Salanter; Rav Chayim Ratzker, author of *Orach Lachayim*; Rav Chayim Yitzchok Shulman, who built up the town's Bikur Cholim society and energetically sought to help the needy; and the martyred Rav Nachum Boruch Ginsburg, author of *Mokor Boruch*, a collection of insights on the

Mishnah, and chairman of the Union of Lithuanian Rabbis.

1939-45: When war broke out between Germany and Russia on June 22, 1941, Jews fled Kovno on foot toward Riga and Vilna along the Kovno-Yanova highway. Many of them, mostly women and children, were killed by German bombs or by gunfire from low-flying German planes. The survivors reached Yanova, but could proceed no farther because the Germans had landed in and occupied nearby Shatt in the Keidan district. Yanova was flooded with refugees from

Rav Chayim Yitzchok Shulman of Yanova.

Kovno and from the nearby towns trying to get as close as possible to the Russian border.

Despite strong Russian resistance, on June 24th the Germans, from their base in Shatt, moved into Yanova and occupied it. They immediately drove the Jews out of their homes and assembled them in the central marketplace. The Germans put two rabbis on display—the rabbi of the city, Rav Ginsburg, and Rav Yeshayohu Levinson, a grandson of the Chofetz Chayim (Rabbi Yisroel Meir Kagan of Radun) and director of the Radun Yeshiva. Rav Levinson found himself in Yanova unexpectedly due to the sudden outbreak of the war. He made it to Kovno and survived until the Germans sent him to Dachau, where he was killed in 1945.

The Germans produced a Communist flag, which they soaked in gasoline. Then they forced the rabbis to hold it while they photographed them. The Jews present were certain that the Germans were planning to set the rabbis on fire. Suddenly artillery shells began to burst. The Russians had opened fire from the Palegon fortress two and a half miles outside of Yanova. The German unit in Yanova was small and quickly withdrew from the marketplace, leaving the Jews there. While the Germans and the Russians fought each other, most of the Jews fled into the countryside. The fight took a terrible toll; in one cellar alone some 70 Jews who were hiding perished as the result of a direct hit. After three days of fighting, the Germans emerged the victorious possessors of Yanova's ruins.

The Jews straggled back into the ruins only to face a decree ordering all non-citizens of Yanova to leave immediately. The local Christians began to rob and murder Jews. The Jews who had left and were headed for Kovno were collected enroute and brought to Kovno's Seventh Fort where they were killed.

Yanova's Jews were forced to work for the Germans, and in addition were fined an enormous sum. Yanova's rabbi, Rav Ginsburg, was brutally beaten—the hair was torn out of his beard—and he was driven to the Kovno Ghetto for Kovno's Jews to ransom. When Rav Ginsburg arrived in the company of two Lithuanian Nazis, his face had been so mauled that he was unrecognizable. When they took him back to Yanova they also took along Kagan the pharmacist. Neither of them was ever seen again.

Soon afterwards, following much abuse, Yanova's men were murdered, followed by the women and children. Twenty families found hiding places in the forests or among Russian peasants who lived in nearby villages. Eventually they were rounded up and taken to Kovno's Ninth Fort. They arrived three days after the liquidation of the Little Ghetto, when more than 2,000 Jews had been murdered, and they were miraculously interned in the ghetto. Nachum Blumberg and his wife were among the Yanishokers who survived the war.

After the liberation of Lithuania, a Jewish woman from Yanova recognized the man who had murdered her husband and many other Jews. He revealed where the rabbi was buried, and in fact his severed head and body were found there. Kagan the pharmacist's body was also found, as was his severed head.

YURBORG

LITHUANIAN NAME: Jurbarkas RUSSIAN NAME: Jurburg

LOCATION: Yurborg—the Germans spell it Jurborg—was in the Rasseyn district. One of Lithuania's oldest towns, it was located along the Niemen River, about six miles from the German border.

JEWISH POPULATION IN 1939: 2,000

JEWISH HISTORY: The Jewish community in Yurborg dates back to the 16th century.

ECONOMY: Most of Yurborg's Jews earned their living from the river. Some Jews—Levenberg and Eisenstat among others—owned steamboats and ferried passengers between Kovno and Smolininken on the German border. Some owned freight boats and carried freight between Memel and Kovno. Others moved freight on rafts. There were exporters, retailers, and craftspeople as well.

Yurborg Jews also made a living from supplying troops garrisoned there. Among them were Jewish soldiers for whom the community operated a kosher kitchen. These soldiers collected money and had a *sefer* Torah written. When it was completed, they paraded through Yurborg's streets, led by Captain Sorokin.

INSTITUTIONS: Yurborg's synagogue, built at the end of the 18th century, had an *aron kodesh* that was a masterpiece of carving. Perfectly carved birds, flowers, and clocks ran the length of the ark from the floor up. This

Yurborg's old synagogue, built in 1790.

*Eliyohu Hanovi's chair, an ornate masterpiece
at the Yurborg synagogue.*

*The ornate bimah at the
Yurborg synagogue.*

Yurborg's Jewish cemetery.

ark was photographed and copies were distributed worldwide. Tourists visiting Lithuania often stopped in Yurborg to see it.

Yurborg's communal institutions included a *hachnosas orchim* (guest) house, a Bikur Cholim society, an elementary school, a high school, a credit union, and two libraries.

SPIRITUAL LEADERS: Yurborg's rabbis included Rav Aryeh Yehuda Leib, who is mentioned in the responsa of Rav Akiva Eger; Rav Yehoshua Zelig Ashkenazi; Rav Moshe Levinson; Rav Yaakov Joseph, later *maggid* of Vilna and Chief Rabbi of New York City; Rav Yechezkel Libshitz, later rabbi of Kalisz; Rav Avrohom Dimant; and the martyred Rav C. Reuven Rubinstein.

Rav Yechezkel Libshitz of Yurborg.

The town's citizens included Torah students and secular scholars: Hirshel Finn; Kalman Friedlander; Pinchos Shachnovitz; Yisroel Levenberg, a charitable man who specialized in secretly helping people who had fallen on hard times; Shmayohu Feinberg, Yurborg's vice-mayor; Alter Simanov; Meir Z. Leviton the pharmacist; Reuven Olshvanger; Dr. Karlinsky; and the *shochetim* Alperovitz and Shmulovitz.

Reb Leibela Yisroel-Boruch was well known in Yurborg. He spent all day studying Torah in the *beis hamidrosh*, while his wife earned what they required. He was first in the *beis hamidrosh* every morning and last to leave every night, always making sure that every pauper had a place to eat. He took special care Friday nights, when there were many visiting paupers, to match visitors with homes so that no visitor went hungry.

His brother Velveka also occupied himself with providing for the local poor. Every Friday he collected *challah*, fish, and meat, and distributed them to poor families for Shabbos.

1939-45: On June 22, 1941, when the Germans attacked Russia, Yurborg's Jews felt the sting immediately. Living so close to the German border, they were under German occupation within a few hours. A Lithuanian police force was established, headed by Levitzkas, a high-school teacher. Its first victim was Reuven Olshvanger. The Lithuanian shopkeepers stopped selling goods to Jews. At day's end they would sell leftover goods to Jews who had waited on a special Jews' line.

On Shabbos, June 27th, the Jews were ordered to carry their books out to the yard of the synagogue by 4 p.m. The patriarchal, grey-bearded Rav Reuven Rubinstein carted his holy books and manuscripts there on the holy Shabbos. At 5 p.m. the Jews were ordered to take the Torah scrolls out of the synagogue. The Lithuanians piled them atop the books and set them afire.

At 11 a.m. on July 2nd, as Jews were standing on breadlines, Germans and Lithuanians began to pull men out of the lines and lead them to the marketplace. Others combed the houses and dragged off Jewish men. By 3 p.m. they had collected 320 men, including Rav Rubinstein, the school principal Yoffe, Dr. Gershovitz, Dr. Karlinsky, and Bregavsky the pharmacist. They loaded the men into trucks and drove them out to the Jewish cemetery where they shot them to death. Farmers in nearby houses watched from their windows as Jews beat each other with branches on orders from the Germans prior to being shot.

While the mass butchery was going on, Lithuanians caught another 80 Jewish men who had been hiding during the initial *Akzion*, and locked them in jail. At 10 p.m. the Lithuanian policeman Botvinskis informed them that they would be shot at 3 the next day. It is noteworthy that not one of them wept. Everyone used his remaining hours to come to terms with his Maker. One of them had a *yahrtzeit* that night and led the *Maariv* prayer, in which all participated with great fervor. The weekday *Maariv* was transmuted into an outpouring of the soul and a pre-death confessional.

Those Jews were not shot that day. But an order was issued commanding all able-bodied men aged 15 to 50 to report daily at 6 a.m. for work. Men over 50 were required to appear twice daily, at 9 a.m. and at 6 p.m. On July 21st, Lithuanians trucked away the 45 over-50 Jews who appeared. On the road to Rasseyn, nine miles out of town, the Lithuanians killed them along with other Jews from nearby towns. Before killing them, the Germans forced these men to write letters to their families saying that they were working and lacked nothing.

On August 1st, Lithuanian murderers arrested 105 elderly Jewish women, beat them brutally, and tossed them into wagons. No one has yet discovered where they were killed or buried.

On the pretext of establishing a labor camp near Tavrig, the Lithuanians assembled the 520 wives and children of the 320 men who had been butchered in the first *Akzion*. They were held under guard for three days in the Yiddish-language elementary school. At midnight they were force-marched to pits waiting for them in the Smolininka woods, where they were machine gunned to death by drunken Lithuanians. The Christian villagers of Passventa related that the earth over the pits was heaving for three days, because so many Jews were buried alive.

About a week later, the remaining 50 laborers were suddenly surrounded at work by Lithuanian policemen and led away to be killed. Three Jews escaped and survived the war: Michalovsky, 18-year-old Davidovich, and an unnamed man.

In fewer than three months, the centuries-old Jewish community of Yurborg was eradicated, root and branch, all its Jews martyred and every sacred object, synagogue, ark and book, burned to cinders and ash.

ZHAGER

LITHUANIAN NAME: Zagare RUSSIAN NAME: Zhagory
LOCATION: The Sventa River, 40 miles from Shavl, divided Zhager into two towns—Old Zhager and New Zhager. It is located in northern Lithuania, a few miles northwest of Yanishok.
JEWISH POPULATION IN 1939: 8,000
JEWISH HISTORY: Old Zhager and New Zhager each had its own Jewish community. Though Zhager is mentioned in 13th-century Lithuanian documents, it never became a major commercial center and did not have a railroad station. The Jewish community dates back to the 16th century.

Many of Zhager's secular men achieved renown. Among them were Professor Mordechai Mandelshtat, Aryeh Leib Mandelstamm, who translated the *Chumash* (Bible) and *Tehillim* (Psalms) into Russian, and the writer Yaakov Dineson. Sidney Hillman, the American labor leader who headed the C.I.O. (Congress of Industrial Organizations) and became an adviser to President Franklin D. Roosevelt, had roots in Zhager and studied in the Slobodka Yeshiva until he was 20 years old.

ECONOMY: The Jews of Zhager supported themselves wholesaling produce and dairy products, exporting geese, vegetable gardening, and through various crafts.

INSTITUTIONS: Zhager had many Jewish institutions, among which were a credit union, a Bikur Cholim society, an old age home, a Talmud Torah, and an elementary school.

New Zhager's yeshiva was founded by Rav Yaakov Joseph, and had an excellent reputation. Old Zhager had a large yeshiva before World War I; its rosh yeshiva was Rav Ben-Tziyon Feldman, and its second rosh yeshiva was Rav Doniyel Zaks, who later became rabbi in Radvilishok.

SPIRITUAL LEADERS: The Jews of eastern Poland and Lithuania had heard of Zhager's sages—among whom were Rav Yisroel Lipkin (Salanter), founder of the *mussar* movement, and Rav Eliyohu of Lida, who was very influential in spreading *mussar*. Zhager's rabbinic roster includes Rav Eliyohu Shik, who served as Lida's rabbi for 14 years before serving as rabbi of Zhager for 11 years; Rav Yehuda Leib Tiktiner; Rav Yekusiel Z. Levitas; Rav Chayim Tzvi Broida; Rav Yitzchok Broida; Rav Chayim Y. Korb; Rav Yisroel Duber Gelernter, author of the chassidic commentary on the Torah *Revid Hazohov*; Rav Yaakov Joseph, who served Zhager after Yurborg, and went on to become Vilna's *maggid* and New York City's chief rabbi; Rav Yehuda Leib Riff; Rav Ben-Tziyon Feldman;

A view of New Zhager's marketplace.

The synagogue in Old Zhager.

*The aron kodesh in
New Zhager's synagogue.*

Rav Yaakov Joseph.

the martyred Rav Yisroel Riff and his son, the martyred Rav Yitzchok.

1939-45: During the German occupation of Lithuania, Zhager's Jews suffered terribly. The Germans established a ghetto in Zhager where 8,000 Jews from Zhager as well as Jews from the nearby towns and villages— Zeimel, Krok, Yanishok, and others—were incarcerated and forced to perform strenuous slave labor, from which many simply dropped dead of exhaustion.

The Germans enjoyed not only physically abusing the Jews, but they also had to have their "fun" at the Jews' expense. Zhager's Jews greatly admired and loved their rabbi, the patriarchal, refined, and righteous Rav Yisroel Riff who was indeed one of Lithuania's great rabbis. Born in 1871, the son of Rav Yehuda Leib Riff, who had served as Zhager's rabbi, Rav Yisroel Riff married the daughter of Rav Refoel Shapiro, the rabbi of Volozhin and dean of its yeshiva. His first rabbinic position was in nearby Kurshan, from which he came to Zhager. Rav Riff's love for his fellow-Jews and his dedication to his community were recognized and reciprocated.

The Germans issued an order that every Jew who passed Rav Riff must spit in his face. Some Jews refused to do so and were immediately shot. When the rabbi saw this he sent word to the entire community: "Suicide is a sin. No Jew may allow himself to be killed by these murderers because he refuses to spit at me. If shaming me makes it possible for a Jew to live longer, then it is my wish that you shame me!"

On the eve of Yom Kippur 1941 toward evening, the Germans led the Jews out of the labor camp, the rabbi at their head along with his son Rav Yitzchok (Old Zhager's rabbi). The melody of *Kol Nidre* accompanied them as they were led to the municipal Nariskis Park, where they were all shot to death.

GLOSSARY

Adar - The twelfth month on the Hebrew calendar, according to biblical reckoning; or the sixth, according to traditional Jewish observance. Purim is on the 14th of Adar.

Adon Olom - "Eternal Lord." A deeply religious hymn that describes G-d's eternal existence. It is sung as part of the daily morning prayers and at the end of the Sabbath and certain holiday services.

Agudas Yisroel - An Orthodox organization headed by rabbis, begun in Europe in 1912 with the purpose of upholding the values of traditional Jewry by preserving the Torah as the main authority in all legal and social areas. The Agudas Yisroel had branches throughout eastern Europe before the Holocaust. Today they are active throughout the world.

Agunah (pl., *agunos*) - A woman who is prevented from remarrying because her husband abandoned her, is missing, or refuses to give her a Jewish bill of divorce.

Akzion (pl., *Akzionen*) - The Nazi operation of rounding up, transporting, and murdering Jews during the Holocaust.

Al Chait - "For Sins." The prayer of confession recited on Yom Kippur, listing sins and asking for G-d's forgiveness.

Aron Kodesh - The "holy ark" or closet in the synagogue in which the Torah scrolls are kept. It is usually decorated with a beautifully embroidered curtain.

Aussiedlungsakzion (German) - The "transferring" of Jews out of their homes and into camps and ghettos. This was done with extreme violence, resulting in many deaths.

Baba Basra - The third tractate in *Nezikin*, the fourth section of the Mishnah, which deals with claims of ownership in real estate, inheritance, and partnership, and with drawing up legal documents.

Bachur (pl. *bachurim*) - Young unmarried man. The term usually refers to young men who study in a yeshiva.

Bar Mitzvah (f. Bat Mitzvah) - "Man of commandments." The occasion on which a 13-year-old boy assumes the responsibility of fulfilling the commandments of the Torah

294 OF LITHUANIAN JEWRY

and is held responsible for his own actions. It is usually celebrated by calling the *bar mitzvah* up to the Torah reading.

Beis Din - A Jewish court of law that rules on civil, criminal, and religious cases.

Beis Hamidrosh (pl., *batei midrosh*) - A "house of learning" and prayer. Between the three daily prayer services, students of various ages study the Talmud, its commentaries, and other Torah subjects in *batei midrosh*.

Beis Hamikdosh (pl., *batei hamikdosh*) - The Temple, a permanent resting place for the Divine Presence. There were two Temples built on Mount Moriah in Jerusalem. The first, built by King Solomon in about 950 B.C.E., was destroyed by the Babylonians in 586 B.C.E. The second was built 70 years later by the Jews returning from the Babylonian Exile, and was destroyed by the Romans in 70 C.E. The only part remaining is the *Kotel Hama'aravi*, the Western Wall. The third and final Temple will be built with the arrival of the Messiah.

Bikur Cholim - An organization that visits the sick and takes care of their needs. Visiting the sick is a blessing that the Talmud says helps the ill recover.

Bimah (pl., *bimos*) - The podium in the center or front of a synagogue from which the Torah is read aloud.

Birkas Hamozon - The Grace after Meals in which one praises G-d and thanks Him for providing sustenance.

Blatt - A page in the Talmud.

Bnei Torah - "Children of the Torah." Refers to those who study the Torah.

Borei Pri Hoadama - "...Who creates the fruit of the earth." This is the blessing recited before eating any vegetation.

Bris (or Bris Milah) (pl., *brissim*) - Circumcision. Jewish law requires all males to be circumcised when they are eight days old. A *bris* affirms that the child is entering a covenant with G-d.

Brocha (pl., *brochos*) - A blessing, recited on food, special occasions, or when one fulfills a commandment.

Chabad - The Chassidic sect which emphasizes the intellectual as well as emotional aspects of a person in serving G-d. Chabad is an acronym for Hebrew words *Chochma*—wisdom, *Bina*—insight, and *Daas*—knowledge.

Chabadniks - Followers of the Chabad Chassidism.

Challah (pl., *challos*) - Braided loaves of bread used for Sabbath meals.

Chometz - "Leavened bread." Eating *chometz* or having it among one's possessions on Pesach is strictly forbidden, in commemoration of the Jews' hasty departure from Egypt that did not allow time for their dough to rise (Exod. 12:34).

Chappenish - "The grabbing time." The period during the first days of the German occupation of Lithuania, when Jews were randomly and violently seized off the streets or from their homes.

Chosid - A pious Jew, usually referring to one who follows Chassidism.

Chassidic - Characteristic of Chassidism, a religious movement that originated in eastern Europe in the late eighteenth century and stressed devotion to the Torah, strict adherence to all laws and traditions, good deeds, and a stronger emphasis on the spiritual life than on the intense study of the Torah and Talmud.

Cheder (pl., *chadorim*) - A religious school for young children where they are taught how to read Hebrew, and study the Torah and Mishnah.

Chevrah Kadishah - A group of men or women who perform the rite of purification on a dead body and prepare it for burial.

Chevrah Mishnayos - An organized group of students and their rabbi who study the Mishnah together.

Chevra Shas - An organized group of students and their rabbi who study the Talmud together.

Cheshvan - The eighth month on the Hebrew calendar, according to biblical reckoning; or the second, according to traditional Jewish observance.

Chumash (pl., *chumashim*) - The Pentateuch or first five books of the Bible: Genesis, Exodus, Leviticus, Numbers, and Deuteronomy.

Daven - To pray. Jewish law requires men to pray three times daily: *Shacharis*, the morning prayer, *Mincha*, the afternoon prayer, and *Maariv*, the evening prayer.

Dayan - A judge in a Jewish court of law.

Der Zamuter Chosid - Yiddish for "that pious Jew from the Zamut," a region in northern Lithuania.

Din Torah - A court case in a Jewish court of law. Halachah requires Jews to bring their civil and religious disputes before a panel of Jewish judges.

Echod - "One," referring to the Almighty. It is the last word of the initial phrase of the *Shema*: "Hear O Israel, Hashem is Our G-d, Hashem is One."

Kel Moley Rachamim - A prayer requesting peace for the soul of the departed. It is recited at the graveside following burial, and is included in services remembering the departed that are recited on Yom Kippur, Sukkos, Pesach, and Shavuos.

Elul - The sixth month on the Hebrew calender, according to biblical reckoning; or the twelfth, according to traditional Jewish observance. Elul is the month before the High Holidays and is the time in which Jews begin the repentance process.

Esrog (pl., *esrogim*.) - A citron, one of the Four Species used in the celebration of Sukkos, along with the palm branch, myrtle, and willow.

Gabbai - A synagogue official, often given the responsibility of selecting congregants to be called up to the Torah reading.

Gaon (pl., *gaonim*) - A genius in the study of the Talmud, or an outstanding scholar and religious leader.

Gehinnom - Hell. The Jewish conception of hell is a place where a soul is purified of its sins through suffering for a finite period of time. The souls of the righteous dwell in *Gan Eden*, the Garden of Eden.

Gemora (pl., *gemoros*) - Talmud, or a volume of Talmud, the edited commentary on and discussion of the Mishnah. It is traditional to study the Talmud before praying.

Godol (pl., *gedolim*.) - A Jewish Torah giant and religious leader.

Hachnosas Kallah - A special charity collected for poverty-stricken brides to pay for their wedding, clothing, and dowry. It is considered to be one of the most meritorious acts of kindness and charity.

Halachah (pl., *halachos*) - Jewish law, which encompasses all aspects of life, including criminal, ethical, religious and moral issues, as well as day-to-day conduct.

Halachist - One who studies the intricacies of Jewish law.

Hamotzi - The blessing recited over bread and grains. It is also said at the beginning of a meal and eliminates the necessity to say a separate blessing over each different food during the meal.

Haskalah - The Enlightenment movement of the eighteenth century, which attempted to move Judaism away from its traditional Talmudic observance and towards a more secular, emancipated life.

Havdolah - "Distinction." A ceremony marking the conclusion of Sabbath or holidays, including blessings recited over wine, fragrant spices and a braided candle. The *havdolah* marks the distinction between the holy day and the weekdays that follow.

Horoyos - The tenth tractate of *Nezikin*, the fourth section of the Mishnah, which deals with misdirections in Jewish law from religious authorities.

Iluy - A prodigy, specifically one who attains high levels of Talmudic study at a very young age.

Jordan Schein - A certificate issued by Fritz Jordan, the commandant of the Kovno ghetto, which certified that a person was a skilled artisan. This temporarily spared his life.

Jude (German) - Jew.

Kab (pl., *kabim*) - A Hebrew liquid measurement equivalent to three gallons.

Kabbalah - Jewish mysticism, originally handed down orally and later arranged in the primary work of Kabbalah, the *Zohar*, which deals with issues such as the essence of G-d, the creation of humans, and destiny.

Kaddish - A prayer for the departed with underlying thoughts of hope for the redemption, customarily recited during the eleven months following the death of a parent and on the anniversary of a parent's death.

Karoim - The Karaite sect of Judaism dating back to the eighth century, which insists on a strict, literal interpretation of the Written Torah and rejects the Oral Law. There were Karaite communities spread throughout Europe before their destruction in World War II. Today about 8,000 *Karoim* remain in Israel.

Kashrus - System of halachic dietary regulations.

Kedushah - A prayer recited as part of the *Shemoneh Esray*, praising G-d using verses from the Prophets and Writings. It is regarded as the angels' prayer, thus when humans say it they are considered to elevate themselves to the status of angels.

Keriah - The act of rending a mourner's garment, usually done opposite his heart.

Kiddush Cup - The cup of wine used to recite the *kiddush*, the sanctification of the Sabbath or holiday.

Kiddush HaShem - An act of sanctification of G-d's name. It usually refers to martyrdom, though it can mean any action that raises the esteem of Judaism in the eyes of the world.

Kinos - Special prayers of lamentation recited in the synagogue on Tisha B'Av morning, composed by medieval poets in remembrance of the destruction of the Temple and other tragedies

Kittel - A long, white robe worn in the synagogue on Yom Kippur and at the Pesach *seder* table. It is also customary for a groom to wear a *kittel* under the wedding canopy during the marriage service.

Kloiz - A small synagogue, in which Jewish men prayed and studied.

Kohen (pl., *kohanim*) - A member of the priestly family descending from Aaron. The *kohanim* performed the sacrificial service in the Temple, and today they bless the congregation on certain occasions.

Kol Nidre - Aramaic for "all vows." The prayer recited on the eve of Yom Kippur that annuls the vows and oaths assumed by an individual regarding himself and G-d.

Kollel - A seminary of advanced Torah study, which usually provides a salary for the married men enrolled.

Kommandos (German) - Units of slave workers.

Kugel - A traditional pudding-like cake, usually made of potatoes or noodles, served on the Sabbath and holidays.

Landsmannschaften - An association of Jewish immigrants from the same town in Europe, formed to provide economic and social benefits for its members. After World War II, many *Landmannschaften* were established in the United States.

Linas Hatzedek - A public guesthouse for travelers. They were common in Jewish communities across eastern Europe.

Lulav (pl., *lulavim.*) - The branch of a palm tree, used in the celebration of Sukkos. The *lulav* combined with the myrtle, willow, and citron comprise the Four Species.

Ma'amodos - Biblical and Talmudic passages prescribed for each day of the week.

Maariv - The daily evening prayers, recited after nightfall. There are three daily prayers: *Shacharis*, the morning prayers, *Mincha*, the afternoon prayers, and *Maariv*.

Machzor - The prayerbook for the holidays that contains special compositions and prayers culled from the Bible, Talmud, and original poets.

Maggid - A local or traveling rabbi who preached simple sermons to draw the listeners to better Torah observance.

Mashgiach (pl., *mashgichim*) - The dean of a yeshiva responsible for supervising the behavior of the students and serving as their spiritual mentor.

Masmid (pl., *masmidim*) - A student primarily devoted to Talmudic study.

Matanos Loevyonim - "Gifts for the poor." A Jew is obligated to give charity to at least two paupers on Purim.

Matzah (pl., *matzos)* - Unleavened bread eaten on Pesach to commemorate the hurried exodus of the Jews from Egypt, during which they ate unleavened bread since it had no time to rise.

Mechuton - A relative by marriage, specifically, the parent of a child's spouse.

Megillah (pl., *megillos*) - A scroll. There are five *megillos* in the Holy Writings. The *Megillah* usually refers to the Book of Esther, which is read on Purim from a scroll.

Melamed (pl., *melamdim*) - A teacher of young children, usually referring to the teacher in a *cheder*.

Menahel - Administrator or director, often referring to a yeshiva principal.

Meshulach (pl., *meshulochim*) - Emissaries sent to distant countries to collect funds for a yeshiva.

Mezuzzah (pl., *mezuzzos*) - "Doorpost." A *mezuzzah* is a small parchment with the *Shema* and two other biblical passages inscribed on it. It is affixed slanted on the right side of the entrance to each room in a Jewish house to serve as a constant reminder of G-d's oneness and our moral duties to Him. Upon entering or leaving the house, it is customary to touch the fingers to the *mezuzzah* and then kiss the fingers.

Mikveh - A pool of water used for the ritual bathing and purification of people and utensils.

Mincha - The daily afternoon prayers.

Minyan (pl., *minyanim*) - A quorum of 10 or more men required for congregational prayer and Torah reading.

Mishloach Manos - Two portions of ready-to-eat food a Jew is obligated to send to at least one friend on Purim.

Mishnah (pl., *mishnayos*) - An early codification of Jewish law and ethics, divided into six sections and subdivided into 63 tractates. The Mishnah contains the Oral Law handed down through the generations from the giving of the Torah until the early third century, when it was compiled by Rabbi Yehuda HaNasi and his fellow scholars. *Mishnayos* is the common term for the tractates.

Misnagdic - Characteristic of *misnagdim*.

Misnagdim - Opponents of Chassidism. The *misnagdim* focused on an individual's knowledge of the Torah and law, while the Chassidim emphasized each person's individual relationship to G-d expressed by much joy and deep emotion.

Mitzvah (pl., *mitzvos*) - A Torah commandment. There are 613 *mitzvos*, divided into 248 positive and 365 negative commandments. The term *mitzvah* connotes any good deed or kind act.

Maos Chitim - "Wheat money." Charity collected annually before Pesach to provide a supply of necessities such as wine and matzah to the needy.

Modeh Ani - The morning prayer recited immediately upon awakening, which thanks G-d for returning our souls to our bodies.

Mohel - A person who is trained in and performs circumcisions.

Moreh Horoah - A rabbinic scholar who is qualified to decide issues in regard to forbidden or permitted things.

Mussar - The study of rebuke to improve one's character. Spiritual and ethical behavior was considered by Rabbi Yisroel Salanter (1810-1883), the founder of the *Mussar* movement, to be the essence of Jewish religious life.

Nedorim - The third tractate of *Nashim*, the third section of the Mishnah, which deals with the making and annulment of vows, especially in regard to women.

Nidah - The seventh tractate of *Tohoros*, the last section of the Mishnah, which deals with women and childbirth.

Nigun (pl., *nigunim*) - A melody or tune to which a prayer is chanted. Chassidic *nigunim* are emotional tunes, often sung without words.

Nisan - The first month on the Hebrew calendar, according to biblical reckoning; or the seventh, according to traditional Jewish observance. Pesach is on the 15th of Nisan.

Parshah (pl., *parshios*) - A section of the Torah, also called a *sidrah*. The *parshios* are the weekly portions read aloud in the synagogue.

Parshas Bechukosy - The tenth and last portion of Leviticus, the third book of the Bible.

Parshas Ekev - The third portion of Deuteronomy, the fifth book of the Bible.

Peios - Sidelocks. Halachah requires that the corners of the heads of Jewish males, above the ears, remain unshaven.

Perushim - Scholars who separated themselves from their families to study.

Pesach - Passover, the holiday celebrating the Exodus from Egypt. The first night of Pesach, as well as the second outside Israel, is celebrated with a ceremonial meal.

Pirchei Shoshanim - A youth organization for children age five to 13 that collected money to buy religious books for schools and houses of study.

Posek (pl., *poskim*) - A rabbinical scholar who rules in halachic issues.

Pushkah - A small container put aside to store money for charity. It is customary to place some charity into the *pushkah* before candlelighting on Sabbath and before the daily morning prayers. One receives great merit as a reward for charity, to the extent that there is a Biblical maxim, "Charity saves one from death (Proverbs 10:2,11:4)."

Rav - "Master." *Rav* is the title a rabbi is given by his Chassidim.

Rebbi - The leader of a Chassidic sect. They were succeeded by their sons or sons-in-law, and thus developed to some degree a Jewish royalty among their followers.

Riboinoi-Shel-Olom - "Master of the Universe."

Rosh Hashanah - The Jewish New Year, also called the Day of Remembrance. It is the beginning of the Ten Days of Repentance, culminating in Yom Kippur, when all people stand before G-d in judgment.

Rosh Yeshiva (pl., *Roshei yeshiva*) - The dean or religious authority of a yeshiva or rabbinic academy.

Sechach - Branches or bamboo poles used to form the roof of a *sukkah*.

Seder (pl., *sedorim*) - The traditional, festive meal eaten on Pesach during which the story of the Exodus is told and numerous acts are performed in commemoration.

Sefer (pl., *seforim*) - Religious book on Torah subjects.

Semichah - Rabbinical ordination. Following an extensive examination in halachah, a student is ordained by a rabbi, given the title "Rabbi" or "Rav," and is then permitted to give a decision in matters of Jewish law.

Shabbos - Sabbath. The seventh day of the week, set aside by G-d for rest since on the seventh day of the Creation, G-d rested. The Jews sanctify the Sabbath by saying *kiddush*, eating three meals, and singing songs that extol the holiness and tranquility of the day.

Shabbos Goy - A non-Jew who provides services for Jews on the Sabbath and holidays, when they may not perform these activities.

Shabbos Mevorechim - The Sabbath before the start of the new month, when we bless the coming month.

Shacharis - The daily morning prayer.

Shamosh - The caretaker of a synagogue who keeps the holy books in order.

Shavuos - "Feast of Weeks," celebrated as the occasion of giving of the Law on Mount Sinai and as a harvest festival.

Shechitah - Ritual slaughter of animals according to Jewish Law.

Shehakol - The blessing recited over foods that are not grains or do not grow on the ground or in trees. *Shehakol* praises G-d by acknowledging that "everything comes by His word."

Shehecheyanu - The blessing thanking G-d for "granting us life, sustenance, and allowing us to reach this occasion." It is recited upon experiencing certain new events, such as lighting the first Chanukah candles, wearing a new garment, reading the Purim scroll, tasting a new food, as well as many other joyous occasions.

Sheilah (pl., *sheilos*) - "Question." Questions on Jewish law are brought before a rabbinical scholar. Many volumes of their answers, reflecting the economic and social positions of Jews during various times, have been published through the ages.

Shema - *Shema Yisroel*. The prayer recited each morning and night, affirming G-d's singular existence and accepting the yoke of divine sovereignty. The initial phrase is translated: "Hear O Israel, Hashem is Our G-d, Hashem is One."

Shemitah - The sabbatical year in the Holy Land when it is forbidden to work the land in fulfillment of Exodus 23:11.

Shemoneh Esray - A prayer of 19 benedictions recited during the three daily prayers.

It is generally referred to as the *Amidah* since it is recited silently while standing. *Shemoneh Esray* literally means "Eighteen," since originally the prayer contained 18 blessings; one was added by later sages.

Shiur (pl., *shiurim*) - A Torah lesson or a class in a *yeshiva*.

Shochet (pl., *shochetim*) - A slaughterer of fowl and animals according to Jewish ritual law.

Shofar (pl., *shofaros*) - A ram's horn, sounded during the month of Elul and on Rosh Hashanah to symbolically awaken the souls to repent.

Sholosh Seudos - The three required Sabbath meals, eaten Friday night, Sabbath at noon, and Sabbath before nightfall. *Kiddush* is recited for the first two meals, and during the third one there is a custom, particularly among the Chassidim, of lengthening the meal as a symbol of saying goodbye to the Sabbath. The third meal is often called *sholosh seudos*.

Shtender - A stand used to rest notes or books while studying or teaching.

Shtetl - Small villages in eastern Europe, almost entirely Jewish. The inhabitants were extremely poor and cut off from the rest of society; they concentrated on Torah study and doing *mitzvos*.

Shul (Yiddish) - Synagogue, house of prayer.

Siddur - Prayer book. The daily prayer book contains the three daily prayers, the Sabbath and festival prayers, services for special occasions such as a circumcision or marriage, and many other prayers and compositions.

Sifrei Torah - Torah scrolls, handwritten by a scribe on parchment from the leather of a kosher animal. The sections are sewn together with threads made from the tendons of kosher animals to form one long scroll. The Torah portions read aloud in the synagogue is read from such a scroll, which is written without punctuation or vowels.

Simchas Torah - Holiday celebrating the completion and renewal of the yearly cycle of portions of the Torah read weekly in the synagogue. The Torah scrolls are carried around the synagogue seven times, with each congregant taking a turn dancing and carrying a Torah. Simchas Torah is celebrated immediately after the last day of Sukkos.

Sivan - The third month on the Hebrew calendar, according to biblical reckoning; or the ninth, according to traditional Jewish observance. The Jewish nation received the Torah at Mount Sinai in Sivan.

Siyum - "Conclusion." A joyous celebration marking the completion of a tractate or scholarly work.

Sukkah - A temporary home built to dwell in during the holiday Sukkos.

Sukkos - Festival of Booths. This holiday, commemorating the booths the Jews dwelled in during the 40 years they wandered in the desert, is celebrated by eating, and even by living, in the *sukkah*.

Tallis (pl., *talleisim*) - A prayer shawl with fringes on its four corners worn during morning prayers.

Talmid Chochom (pl., *talmidei chochomim*) - A scholar learned in the Torah. Jewish tradition regards the Torah as the most precious commodity in the world, so those who devote their lives to the study of the Torah are considered the elite of the Jewish nation.

Tamuz - The fourth month on the Jewish calendar, according to Biblical reckoning; or the tenth, according to traditional Jewish observance.

Tefillin - Phylacteries. Two black leather boxes containing Torah passages written on parchment, fastened to the head and left arm with black leather straps. They are worn at the weekday morning services by Jewish men age 13 and up, who are commanded to do so in the Torah.

Tehillim - The Book of Psalms. Poems and songs of praise to G-d, many of which are included in the daily prayer liturgy. Written by King David, the psalms are often recited during times of trouble or danger, and their soothing words usually calm those who recite them.

Teshuvah - Repentance, a return to the Torah after sin. Judaism allows any person to repent at any time, never believing it is too late. The 10 days beginning with Rosh Hashanah and concluding with Yom Kippur are considered to be the primary time for repentance.

Tiferes Bachurim - An organization of young men who met every night to study Talmud, the Bible, and halachah.

Tisha B'Av - The ninth day of the month of Av, anniversary of the destruction of the two Temples in Jerusalem. Throughout the generations, this date has been a day of mourning, sorrow, and fasting for Jews, and it has been a date often chosen upon which to carry out harsh decrees against the Jews.

Torah - The Five Books of Moses. The study of the Torah is considered the highest level of worship to G-d, and one who is learned in the Torah is considered the elite of the Jewish nation. More generally, Torah refers to all of Judaism's teachings, religious and ethical, and its culture.

Tosofos - Additions to the traditional commentary of Rashi, the famed twelfth century commentator, on the Talmud. The Tosafists are the students of Rashi and their students, ranging from the twelfth to fourteenth centuries in northern France. Their method of study—to point out discrepancies and then resolve them—has been greatly analyzed and studied by students of the Talmud.

Tzaddik - A righteous man. A rabbi or Torah giant is often referred to as a *tzaddik* to emphasize his righteousness and noble character.

Tzitzis - Fringes tied to a four-cornered garment to fulfill a Torah commandment.

Viduy - Confession of sins. It is recited repeatedly on Yom Kippur and on a person's deathbed.

Wehrmacht (German) - The armed forces of the German army.

Yahrtzeit - The anniversary of a death. On the eve of the Jewish date of the death of one's parent it is customary to recite prayers for the dead and to light a special candle, which remains burning until sunset on the following day.

Yemach Shemom - "Their name should be erased." This is said when mentioning an evil enemy of the Jews, as if to contribute to the wiping out of that enemy.

Yeshiva (pl., *yeshivos*) - An institute of Torah learning, devoted primarily to Talmudic study. In eastern Europe, the *yeshivos* were usually supported by the community and provided housing and meals for students.

Yeshiva Ketanah - An elementary or preparatory school where the study of the Torah predominates.

Yevamos - The first tractate of *Nashim* the third section of the *Mishnah*, which deals with levirate marriages.

Yiddishkeit - Yiddish for "Judaism," implying a way of life adhering to G-d, the Torah, and rabbinic teachings. Yiddishkeit implies a halachic and moral observance of traditional Judaism.

Yom Tov - Literally means "Good day"; a holiday. Holidays, are celebrated with feasts, prayers, and joy.

Zevochim - The first tractate of *Kadoshim*, the fifth section of the Mishnah, which deals with the sacrificial offerings in the Temple.

INDEX OF NAMES

This index includes names of people mentioned in both parts of this book and many of the town names.

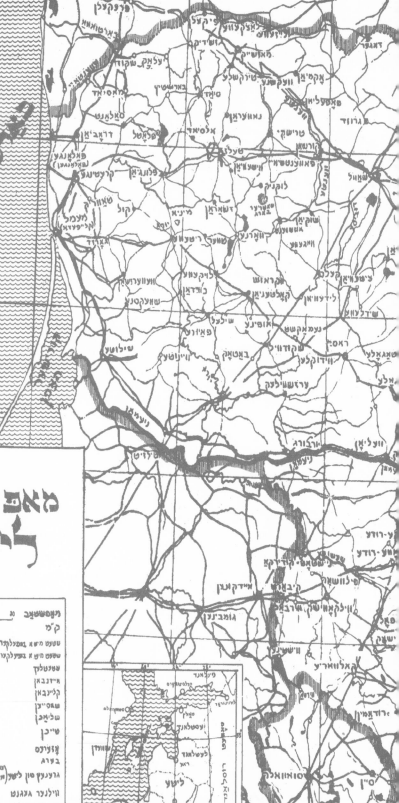

מאפע פון
ליטע